THE MEANING OF APHRODITE

Paul Friedrich

The Meaning of
APHRODITE

The University of Chicago Press

Chicago and London

The University of Chicago Press, Chicago 60637
The University of Chicago Press, Ltd., London

© 1978 by The University of Chicago
All rights reserved. Published 1978

Printed in the United States of America

82 81 80 79 78 9 8 7 6 5 4 3 2 1

Library of Congress Cataloging in Publication Data

Friedrich, Paul, 1927–
   The meaning of Aphrodite.

   Bibliography: p.
   Includes index.
   1. Aphrodite. I. Title.
BL820.V5F74   291.1'3   78–3177
ISBN 0–226–26482–3

Paul Friedrich is Professor of Anthropology and
Linguistics at The University of Chicago

for Deborah

Contents

ILLUSTRATIONS

MAP AND CHARTS

viii

Acknowledgments

The Meaning of Aphrodite reflects my lifelong debt to three models of polymath, interdisciplinary research: the anthropologists, Clyde Kluckhohn and Ralph Linton and my father, Carl Friedrich. The book also reflects the educational experience of four years of team-teaching a yearlong Introduction to Homeric Greek with my friend and colleague James Redfield, in the course of which, by presenting and criticizing each other's ideas, we created a network of new and complex intuitions for studying Homeric language and culture. Early drafts and versions were intermittently presented during two years of the course (1974–76), with Redfield usually attending. More particularly, the entire Greek texts of the Homeric Hymns to Aphrodite and Demeter were meticulously reviewed by the class during the spring of 1976, and I am indebted to all of the dozen students and the coinstructor for that experience. A seminar on Sappho in the winter of 1978 proved crucial. Otherwise, most of the text was reviewed or discussed more than once in my course on general mythology.

The first comprehensive version of it was presented in the spring of 1975 at a Brown University symposium, Anthropology and the Classics, and I remain grateful to William Beeman and William Wyatt for thus getting me to "put it together." Other versions were presented to the Chicago Homeric Society and the Hellenic Civilization program. From lectures and courses I particularly recall comments by these anthropologists and classicists: Beth Brown, Janet Fair, Beth Goldring, Ida Levine, Bruce Livingston, Michaelyn Park, Richard Scherl, Murray Stein, Beauregard Stubblefield, Sharon Stevens, Harry Levi, and Ernestine Friedl. For their comments on various stages and parts of the manuscript I wish to thankfully acknowledge the classicist Myra Derkatch and the anthropologists Robert Bourgeois, Larry Martin, Elizabeth Coville, and Miguel Civil (Sumer), Dan Garrison (Homer), Cyrus Gordon (parts of chapter 2), Wendy O'Flaherty and William F. Wyatt, Jr. (parts of the

Indo-European material), Ray Fogelson, Richard Wortman, the poet Tess Gallagher (chapter 9), and Nancy Spencer, for her research on the Minoan and Mycenaean periods. My daughters, Maria and Su, read early versions and gave crucial advice. Arthur Adkins' page-by-page commentary on a late stage of the manuscript was uniquely helpful. I am particularly thankful to Margaret Egnor for her perspicacious and sympathetic comments on various stages of six chapters. Naturally, none of these persons is responsible for my positions, some of which differ from some of theirs.

All the translations from the early Greek, unless otherwise indicated, are by me (granted that I may have inadvertently used, without specific mention, another's translation of some short passage). The exceptions are Barnstone, some of whose superb renderings of Sappho I could not resist using, and Lattimore, whose translations of Pindar, though often not literal, seem to have brilliantly captured or recreated the spirit and sense of this mind-boggling poet. I have also done the Sanskrit translations (guided by the German of Geldner); the exception is Hymn 1. 113, newly translated for this volume by James Fitzgerald.

Above all, I stand indebted to my wife, Deborah Friedrich, herself a trained mythologist, philologist (Germanics), poet, and comparative-literature expert, who has been carrying out a closely related analysis of the Odin figure of Old Norse myth (as her doctoral thesis). She shared in the formation, in particular, of chapter 6. She also read my first complete text, as well as the final version, and gave many comments at all levels (including the critical first one, when the author has but a tiny bright idea). We have had many wonderful discussions of the problems dealt with in this book and in my closely related volumes of poems.

Last, I thank the University of Chicago, both the Department of Anthropology and the Lichtstern Fund, for secretarial help and for research time.

Останься пеной, Афродита,
Слово в музыку вернись . . .

Remain foam, Aphrodite
make the word music . . .
Osip Mandelstam

We ought not to be awake. It is from this
That a red woman will be rising

And, standing in violent golds, will brush her hair.
She will speak thoughtfully the words of a line.

She will think about them not quite able to sing.
Besides, when the sky is so blue, things sing
    themselves,

Even for her, already for her.

Wallace Stevens

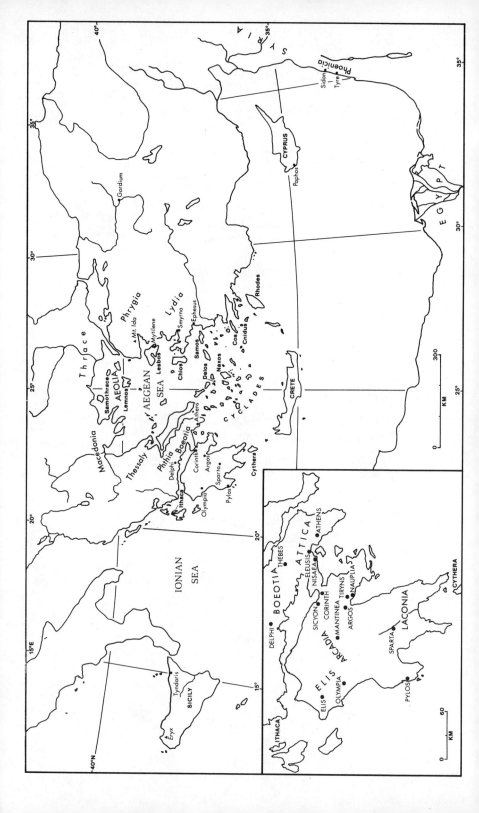

1

Introduction

Let us recall that for complexity and inherent interest the myths and religion of the early Greeks are on a par with those of Christianity Judaism, Buddhism, and the other great systems. More particularly, the Greek system stands out because of the number and stature of its female divinities, so diverse in their personal, moral, and aesthetic characteristics, and for what it says or suggests about "the feminine." Within this general matrix a central problem is that of the meaning of Aphrodite, a meaning that interconnects female sexuality, tenderness, procreation, subjectivity, and other complexes of symbols to be discussed below. The origins and structure of these symbols also raise fundamental questions about the values, of both early Greece and our own time.

The Avoidance of Aphrodite

Let us turn first to certain misconceptions about Aphrodite and to the way she is avoided by the many specialists who, in the course of their books on Greek myth or religion, typically allot only a few words or phrases to her, and these often disparaging ones; one of the main authorities speaks of "a pretty figure of mythology and folk-tales whom no one is known to have worshipped in the whole ancient world." Another in his authoritative article limits himself to "the foolish creature who complained of Diomedes and was caught in her husband's chains."[1] I refrain from needlessly pillorying these two particular experts by naming them, because they are no worse than dozens of others. And I hasten to identify some isolated, exceptional nonavoiders, such as Otto (1954), Detienne (1972), and Seltman, who puts the issue very well: "Of all the Twelve Olympians she is the most alarming and the most alluring, so much so that many writers have tended to edge away from a discussion of her. It is not that they write against Aphrodite, but rather that they avoid her as a topic" (1956: 79).

1

I am hitting this avoidance because the authorities create a problem with many ramifications. To the extent that they say anything at all, they usually categorize Aphrodite as foreign, "Oriental," immoral, and the like as part of a general rejection of what she meant and still implies (while at the same time accepting with urbane amusement the rapacious lust of Zeus and other male divinities). The avoidance of Aphrodite and her associations reflects deep cultural and religious biases. It seems that one has few adjustments to make when coming from the Old or New Testament to Zeus or Athena but a great many with respect to Aphrodite if she is to be taken seriously as a religious figure symbolizing profound values and great ambivalences and who, for the Greeks, merited the epithets "revered" and "awe-inspiring."[2]

Recent points of view, both popular and scholarly, tend to reduce Aphrodite, including the Homeric Greek one, to a fun girl or a patroness of prostitutes and to equate the Sapphic Aphrodite with the physical side of Lesbianism. Obviously, classicists, the upper classes, youth, anthropologists, the literati, and yet other groups that come to mind do not eschew the obscene, the perverse, the erotic—in fact, many delight in it—but they are made anxious and puzzled by the conjunction of meanings, particularly the religious ones, that constitute the early Greek "meaning of Aphrodite." That the literati, in contrast to many poets, often avoid Aphrodite is illustrated by an excellent recent anthology, *Myth and Literature,* where, in 391 pages, she is never mentioned.

The love symbol, Aphrodite, has been proclaimed as having universal human relevance: "Who would gainsay that Aphrodite exists? . . . It would be downright absurd to maintain that one does not 'believe' in Aphrodite, the goddess of love. It is possible to neglect her, to pay no respect to her, as was done by the huntsman, Hippolytus, but Aphrodite is present and active none the less" (Snell 1960: 25). We may smile condescendingly at this author's ebullience, but we might also grant the soundness of his intuition of the special significance of Aphrodite in antiquity, since it is actually supported by the leading authority on the ancient cults, who wrote that her worship was "perhaps as widely diffused around the Mediterranean lands as that of any other Hellenic divinity" (Farnell 1897: 658) and who documents her worship at scores of sites, mainly classical and Hellenistic. If the large exhibits in the Louvre today are at all representative, and I think they are, Aphrodite was more important in popular cult than any of the other goddesses.

We know she was worshiped not only at such obvious places as Cyprus and Corinth but throughout northern Greece (e.g., Thebes) and in Attica (Athens), Sicily, Asia Minor (e.g., Smyrna), and the Greek islands. But beyond these facts of distribution, Snell's remark points accurately to the potential importance of Aphrodite in the field of comparative religion and a yet wider spectrum of human emotional concerns. There are other love goddesses and love-and-war goddesses in the myths of the world but none so complex and interesting as the early Greek Aphrodite.

ORGANIZATION OF THE ARGUMENT

In this book I will try to fill a major gap in the study of myth and religion. Taking a position that combines those of the cultural anthropologist, linguist, humanist, poet, and specialist in Homeric Greek, I will explore in what I believe is a novel manner *how the meaning of Aphrodite arose, how it is constituted,* and *how it is motivated.* I will inquire into the constituents that make up this figure, seen as a complex, goal-oriented system of meanings. By "goal-oriented" I mean that this system, like other systems of language and culture, has implications that tend in a certain direction, that is, that the meaning of Aphrodite has what biologists call a teleonomy or what the linguist and poet, Edward Sapir, would have referred to as "drift."

I have organized the book as follows. First I view the meaning of Aphrodite in its prehistoric and historic origins and then review the most relevant texts for the nonspecialist, annotating at some points. Next I turn to the complex and often vivid network of meanings that can be gotten from those texts. Special attention is given to Homer, the richest and most authoritative source, and to Sappho, because she took the subjective and sensuous aspects of Aphrodite to a new and more intense level of significance. Toward the end of this historical and structural study of symbols I deal, in a separate chapter, with the religious meaning of Aphrodite, particularly as that is created through her interstitial or "liminal" dynamics (for this I draw on some recent theory in symbolic anthropology with a focus on liminality, as set forth by Victor Turner and adapted by me). The meaning of Aphrodite is then compared with the meaning of Demeter, who seems to have filled an emotional gap in the Greek mythic system. My final chapter draws together many of the earlier threads through a humanistic psychological discussion that tries to open up the question of the relation between "sex/sensuousness" and "maternity/motherliness." Throughout I am concerned with the bearing of Aphrodite on poetry, especially that of Homer and Sappho, and with the relations between poetry and myth. Many of the poetic implications of this book are developed in my volumes of poems.

I am also concerned with both the universal and the contemporary American meanings of Aphrodite, notably as these bear on our understanding of the psychology of women. Aside from their intrinsic interest, the questions have a methodological import. Since the meaning of Aphrodite has been neglected by many persons because of their own preconceptions, I shall try to be explicit and "vulnerable," in the constructive sense of making it as easy as possible for others to perceive the fallacies in my reasoning and the flaws in my preconceptions and so move on to more enlightened and humane positions.

ASSUMPTIONS AND CONTENTIONS

I also wish to make clear, as comprehensively and forcefully as I can, what I assume and what I am arguing. This will overlap—as is inevitable—with what I have just been saying.

The Indo-European *vs.* the Semitic Origin of Aphrodite

The first fifth or so of my book grapples with a loaded controversy between what could justifiably be called the "pro-Indo-European" and the "pro-Semitic" partisans with respect to the origins of Aphrodite. Today, as for centuries (actually, millennia, beginning with Herodotus), there are people who insist that she is exclusively Near Eastern or even "Oriental" (e.g., West 1966). Others have been just as categorical about an exclusively Greek, that is, early Indo-European, provenience (e.g., Boedeker 1975), while granting an eventual influence from the Semitic (mainly Phoenician) tradition. Such strong partisanship may reflect underlying ethnic prejudices; otherwise, as with the two scholars just named, we appear to have a reasonably objective judgment arrived at after a responsible and scholarly analysis. I am arguing, however, that both *parti pris* are wrongheaded or, on another plane, are partly right; for both sources, the Semitic and the Indo-European, gave substantial input into the great figures of Aphrodite that we find in Homer and Sappho. Indeed, this eventual Aphrodite reflects the syncretic and cybernetic process that involved other sources, including Old Europe, Sumer, and Egypt. My syncretic-cybernetic position is buttressed by the (currently unfashionable) theories of diffusion and borrowing (e.g., that of Boas 1916, in Boas 1940). More importantly, it reflects a deeper ethical concern for the constructive and mutually enriching interaction between peoples of differing backgrounds.

Diachrony *vs.* Synchrony

Second, most of the book deals, albeit intermittently, with many interrelations between prehistoric origins and early history and, on the other hand, the system of Greek cultural symbols at a given time or "time horizon," mainly that of the eighth to early sixth centuries as evidenced by Homer and Sappho. I repeatedly and extensively ask such questions as Where did the Aphrodite gestalt originate? Is her lily symbol from the Phoenicians? Is her mother, Dione, of Proto-Indo-European provenience? The attitude reflected in such questions contradicts the many mythologists who want to ignore or at least neglect the past, particularly the remote, prehistoric past, which is said to be murky and inferential (which it is) and hence of no value for constructing models for the analysis of myth (which it isn't). But my historicist assumptions also fly in the face of the equally large number who want to ignore the systematic synchronic study of values, including religious or sexual ones (e.g., Nilsson). My contention is that, by looking hard at dynamics *in time and through time* and, on the other hand, *within one given time horizon,* we can attain to insights that are denied to the advocates of an exaggerated historicity, on the one hand, or of an extreme "synchronic" position, on the other. In these theoretical terms, then, my book is devoted to exploring the history of a structure and the structure of a history and so illustrates what Jakobson once dubbed a "panchronic" (diachronic-cum-synchronic) approach. In other words, I assume that something may be defined in terms of what it came from, and also its internal organization at a given time, and the interaction between these two realities.

Structuralism

Third, the middle and later parts of my book go into what I have called "the structure of meaning" of Aphrodite in eighth- and seventh-century Greece. But what do I mean by the fashionable word "structure"? I assume, to begin with, that structure may be primarily aesthetic and of great inherent interest as such, even if we do not necessarily know or assume much about rituals or other social contexts (about which we know *relatively* little in the case of the early Aphrodite). So I base myself mainly on texts, which I review, translate, annotate, and so forth, in order to explore the structure. In other words, I agree with Kirk and others that myth, like language, has the function of communicating a content—in this case, an aesthetic content.

The form of this structure is a network of significant dimensions of meaning. Some of the labels of these dimensions, such as fertility-creativity and "subjectivity," not only sound complex but in fact refer to realms of meaning that *are* extremely complex. Many of the dimensions discussed in chapter 4 are explicitly conjunctive ("fruits *and* flowers," "friendship *and* intimacy"). But even features that sound simple, such as the "goldenness" of "the golden Aphrodite," turn out to refer to meanings that are intricate. In each case I have tried to specify the categories and subcategories as finely as possible in terms of early Greek culture, without, however, drawing axiomatic lines between them or between this system and such considerations of "external history" or recent theory as seem relevant.

Another assumption about this mythic structure or structures is that, as noted, its overall shape or gestalt is that of a network (in a loose but mathematical sense). Within this network the specific shape may, in principle, be of any sort: paradigm, braid, taxonomy, chain, and the other possibilities. What Vigotsky has shown for the "preconceptual thought" of children is true also of the culture of adults: the dimensions of thought and emotion are of so many basic types that no theoretical limit can be set—no more than for snow crystals. This assumption of rich variability I counterpose to the widespread position that myth is organized primarily or even exclusively in terms of certain kinds of analogical relations.

My last assumption about the form of mythic structure is that great and perhaps maximum richness of insight can be obtained from one or two complex, clearly defined, and more or less bounded sets of excellent texts, such as the poetry of Homer and Sappho. This means, of necessity, that I see little profit in drawing a sharp line between myth and literature or even between natural and poetic language. It also means disagreeing with the structuralist canon of method by which a great number of (usually short) variants of the same text are compared in order to arrive at allegedly "deep" insights into a system such as myth. The importance these structuralists place on having large numbers of variants seems to justify—at least for them—the use of texts drawn from an enormous area or even from discontinuous areas (e.g., whole sections of South America) and separated originally by enormous spans of time (e.g., 1,500 years).

The Theory of Liminality

Fourth, I assume that myth is basically about emotion. But how does one get at these emotional wellsprings? One way is through the vivid imagery in the texts themselves, and that is one reason why the major appearances and epiphanies of Aphrodite and Demeter are carefully translated or closely summarized and partly annotated below. A second way to capture the emotional basis of myth is through the relatively recent theory of liminality, that is, of interstitial and marginal states and processes. This theory has been worked out mainly by Victor Turner, who draws widely, as I do, on social anthropology, psychoanalysis, literature, and other sources. His theory can be adapted to present needs, as can some of the concepts in Lévi-Strauss, without accepting the latter's rationalistic or "intellectual" premises. In my almost entirely original theory of the liminality of Aphrodite I argue that she asserts or even demands a crossing-over between emotional antitheses or a simultaneous affirmation of them.

Psychological Theory

Fifth, everyone would have to agree with Kirk that Greek myth is "unusually rich in characters, in personnel" (Kirk 1975: 248); in fact, what mythology or literature is richer in archetypes, implicit characterology, insight into the human psyche? Elizabethan and nineteenth-century Russian, for example, do not surpass it. For these reasons the mythology of Greek myth (more than that of the American Indians) should draw on psychological theory, and I have done so. And by an inevitable circularity, psychological theory, particularly that of Freud and Jung and their epigones, has drawn heavily on Greek myth, not only as data but because, as Ann Amory put it so well, "In the Homeric poems the relation between gods and men is not only a convention of marvellous poetic power, but reflects an intricate, subtle, by no means primitive view of man's psychology" (1963: 111).

I want to explore the emotional and psychological meanings of Aphrodite and Demeter, and that in a concrete manner. As experts will agree, my position is "Freudian" (or "Jungian") only insofar as the insights of these and other psychologists and humanists reflect or have contributed to our informed, educated, or "hard-life" understanding of human nature, sexual symbolism, and so forth. The symbolism of orality and castration, for example, that I occasionally probe will seem Freudian only to those who equate "Freudian" with "sexual." You do not have to be a Freudian to get the jokes in Aristophanes (in fact, you miss some of the fun if you are). In short, while I have read widely in technical psychology and have found it helpful, my statement, or book, does not claim to be psychological in a technical sense.

In the central and final portions of the book I have tried to sketch the outlines of two emotional complexes, one including sex and sensuousness, the other such things as maternity and motherliness. Both involve tenderness and intersubjectivity. What is the content of these complexes? How are they related to each other? Do they arise from the same source? If so, what is its nature? And, if so, why are they held apart from each other so often in myth and high literature? How can our study of these ancient symbolisms add to our understanding of the psychology of women that is gained from our own lives and the scientific efforts of Horney, Deutsch, Chodorow, Mead, Rossi, and the many others working and publishing on female psychology? The disjunction of sex/sensuousness and maternity/motherliness in myth and literature suggests that we have a suppressed lover-mother archetype, and I discuss this in chapter 9.

The widespread disjunction between these complexes leads us to one of the fundamental problems of the anthropologist and classicist: incest—in this case involving a conjunction of the roles of parent and lover (e.g., mother and lover and daughter and lover). We seem to be left with a universal and unsolvable conflict between the social forces that unify the roles and those that keep them discrete. I assume that these age-old questions are as packed with interest as they ever were.

Anti-Parochialism

A more general assumption is methodological and ideological. Throughout this book I have tried to cross boundaries, to poach in well-stocked scholarly preserves, to break up standard categories of analysis, and to explore and integrate the insights of many diverse but indispensable fields, such as psychology and Indo-European linguistics. This reflects my own background, a horror at parochialism, academic vested interests, and prejudice of any sort, and a personal belief in a pursuit that transcends particularities in the search for knowledge and the heart's meaning.

2

The Origins of Aphrodite

Let us begin with the origins in the remote past of the symbolism of Aphrodite, with the details of her background in prehistory and early history (some readers may want to go directly to the summary on pages 49–53, below).

How does one decide what matters? In research into prehistory, as in structural analysis, there is no simple, programmable procedure for discovery, for hitting on the variables that are going to have discriminatory power. On the contrary, one develops a feeling for the subject, learns languages, analyzes texts, reads secondary sources, tries out approaches and new models, and, in the course of it all, gradually sorts and sifts out variables and hypotheses that are increasingly realistic and sensitive to one's materials. In the present case my study of the sources in the six constituent systems (Old European, Sumerian, etc.) led to a gradual isolation of a half-dozen or so themes or dimensions that are frequent in that data and also charged with meaning or power: fertility, motherhood, sexuality and sensuousness, astrality, and war and destruction (these are crude labels for complexes to be explored below). What tests this system of dimensions through time are such familiar criteria as internal consistency, accuracy in the use of textual evidence, and the degree to which the analysis adds insight to previous statements on the same subject.

OLD EUROPE

The first serious source is what has been called Old European civilization, a congeries of southeast European cultures that date from about 7000 to 3500 B.C. and that have been illuminated through the analysis, much of it fairly recent, of over 30,000 figurines from about 3,000 sites (see, e.g., Gimbutas 1974a, upon which much of what follows is based). This analysis of the figurines has added a great deal of empirical depth to earlier hypotheses of a pre-Hellenic

HISTORICAL PERIODS OF THE NEAR EAST AND THE EASTERN
MEDITERRANEAN

GREECE			NEAR EAST
	Old Europe 7000–3500 B.C.		
Proto-Indo-European 5000–3000			
	Early Helladic 3000–2000		Sumer 3000–2100
Pre-Greek 2000			Babylonian-Akkadian 2400–600
		Hittite Empire 1900–1200	
Middle Minoan (Cnossus) 1600–1200	Mycenae 1600–1200		Canaanites under Sidon 1600–1300
		Troy falls 1225	Decline of Sidon 1200
	Dorian Invasions 1150		Phoenicians under Tyre 1000–700
	Dark Ages		
	Homer, Hesiod 8th century		
	Sappho 600		

stratum in which women and goddesses supposedly played a pre-
ponderant and dominant role (e.g., Harrison 1912). While the new
evidence falls far short of giving a specific or unambiguous source
for Aphrodite (as if that were possible), it does provide us with
a rich context of symbols that probably contributed to the eventual
Greek meanings in question.

Let us begin with the fundamental ideas of origins, as these have
been inferred from archeological remains. One primary concern

of the Old Europeans was water, and it is represented as oceans, rivers, or rain by means of meanders, labyrinths, and other ideograms in the Old European "script."[1] Water was presumably seen as the primary source of life; from it emerged water birds, water snakes, horned female snakes, and, eventually, eggs and other entities for which there is archeological evidence.

The great majority of Old European figurines depict females, but these vary in important ways. The Great Bird goddess sometimes appears as a hybrid of a bird and a woman, or of a woman and a fish, or of all three at once. The archaic Bird and Snake goddesses are often sexually ambiguous: a fish, for example, may stand for a vulva as well as a penis, or a long phallic neck may rise from an avian body, while round protuberances suggest testicles and scrotum as well as breasts. Interpreters of the Old European civilization sometimes ignore such androgyny and other precedents for Aphrodite (who, for example, is hardly mentioned in Gimbutas 1974a).

By "other precedents" in Old Europe I refer to such things as birth from waters, the prehistoric egg and snake motifs, and the posture of the woman cupping her breasts in her hands—the stereotypically aphrodisiac pose of pre- and postclassical times (which pose, incidentally, has certain maternal implications). Many archaic Greek representations of Aphrodite have birdlike heads or eyes. Aphrodite herself can be seen as a humanized and rationalized descendant from the Old European Water Bird—the queen of water birds.

The Old European figurines are usually of females, and it seems likely that a female goddess incarnated the creative principle. A large percentage of the figurines (nearly half in some Neolithic sites) are of a clearly maternal figure exhibiting in various combinations such features as apparent pregnancy, large hips and buttocks, a seated position on a "throne," with the hands held down along the sides or crossed over the belly, and association with a child or smaller figure that can sometimes be identified as a female but never as a male.[2] Conventionalized figurines of the "Mother" goddess, seated or squatting, also predominate in the Neolithic of Crete (Childe 1958: 17–18). These several Neolithic figures seem to point toward Demeter and the Demeter-Persephone, who are deemphasized in Homer but are very important in the more popular religions and who, in one form or another, have survived to the present day.

The great goddesses of Old Europe were largely replaced by the divinities of the invading Indo-Europeans (during the early second millennium before Christ). "Some of the old elements were fused together as a subsidiary of the new imagery, thus losing their original meaning. Some images persisted side by side, creating chaos in the former harmony" (Gimbutas 1974a: 238). But much of the religion and myth of Old Europe appears to have survived in Crete, the Aegean islands, and southern Greece in the imagery of butterflies, snake goddesses, and the bull-and-bee cults of Minoan civilization. Much survived in Mycenaean art, from which it developed through the Greek Dark Ages into the familiar goddesses: ox-eyed Hera, Artemis of the quail, moon, and stag, Athena of the eagle, snake, and owl, and also the water-born Aphrodite, associated with the dove and the goose or swan. At various points in myth the goddesses appear as swans, vultures, or woodpeckers: "bird epiphanies have always been popular in Mediterranean lands" (Seltman 1956: 32). Old European religion was also preserved in many specific cults of the Greek states, cults that often involved the snake, the sow, and the bull as their central symbols. It was mainly through Greek mythology that the images and the myths and artistic concepts of Old European civilization evolved into integral parts of the cultural heritage of the Western world.[3]

THE SUMERIAN INANNA AND THE SEMITIC ISHTARS

The second serious antecedents for Aphrodite are the regal figure of the Sumerian Inanna, the Ishtars of older Akkadian, and the many Ishtars and Ishtar-like figures of the entire Semitic area. This "Oriental" theory of Aphrodite's origins goes back at least to Herodotus, who said that the Phoenicians first brought her cult from Askalon to the Greek island of Cythera. His statement is supported by considerable evidence, which is sometimes, however, misused; for example, Aphrodite's siding with the Trojans and her bonds to Anchises and Aeneas, while Oriental in some ways, must be balanced against the probability that the Trojans themselves spoke Greek or some closely related Indo-European language. Other ancient authorities, such as Pausanias, are contradictory or unclear as to the Greek or Semitic origins of Aphrodite.

Many persons, since Herodotus, if not earlier, have espoused the Oriental theory. Farnell, still the preeminent source on Greek cults, strongly advocated a purely eastern origin in much of his generally excellent chapter on Aphrodite (1897: esp. vol. 2, pp. 618–29).

Another conspicuous authority, James Frazer, argues for an eastern origin and identifies Aphrodite with Astarte so closely that he usually applies her name to the Phoenician deity (1951). Quite recently, West concluded his review of the evidence (three complex systems are dealt with in twelve pages) with the pronunciamento that "Greece is part of Asia; Greek literature is Near Eastern literature" (1966: 31). Despite its superficiality in terms of cultural history, this judgment will probably be accepted by many persons because it is attached to the most authoritative recent scholarly edition of Hesiod. Even Otto accepted the exclusively Oriental (here Semitic) origin, although at the same time he held the following extreme view about the way the Greeks remade the materials: "The queen of heaven as she is celebrated in the Babylonian poems is utterly foreign, not only to the Homeric but even to the Orphic hymns" (1954: 92). I return below to this sentimentalizing, but now let us take up Inanna and Ishtar (drawing heavily, often without specific reference, on such authorities as Albright, Gordon, Kramer, and Rawlinson—I make no particular claim to scholarly expertise in this area).

Inanna appears at the dawn of history as the dominant divinity of the Sumerians, architects of the most innovative civilization after the Neolithic (circa 3000–2000 B.C.; Kramer 1958). The cuneiform sign for her actually dates from at least the beginning of the third millennium (Civil; personal communication), and her hegemony lasted all through it; however, 95 percent of the Sumerian evidence stems from Semitic sources of the nineteenth and eighteenth centuries B.C., and the translations of the Sumerian come later yet. Her main city was Uruk, but cult centers were spread throughout Sumer and Akkad.

Inanna is symbolized by bounteous crops, full storehouses, and grain, apples, and lettuce, which she "pours forth from her womb" (in the texts, moreover, lettuce is taken to symbolize her pubic hair and/or vulva). Some interpret all the crop and storehouse symbolism as a part of the Sumerian "obsession" with fertility (Kramer 1969), whereas others see it as standing primarily for prosperity. One decisive fact is that Inanna is never maternal and that procreation and generation are patronized by various important mother goddesses, with whom she should not be confused. One of these, the goddess of the primal sea and creatrix of the earth, suffered a sharp decline toward the end of the Sumerian period. The sharp dichotomization between sexuality and maternity anticipates at the very outset of this study a basic issue, to which the concluding chapter is devoted.

Inanna's main function is sex. Striking in a comparativist perspective is the full and frank eroticism in these ancient writings, which describe her lips, bosom, and high and tangled hair, her lap of honey, and many other details, particularly in connection with her vulva and its hair, which is likened to a horn, a boat of heaven, a new moon, fallow land, and, as noted, to lettuce or a field of lettuce. As one song goes, "My brother brought me into his house / Laid me down on a fragrant honey bed / My precious sweet, lying on my 'heart' / My brother did it fifty times / One by one, 'tongue-making.' "[4] In addition to such sweetness there is often a more crudely carnal quality about her. Her appetites are "insatiable" and lead her to copulate with horses, she is patron goddess not only of kisses but of masturbation,[5] and not only is she a patroness of prostitutes but she is herself a prostitute some of the time, visiting "taverns" and converting her own temples into such establishments.

As a war goddess, battle was her game, skulls her playthings. She "attacks again and again in an all-pervading storm" before which "the gods flee Inanna like bats fluttering to their clefts" (Kramer 1969: 43, 47). Her martiality is diagnostic.

Her last important attribute was astral. Inanna is the daughter or sister of the sun and was identified with the planet Venus. She was "Inanna of the dawn" and "the lady of the Evening Star."

The early Inanna already had a multiplicity of minor attributes and functions, the list running to over a hundred and including sheep-herding, black clothing, music, traveling, hard work, carpentry, the family, wisdom, victory, and so forth (Farber-Flügge 1973).

Some of her major and minor features anticipate the Homeric (and, even more, the post-Homeric) Aphrodite. These include the gold of her bracelets and ornaments and the emphasis on cosmetics and her own natural beauty; and, like Aphrodite, she was washed and anointed by attendants, was labeled "deceitful," and was accompanied by a train of singers, dancers, and other consorts. She is astral, a patroness of carnal love, and is a symbol of fertility and prosperity. Inanna's martiality, on the other hand, points toward the dangers of the Canaanite-Phoenician Ishtars and, yet later, those of the Homeric goddess.[6]

Inanna overlaps with the Ishtars of the Semites because the two civilizations to which they respectively belong—Sumer (3000 to 2000 B.C.) and the Akkadian-Babylonian (starting in the middle of the third millennium)—overlap in time, space, and inhabitants. The Semitic Ishtars differ considerably from one another, but they have enough in common for me to speak of them collectively as "the Semitic Ishtars" or "the generic Ishtar."

One of our earliest documents on these figures is a transitional one, the remarkable "celebration of Inanna" by the Babylonian Enheduanna, daughter of Sargon I, and the world's first known woman poet or, indeed, known poet of either sex (circa 2300 B.C.). Inanna is already primarily a dragon in this poem, a devastator of the lands, crushing vegetation, destroying by fire and flood, terrifying mankind, filling rivers with blood, raging, malevolent, smiting, devouring, and, be it observed, destroying love among those who do not pay her homage (Hallo and Van Dijk 1968: 15–31). Homer specialists will be interested in the line that runs "you who devour cadavers like a dog" because it is reminiscent of the bitch of Troy— not that Helen ate corpses but because (as is further discussed below) she is the only protagonist in the epics who calls herself (himself) a dog as well as being so called by others. On the other hand, "there is no Greek equivalent to the blood-baths initiated by the warrior goddesses like Inanna/Ishtar, her Canaanite equivalent Anath, or the Egyptian goddess Hathor or Sekhmet" (Kirk 1975: 225).

The Enheduanna text may be as highly idiosyncratic as some of the male views of this supreme goddess presumably were, but it seems more likely to me that it approximately reflects the standard doctrine of which she was an official priestess. It also can be argued that many of the passages in her celebration can be read as metaphors of the dangers and ravages of love. But to metaphorize with that intensity and complexity from a basis of war and disaster says a great deal about the attitudes toward love and sex.

A second very early document on Ishtar is the great Gilgamesh Epic. The earliest complete text dates from the seventh century, but it was probably first "put together" about 2000 B.C., although even this is speculative and the actual date may be several hundred years earlier. The great majority of the texts are in Akkadian and hence Semitic, but the epic as a whole seems to have evolved from a Sumerian original. To be more specific, of the few Sumerian fragments that we have, some agree with the later Akkadian versions almost verbatim, whereas others differ considerably (Heidel 1973: 2). The story of Gilgamesh was probably known all over Mesopotamia and transmitted without much alteration for two millennia.

Still insufficiently appreciated, it is a masterpiece dealing with ultimate questions of friendship, love, civilization, nature, death, and immortality. (It does not seem to have been suggested, at least in print, but I am sure that the Gilgamesh Epic was created by one person.)

Ishtar conspicuously patronizes carnal love in the Gilgamesh Epic, and there is emphasis on the sheer quantity of her lovers. At one point she is mocked and cursed by Gilgamesh, who says, "What lover [of thine is there whom thou dost love] forever? What shepherd of thine [is there] who can please [thee for all time]?" (Tablet VI. 42, 43, in Heidel). He then lists her many lovers, ranging from Tammuz, who was taken into the underworld, to a shepherd whom she turned into a wolf, to lion and horse lovers, who are trapped and whipped, and others who suffer dire fates at her hands; these punishments reverse the order of nature and culture, as Kirk has astutely noted (1975: 148). These passages emphasize the dangers, usually mortal, to any man who enjoys Ishtar: he experiences the "evil deeds" and the "evil curses" of Ishtar.

Ishtar is attended by "girl devotees, the prostitutes and courtesans" (VI. 164–65) who are an integral part of a larger system. At the outset of the epic, for example, a courtesan (or "harlot") from the city is selected by Gilgamesh to civilize a wild and hirsute monster (his eventual friend) by seducing him (uncovering herself and "inciting his lust") and making love with him, as it turns out, for six days and seven nights. This incident, like Ishtar's entourage, underscores the connection between artful, or sophisticated, sensuousness and civilization—a point missed by scholarly commentators on these texts but one that will prove crucial below, in the analysis of Aphrodite. The Babylonian Ishtar is also vengeful and, after being spurned by Gilgamesh and insulted by his friend, has the latter slain by her father. In this epic and in Babylonian literature in general she becomes very much a goddess of war and violence. By the middle of the second millennium B.C. the war functions of Ishtar had increased greatly, especially, again, in the north Syrian area, where she was characterized by violence, a lust for revenge, and the drive to power.

Variants of the Ishtar figure appear in many parts of the Near East. A conflated Inanna-Ishtar rite of marriage probably underlies the wedding rites of the Song of Solomon (Kramer 1969, chap. 5) and the obscure references to a "queen of heaven" in Jeremiah

7:18 and to a Tammuz in the Vulgate of Ezekiel. Inanna-Ishtar was also the source of the Hittite goddess who is denoted by the same ideograph (borrowed from Akkadian). She was a dominant deity, depicted with wings, golden accoutrements, a lion, and two attendants; "she" is sometimes male and is primarily a patron(ess) of war. The Phoenician variants of Ishtar sorely tempted the ancient Hebrews, notably Solomon, who, as the King James version has it, "went after Astaroth" (1 Kings 11:5) or, to be more precise, "walked in the way of Astaroth." He also got some of his 700 wives and 300 concubines from the Phoenicians.

Of the Semitic variants the one most relevant to our problem is the Ishtar of Canaan-Phoenicia. Granted the differences that are due to the passage of time, I would agree with Albright that "the Canaanites and Phoenicians were one people so far as their language and cultural tradition went" (1953: 68). Our principal sources for this system are the remarkably rich and variegated texts from the site of Ugarit, often designated by the Arabic name Ras Shamra, that were discovered in 1928 and deciphered a year later. Ugarit, in northwestern Canaan, was open to influences from Egypt, Mesopotamia, the Hittites to the north, and the Mycenaean Greeks and others to the west; the texts date from about 1400 to 1200 B.C. They show three goddesses who, although related and sometimes confused by outsiders, seem to be distinguishable: Astarte, the chief of these goddesses, is quite close to the second, Anat, while Asherah, queen of the sea, was consort of the high god, El, and is in many ways quite different from the other two (the name we use is a plural form from Hebrew, where false gods are often referred to in the plural; the Ugaritic is never plural).

Anat is called "the virgin," not in the sense of a *virgo intacta* but of a hale and desirable woman. She is equal to a warrior in strength and ferocity and is conspicuously cruel and bloodthirsty:

> Anat gluts her liver with laughter
>   Her heart is filled with joy
>   For in Anath's hand is victory.
> For knee-deep she plunges in the blood of soldiery
>   Up to the neck in the gore of troops.
> Until she is sated she smites in the house
>   Fights between the two tables
>   *Shedding* — — — — the blood of soldiery

. . . .

She washes her hands in the blood of soldiery
Her fingers in the gore of troops.

(Gordon 1966: 51)

Or: "Under her are heads like vultures / Over her are hands like locusts. . . . She piles up heads on her back, / She ties up hands in her bundle. / Knee-deep she plunges in the blood of soldiery" (ibid.: 50). Anat is vindictive and "directly violent" (Kapelrud 1969: 114).

Sex is her main preoccupation, and her intercourse is described:

he] is passionate and takes hold of [her] vagina
she] is passionate and takes hold of [his] testicles
Aliyan] Baal makes love by the thousand.

(Gordon 1966: 90)

Despite the evidence, some have argued that although she "represented love and fertility . . . she was no special goddess of these phenomena" (Kapelrud, ibid.), but other major authorities would agree that "sex was the primary function" (Albright 1953: 77). The name Anat itself has been cogently derived from a root that usually means "to answer" but can also mean "to perform the sexual act" and even (in a common variant) "to rape" (Cyrus Gordon, personal communication). We must also keep in mind that—the implicitly pejorative wording of some scholars notwithstanding—the martiality of Anat was considered a positive and even heroic quality and can sometimes legitimately be taken as a metaphor for strong sexuality. All three of the Phoenician goddesses were concerned with war as well as sex, although the priorities and ambiguities of these functions fluctuate over time.

Even aside from their being mingled with war motifs, the love and sex symbolism of these Canaanite-Phoenician goddesses is complex and many-valued. The early Sidonians worshiped a sensuous Astarte (or Asherah?), depicted as a naked woman in the prime of her years, often with emphasis on the erotic zones. The lily that she held symbolized her charm, the serpent her fecundity. Rawlinson says of the later, Phoenician version that "sometimes . . . her figure has that modest and retiring attitude that caused it to be described . . . as the 'Phoenician prototype of the Venus de Medici.' " Just a bit later, however, he says that she was "rarely, however, represented with the chaste and modest attributes of the Grecian Aphrodite-Urania, far more commonly with these coarser . . . ones which characterize

Aphrodite Pandemos . . . ; her aphrodisiac character was certainly the one in which she most frequently appeared. She was the goddess of the sexual passion" (Rawlinson 1889—whose view, based mainly on artifacts, is a valuable supplement to the more recent text-based interpretations).

These sexual passions were variegated. Heterosexual love was of course primary, and in some places a woman was expected to prostitute herself for one day, just before her marriage, in a temple to Astarte—but only to strangers, and with the proceeds to be spent on sacrifices (see, e.g., Frazer 1951: 384). In Phoenicia, too, it was common for worshipers to have sexual relations with the priestesses in the temples and groves of Astaroth. Such priestesses are probably being referred to in the Old Testament when it is said that the prophet Josiah "brake down the houses of the sodomites, that were by the house of the Lord, where the women wove hangings for the grove" (2 Kings 23:7). In Heliopolis, in Syria, every maiden had to prostitute herself to a stranger in the temple of Astarte (Frazer 1951: 384).

To the aphrodisiac features were added others, of a female or yet more general nature, to form a syncretic version that has been summarized as

the embodiment of the receptive and productive principle. [Astarte] was the great nature goddess . . . regent of the stars, queen of heaven, giver of life, and source of woman's fecundity. . . . Most commonly she appears as a naked female, with long hair, sometimes gathered into tresses, and with her two hands supporting her two breasts . . . or [as] a mother . . . nursing her babe, [or she] holds a dove to her breast, [or] takes an attitude of command with the right hand raised (Rawlinson 1889: 327).

Her temples were usually in groves and connected with tree worship. She was also a goddess of navigation and the sea, "She who walks the sea." In Canaan-Phoenicia the maternal, procreative, and other functions were also conjoined with a bloodthirsty and aggressive martiality, although to a lesser degree than among the Assyrians. By the early first millennium the West Semitic Ishtar had become a highly generalized goddess in the tradition that was already well under its way by the time of the Gilgamesh Epic.[7]

This sketch of the Western Semitic Ishtars bears critically on the facts of cultural interaction between the Phoenicians and the Greeks. During its dominance (1600–1300) the city of Sidon was a prestigious center of culture and was a source, for the Mycenaean Greeks, of purple dye, fine metalwork, and the most refined textiles. From about 1300 onward the Phoenician cities continued to interexchange heavily with the centers of Mycenaean culture. The Mycenaean civilization was already mighty, comparable in some ways to Babylon, the Hittite empire, and Egypt; for example, it was certainly inferior in population and the industrial arts but was about equal in military strength and probably superior in the verbal arts (judging from what remains of Babylonian, Egyptian, and Hittite poetry as contrasted with that of ancient Greece and the related Indo-European poetry of the Indo-Iranians).

The general lot of old Canaan did alter drastically after about 1200 B.C., when nine-tenths of the land was seized by the Israelites and others. The Canaanites then reconstituted themselves as a set of cities and eventually prospered. After about 1000 B.C., under the hegemony of Tyre, they moved into a second efflorescence of wealth and culture before sinking into a protracted decline, about 700, under a combination of Assyrian military aggression and Greek commercial competition. These changing fortunes of the Phoenicians were related closely to those of the Greeks.

The power of the Mycenaean kingdoms had also fallen during the twelfth century as a result of the Dorian invasions; but after the so-called Dark Ages in Greece there was a recrudescence of cultural life and the beginning of intense colonization as the Greeks established cities from Gibraltar to the Black Sea. Internal growth and external expansion were accompanied by active trade and improvements in technology, which enabled the Greeks to compete favorably with the Phoenicians even while the latter were still the dominant trading power in the Mediterranean (i.e., before the decline described above).

Greek-Phoenician relations were complex. The sort of cultural stereotype of Phoenicians we find in Homer reflects ethnocentric hostility (e.g., about Phoenician trickery and baby-stealing) mixed with admiration for cultural products; the finest gift of guest-friendship was still "Sidonian" textiles and metalwork. In Book Six of the *Iliad* the great queen of Troy, Hecuba, selects a richly embroidered Sidonian robe as an offering to Athena, one that was "fairest in its many-colored embroiderings and the largest; like a star it shone, and lay beneath the others" (*Il.* 6. 288–95). In Book Twenty-three, Achilles selects as a prize for fleetness of foot "a mixing bowl of silver, a work of art; six measures it held and in beauty far surpassed all others on earth, since Sidonians skilled in craftsmanship had wrought it well" (23. 741–43). In the *Odyssey* (4. 613–19), Menelaus gives away, as the finest treasure in his house ("the most beautiful and the costliest" or "most-honored"), a mixing bowl of Sidonian origin (see also *Od.* 15. 459–69). Of course, acquiring rugs and silver bowls does not necessarily imply borrowing religious ideas; the tycoons of Wall Street have not borrowed one speck of Armenian Orthodoxy (to go with the rugs). But in the present case the rich evidence that the Greeks viewed Phoenician material culture positively is clearly part of a larger fabric of attitudes and cultural exchanges that also involved the plastic arts, verbal culture (the Phoenician alphabet was adapted by the Greeks about 1000 B.C.), and, in all likelihood, some religious ideas, notably those connected with the meaning of Aphrodite. Some sense of this more pervasive attitude and exchange is provided by Pindar's "This melody is sent you like Phoenician wares over the grey sea" *(Second Pythian).* As has long been established—and is indeed common sense—myths tend to be shared along trade routes (Boas 1896: in Boas 1940, p. 428).

Early exchange between the Mycenaean Greeks and the Phoenicians is also reflected in the myth of Cadmus, the legendary founder of Thebes and introducer of the sixteen-letter Phoenician alphabet. Zeus married him to Harmonia, a daughter of Aphrodite by Ares, and at the wedding gave to the bride the peplus and necklace he had been given by Hephaestus, the husband of Aphrodite. It was through a daughter of this marriage, Semele, that Aphrodite became the grandmother of Dionysus. Cadmus himself was a Phoenician. Such a myth is not a historical record, of course, but it *is* part of the cultural map or charter for a given society and so bears on one of my main goals—to understand the meaning of Aphrodite in eighth- and seventh-century Greece.

The interactions and syntheses in myth are paralleled by some of the evidence from cults and by the archeological remains. In general, the Cypriot cities were closely related to Mycenaean Greece and were unquestionably interacting with Semites throughout the middle of the second millennium B.C., although strictly Phoenician settlements on Cyprus are not actually attested until about 1000 B.C. According to Herodotus, writing half a millennium later, the worship of Ishtar and its associated temple prostitution flourished in these part-Greek, part-Phoenician communities (see Appendix 3). From here they were carried, "certainly by Phoenicians," to

Cythera and then to Corinth, where a large number of courtesans lived "high up on the splendid summit" (Seltman 1956: 82). Many poets wrote to or about these women; Pindar's light piece is included below as Appendix 4. Also well known was the center in Sicily, with its temple and numerous hierodules high up on Mount Eryx, 2,465 feet above sea level; here the goddess was known as Ishtar under the Carthaginians, as Aphrodite under the Greeks, and then, under the Romans, as Venus.

In all such cases the hierodule *represented or incarnated the goddess* (in contrast to India, for example, where the *client* represents a god). The tendency for the centers to be on or near the summits of hills or mountains seems to be connected with the fact that other centers, not so located, still look toward mountains having a profile of a certain crescentic shape (a matter exhaustively researched by Scully [1962]). This imagery would seem to have its antecedents in Old Europe, as already noted, and in the Minoan and Mycenaean religions, where, as will be discussed below, the "horns of consecration" constituted one of the two basic symbols and may have been connected with an early Aphrodite cult that has been seriously neglected. (Granted that these horns may also stand for the sanctity of the altars.) The mountainous sites symbolize one of the key aspects of the religious meaning of Aphrodite: her interstitiality or, better, her "liminality" (the main subject of chapter 6, below).

Let us now draw together the sketch of the Semitic Ishtars and the facts about interaction between Greeks and Canaanites-Phoenicians. The essential elements are three. First, the cultural status of both groups was high during both the Mycenaean epoch and the eighth and seventh centuries. Second, their interaction and competition as artisans and traders must have been intense, and one can assume a great deal of cultural exchange during the centuries before Homer, including the exchange of myths and songs via bilingual bards. Third, the Greek Aphrodite is, in the Indo-European context, comparable primarily to the dawn goddess of Sanskrit literature (analyzed below, in this chapter). She also contains elements that are Semitic. The Phoenician goddesses of love and war, on the other hand, share critical features with the Greek goddess (such as patronage of navigation). Early Greek religion, then, was significantly Semitic in origin, and, on the other side, "the Canaanite theogony, especially in its later, Phoenician form, resembled the Greek theogony much more than the Babylonian" (Albright 1953:

91). Rather than a simple diffusion of *eros ex oriente* or a simple evolution from Proto-Indo-European, we have here a partial synthesis between two different cultures in one area: the Indo-European Greeks and the Semitic Phoenicians.

THE MINOAN AND MYCENAEAN EVIDENCE

Many basic patterns present in Old European religion were inherited by the subsequent Minoan religion of Crete, which lasted from about 3000 to 1000 B.C. My discussion refers mainly to the Middle and Late Minoan of the second millennium B.C., starting about 2000. During this period, Crete, some authorities feel, was "the greatest artistic center in the Eastern Mediterranean" (Gordon 1975: 161). My general and rather amateur discussion below is drawn from Budge, Chadwick, Gordon, Hawks, Hutchinson, Nilsson, Rose, Spencer, and E. Vermeule (see bibliography); I have not attempted to give all the specific references.

Most authorities agree that the substantial majority of physical representations are of females, whether these be human votaries or "plausibly divine figures." Rose goes so far as to claim that "goddesses formed the principal object of worship" (Rose 1969: 464). Others (e.g., Gordon 1966: 31) take the same materials to be evidence for a female fertility cult at the popular level. The positions are not necessarily exclusive, and we are still left with the incontestable importance on Minoan Crete of females in what appear to be religious contexts.

There are three main goddesses. First, there is an all-embracing earth goddess or Great Mother figure, who is usually squat and seated, with full breast and buttocks; occasionally she is a cow goddess. The second most frequently found representations are of the so-called Mistress of Animals or Mistress of Wild Things, who is depicted with animals and monsters of various sorts and seems ancestral to Artemis; there is a Master of Wild Things, also, but he is much rarer. Third is the snake, or household, goddess, well known to nonspecialists because of one remarkable ivory statuette but in fact rarely represented. The snake goddess is part of a larger set of evidence for a cult of domestic snakes, which some scholars are tempted to connect with ideas of the underworld. The snake goddess is identical with or overlaps with the Mycenaean palace goddess, who in one instance is symbolized with a shield, a tree, and a bird. Most of the components of this snake or household or palace goddess seem ancestral to Athena. Finally, there is some evidence for a Minoan cult of a fourth and relatively minor goddess of childbirth. The scheme just given should not obscure the fact that there was considerable overlap, not only between the Great Mother and the Mistress of Animals but between the snake-bearing palace goddess and the snakes of an Aphrodite figure whom we shall soon consider.

The goddesses inferred from archeological sources may be compared with the names in Linear B (the ancient script deciphered in 1953). On both Crete and mainland Greece we find a Diwiya figure, the female counterpart of the high god, Zeus, and there is also a Mistress, who was probably the antecedent to Demeter (one of her epithets is "equine"). Crete also had an Athana Mistress (i.e., Athena), priestesses of the winds, Furies, and a goddess of childbirth.

In addition to the predominantly female gender of its divinities, the Minoan religion was typified by two main symbols, which verge on being master symbols: the double ax and the "horns of consecration." The former was its "most conspicuous sign" (Nilsson 1950: 194), and it appears nearly ubiquitously, on pots, buildings, and many shrine sites—but *never with a male figure* and often with female ones (Nilsson 1950: 226). These axes are of various sizes; some of them are usable, but many, very thin and made of precious metal, are probably cult objects. Some scholars limit themselves to asserting a "clearly religious function" for the double ax, others regard it as part of a Cretan cult of hoplolatry (weapon worship), while yet others perceive the obvious symbolic and metaphoric connections between this image and the other female symbolism in the religion—the butterflies and bees and the dominance of female votaries and goddesses. The other main cult weapon is the figure-8 shield, which resembles the double ax in its shape and presumably symbolizes closely related concepts. "Ax-amulets" abound as far back as the Cretan Neolithic.

The second main symbol, the so-called horns of consecration, is also extremely common and is *almost always* depicted with female figures. These horns may be connected with the bull ritual and the celebrated tauromachias of ancient Crete, but it should be remembered that the bull itself was part of the female-dominated symbolism; one instance of this is the bee or the butterfly born from the bull's dead carcass (as retold, for example, in Virgil's Fourth Georgic). The horns may have been lunar symbols (and in Sumerian imagery, as noted above, connections are drawn between the moon, the horn, and the vulva). Both the horns of consecration and the double ax are remarkable for their bilateral or dualistic quality, as are a number of other components of this system. There is also excellent evidence of tree worship, especially of plane trees. Birds are often attached to the sacred figures or appear as epiphanies of female divinities.

Having reviewed the overall Minoan evidence, let us turn to some particulars that may possibly foreshadow Aphrodite. Their weak and fragmentary quality has led most scholars to avoid certain valuable implications. It is striking how few centers of Aphrodite worship have been excavated (or even found). As for written evidence, Chadwick's latest, authoritative word on Linear B is "no trace of Aphrodite" (1976: 99), but earlier (1970: 124) he also said that this absence may have been due to "mere chance," because of the fragmentary nature of the evidence. I wish to emphasize that what follows are hypotheses, not necessarily about direct forerunners of the cult of Aphrodite but of the imagery that contributed to it.

First, the many graceful nudes in early Minoan and Cycladic excavations seem more ancestral to her than to any other Greek goddess. Such nude figures have been found in Cyprus, dating as far back as 1800 B.C. For full Mycenaean times (about the fourteenth century) a remarkable series of goddesses has been found at Ceos in the Cyclades, "one of the most remarkable finds of Aegean archeology" (Vermeule 1964: 217). These figures range in height from life-size to one meter. The details of their dress (e.g., the bell skirts) and, even more, the absence of dress, their "drooping breasts" and "narrow lissome waists," their hairdos and "genuine archaic smile" would seem, when taken together, to suggest Aphrodite. Classical archeologists, on the other hand, tend to call them "a curious experiment" or even "grotesque."

Second, one major site at Cnossus is thought by most authorities to be the shrine of a dove goddess, although, as Hutchinson astutely notes, the "doves" are usually identifiable only as small birds. Nevertheless, the many finds of what appear to be doves have to be taken together with other finds—of phallic goddesses, poppy goddesses, snake goddesses, and mountain-peak sanctuaries—as possible components of an Aphrodite cult. The dove was, of course, diagnostic not only of Aphrodite but of the Semitic Astarte. In evaluating these dove goddesses and the like we also have to bear in mind that almost all the available evidence comes from palaces, whereas it is reasonable to suppose the existence of a distinct popular culture in which the worship of Aphrodite was relatively important; most of this pre- or proto-Aphrodite cult may have lived in the perishable huts of the ordinary folk.

Third, the close economic and cultural ties between Crete, Mycenae, and Egypt, which are universally accepted, were probably accompanied by a considerable exchange of religious influence. Specifically, the Egyptian Hathor was a major cosmic goddess of the power of nature, of conceiving and bringing-forth. She is often depicted as a cow or with cow's horns. While cruel and literally bloodthirsty in some contexts (as when sent to spread destruction among men), she is generally benign and helpful, a protector of infants. Since she was also the patroness of music, dancing, and love, the later Greeks identified her with Aphrodite. There must have been some cybernetic relation between this figure and the Semitic Ishtars and the Greek pre-Aphrodites.[8]

The relation between Crete and Mycenae is crucial. Most specialists concur on the close contact and affinity between the two religions. Goddesses, for example, are conspicious in both, and the representations at Tiryns and Thebes in fact are of goddesses only. The king in both areas was probably also a priest, and the temples of later Greek goddesses were sometimes built on great Mycenaean sites: Athena's at Tiryns, Hera's at Mycenae and Samos, and Demeter's at Eleusis. In many classic temples on Mycenaean sites, however, the fact of continuity has to be established, and few if any scholars today would follow Arthur Evans and equate the two religions.

Let us turn to the Mycenaeans. They came with a distinctive Indo-European tradition that was then partly synthesized with that of the Minoans. The main difference between the two religions is found in the lack of "independent" (i.e., purely sacred) shrine sites and complex shrine paraphernalia in the Mycenaean sites. The priests are on a par in number and function, and there is animal sacrifice in both; the famous scene from the *Odyssey* (3. 5) of Nestor's people sacrificing on the beach at Pylos corresponds well to what we infer archeologically (and was probably a direct inheritance from Proto-Indo-European). The Mycenaean gods somewhat outnumber the goddesses, and there are specific differences in the statuses of the divinities. Zeus, Poseidon, Enyalios (that is, Ares), Apollo, Hermes, and probably Hephaestus all occur in the tablets found at Pylos in southwestern Greece. Poseidon was the main god, as one would expect among a sea-faring people. On the other hand, only one of the rings found at Pylos bears the representation of a god, and the goddesses predominate in some contexts —notably the great Mistress and the Two Queens, whom I assume to be ancestral to Demeter. The tablets mention a Hera (who contrasts with the Mistress in one context), and Artemis, and Poseidonia, the consort of Poseidon. The female divinities who have been posited on archeological and philological reconstruction generally correspond to the names in Linear B.

Probably the most fascinating and significant archeological evidence is the repoussée figure of a goddess found in shaft grave III (dated about 1600–1500 B.C.) at Mycenae. It was unique in being nude. This nudity, together with the attachment of three small birds (doves?) to her head and shoulders led Schliemann—correctly, I think—to conclude that the goddess was Aphrodite. Even the cautious Nilsson admits that "the nudity is . . . very remarkable, and after the cessation of the nude idols of the early Minoan and Cycladic age is unparalleled in Minoan-Mycenaean civilization, except for the enthroned nude idol from Delphi" (1950: 397). Also at Mycenae is a "Dove Shrine," and other phallic, dove, and poppy goddesses have been found in other parts of Greece, dating from the same period. Given the intense cultural interaction between the Mycenaeans and Phoenicians, the possibility cannot be excluded that these particulars reflect the influence of the (semi)nude and dove-attended figures of Astarte.

From a conservative and rather superficial point of view, the evidence I have just adduced for a cult of Aphrodite in Mycenaean religion consists mainly of representations of bees and butterflies. From the point of view I have been taking, these same *realia* are *symbols* of an underlying cultural system that I assume to have been *typologically natural,* in the sense of largely conforming to living cultures we know about or to dead cultures for which we have ample texts. In terms of such a symbolic approach the scholar should feel encouraged to draw the obvious connections between the rather strong evidence for the role of females in ritual and the possible meanings of such symbols. The same shape may stand for butterflies in one context and an ax in another. We have to assume that shapes, like words, have different meanings in different contexts— that, to use the fashionable term, they are "multivocal." These assumptions bear most centrally on the symbolism of androgyny and female sexuality in the Minoan and Old European remains, as in the case of the figures with their hands on their breasts. In sum, the diverse ambiguities of much of our evidence should encourage a reliance, not on the specific archeological specialist, whose imagination is often very limited, but on a general model of interpretation that explicitly entertains such ambiguity as part of a scheme that is realistic in its complexity.

Let us pull together the foregoing discussion of these two great civilizations of the eastern Aegean. I would agree with Rose that "we have evidence, scrappy but suggestive and highly interesting, of two pre-Homeric strata of religion: the Minoan, carried by a people of non-Indo-European speech or antecedents, and the Mycenaean or Achaean, belonging to the Greek-speaking invaders" (1969: 475). It was in Late Helladic times, in centers such as Tiryns, that the Mycenaean Greeks carried out the early stages of their synthesis of the male-dominated Indo-European pantheon and the Minoan (and, ultimately, Old European) one, in which females were relatively prominent; in each case there was a considerable input from the Semites. By the time Mycenaean Greece collapsed before the Dorian invasions from the north, it had already created much of the Olympian pantheon and all of the "pre-Olympian" one, and, I emphasize, the latter unquestionably includes Aphrodite as well as the Graces and the Nereids and other figures associated with her. The term "Mycenaean" should be taken to refer to this original synthesis.

THE INDO-EUROPEAN EVIDENCE

Introduction

The fourth source for the Aphrodite figure is one that partisans of the "Oriental" theory have naturally been loath to entertain. The man whom many regard as the major scholar of all time in the field of early Greek religion, Martin Nilsson, wrote that "our knowledge of the religion of the invading Greeks almost amounts to one word only, but this word is very important—the name Zeus, which the Greeks shared with the Indians" (1950: 4; aside from its crass philological inaccuracy, the statement also advertises the author's "patrilineal" bias). Actually, the Indo-European background for the Aphrodite figure consists of several elements: first, possibly, the symbolism of water and water nymphs, second, the features of a

THE INDO-EUROPEAN LANGUAGES
(Partial Stemma)

	Anatolian	{ Hittite / Lydian	
	Indic	Rig Vedic Sanskrit	Classical Sanskrit
	Iranian		
	Armenian		
PROTO-INDO-EUROPEAN	Greek	Homeric Greek	
	Italic		Latin
	Slavic		
	Baltic	{ Lithuanian / Latvian / Old Prussian	
	Germanic	{ Old Norse / Old English	
	Celtic	Old Irish	

solar religion, and third, the complex and definitely established Proto-Indo-European goddess of dawn, *awsos* (strictly, **áwsōs*).

Proto-Indo-European Water Nymphs

"Water" is one of the basic units in Proto-Indo-European, and the two reconstructed words for it are well established. Aquatic supernaturals are also important in the reconstructible symbolism and loom large in central and east European folklore. The Slavs, in particular, had many water nymphs and other daemonic females who dance by night, capture young men, and the like. Most specialists would agree that such water spirits are Common or even Proto-Slavic. The evidence is often admittedly rather late, but the nineteenth-century peasants from whom much of it was obtained preserved many extremely archaic features in their culture. These Slavic water spirits were almost invariably associated with abnormal or unnatural death—by abortion, hanging, suffocation, suicide, miscarriage, death before baptism, and, above all, death by drowning. The spirits could be the souls of the victims or the instruments of their death—somber connotations that seem akin to "the perils of the soul" inflicted by Aphrodite that I will discuss below (my main source for Slavic materials has been Moszyńsky 1967: vol. 2, esp. pp. 508–88).[9]

Water nymphs are also widely distributed in Baltic and Germanic mythology, where they are often associated with water birds and talking birds (usually feminine in gender). The principal Norse goddess, Freya, has a feathery cloak (of hawk or falcon feathers). Frigg, the wife of the chief of the gods, Odin, likewise has a feather coat. Swans, swan maidens, nymphs, and goddesses of wells and streams are widespread among the Celts (e.g., Ross 1967: 218–19). Many if not all of these diverse north European spirits would seem to be directly or indirectly cognate to those referred to in the Rig Veda and the Homeric texts. Of course, water nymphs and swan maidens are common in many non-Indo-European mythologies (Boas 1940: 463), but this does not make them less probable for the early Indo-Europeans; on the contrary, it makes them more probable. I think we can reasonably assume a variegated set of water nymphs and water-bird nymphs for the Proto-Indo-Europeans and that these figures constituted a symbolic antecedent for the Greek Aphrodite, with her swans, ducks, and geese (discussed in chapter 4 under Dimension 3: Birds). But the case is not particularly strong, and it is less relevant than the solar imagery, to which I now turn.

The "Solar" Hypothesis

A long line of scholarship in the fields of myth and archaic religion, some of it valid or at least original, has been "solar." The "solar" hypothesis is part of a more general one, according to which the main source of myth-making is the need to account for natural phenomena. Within this "naturalist" theory, celestial phenomena of all sorts are perceived as central—above all, the *sun,* but also associated matter, such as fire, the sun's rays, its heat, its effects, its course through the sky, its colors of tawny and golden, and, of course, its *dawn.* At another, deeper level it is argued that solar phenomena have been the main stimulus and even the main goal in man's quest for religion and poetry. Much of the tangible evidence, and there is quite a bit, comes from primitive cultures in various parts of the world, but a great deal has also been garnered from the earlier phases of Indo-European, particularly Indic and Iranian. Some of the pioneer research was done by Adalbert Kuhn, whose elegant book on "the descent of fire" (1886) still inspires respect. But the most conspicuous proponent was unquestionably Max Müller, who in the course of a lengthy career poured out the details of his "solar theory" in a series of articles and books that almost kept pace with the countercurrent from his equally prolific antagonist, Andrew Lang.[10] I find it necessary to deal in brief with the solar theory (really a hypothesis) because of my more essential hypothesis that the Proto-Indo-European goddess of dawn was one of several main sources for the Greek Aphrodite. Because of the violent feelings that are sometimes still aroused by *any* positive attitude toward even a *solaroid* theory, I think I should be fairly explicit about my limited connections with it.

Many persons today, mainly in Great Britian and working in the history of religion, seem to be overwhelmed by what were indeed excesses of the solar position: its many untenable etymologies, its distasteful romanticizing of dawn and the sun, the obvious Anglo-Saxon and Germanic (including Scandinavian) racism (e.g., in the works of Cox), its frequent indifference to comparative ethnographic evidence, its overemphasis on the Indic evidence, its position that "diseases of language" determine the growth of myth, and, perhaps above all, the obsessive way in which it pushed solar implications beyond obvious limits—a trespassing that generated a whole series of scholarly and journalistic articles and also a good bit of rather inane Oxonian fencing and pedantic repartee. The sins and peccadilloes of the solar crowd were indeed manifold.

Today solar mythology has been eclipsed (Dorson 1955), not only by the antisolar theorists in comparative religion but by the equally extreme and lopsided theories of more recent decades, particularly the structuralism of Lévi-Strauss and the comparative mythology of Dumézil. But my review of much of the evidence suggests that there were some kernels of truth in the solar hypothesis and that it is to everyone's loss if these are lost sight of in the controversies, especially the more trivial ones. Though they are of limited value, I would single out a few of the early etymological suggestions, the enormous amount of cross-cultural evidence on solar myths (e.g., Haas 1942), and, perhaps above all, the quality and quantity of the evidence on the character of Vedic religion. Not only does the Rig Veda have several solar divinities—Savitar, Sūrya, Ushas, and others—but most of the other members of the pantheon are to some degree solar as well. There is a great deal in the Rig Veda about sun, fire, and light, as can be seen from any large sample of the hymns. I think it is also beyond dispute that early Greek religion, particularly as reflected in the Homeric texts, contains an enormous number of complex and intricate connections with Vedic religion and, more specifically, a great deal about sun and fire; Whitman, for example, devotes an entire chapter to "fire and other elements" in his excellent book *Homer and the Heroic Tradition,* even though he does not have the solar hypothesis in mind. To put it simply, someone with no inkling of the solar hypothesis would probably come up with it after carefully reading and comparing the Vedic and Homeric texts. My own decision, therefore, has been to spell out the decisive connections among the three main traditions that bear most directly on the meaning of Aphrodite; these are the Baltic sun goddess, the Vedic Dawn and Sun Maiden, and the early Greek goddesses Eos (dawn) and Aphrodite. I shall filter out the irrelevant aspects of the solar hypothesis but at the same time shall not allow the antisolar positions to skew my analysis in the other direction. In what follows, the order of events is, first, a discussion of the excellent mythological case for the ancient Proto-Indo-European status of the Divine Twins (the lovers and brothers of Dawn), followed by a brief summary of the Baltic evidence; then will come rather detailed treatments of the two main dawn goddesses that we have in actual texts: the Vedic Ushas and the Greek Eos, and, finally, the linguistic and philological case for the well-established Proto-Indo-European terms for dawn/Dawn.

The Divine Twins

The case for the Proto-Indo-European goddess of dawn is deepened considerably by that for the closely related Divine Twins; the evidence for each comes mainly from the same four stocks: Indic, Greek, Italic, and Baltic. This comparative evidence more or less supports over a dozen features which are themselves arranged in a structure of interesting complexity. My discussion owes a great deal to Ward (1968), to both his synthesis and his bibliography. Let us review the main features.

1. *The astral feature.* The three sets of myth are all, to a significant degree, connected with the natural phenomena of Venus, that is, the Morning and Evening Star. A common variation on this theme, particularly in Vedic, is the morning and evening *twilight;* the Twins are bright and shining, also ruddy or red.[11]

2. *The lunar feature.* In the Vedic poems the Twins compete

with the Moon, one of the forms that is taken by Soma, a principal divinity in the pantheon. In early Greek, on the other hand, the Moon is a sister of Dawn. In Baltic the moon god is male and is the principle lover of the female Sun, whom the (here female) morning and evening stars also attend.

3. *The aquatic feature.* The Twins are associated with water. They conduct man across water in the Vedas. They are frequent in the Greek texts as patrons of seamen and ports; they were among the Argonauts; they appear in the hymn dedicated to them as the saviors of a foundering ship. In Baltic folklore they also rescue men at sea, and they use boats of applewood.

4. *The bird feature.* The chariots of the Twins are drawn by birds, bird-horses, or winged horses. In the Vedic tradition the birds are typically swans, and in Greek mythology it is in the form of a swan that Zeus rapes Leda and so sires the Twins.

5. *The equine feature.* The Vedic term for the Twins, *Aśvins* (pl.) is transparently derived from the word for horse *(áśva)*—itself with an excellent Proto-Indo-European pedigree. They are born while their mother, Saranyū, is in the form of a mare. In both Vedic and Homeric texts the Twins appear on red, winged horses, while saving ships. The early Greek Castor and Polydeuces and their Latin counterparts, Castor and Pollux, are horse-tamers and charioteers, appear mounted on or drawn by horses, and are the owners of white horses.

6. *The paternity feature.* In the Vedic and Greek texts there is some evidence that the Twins were thought to derive from different fathers, one, for example, being the son of Zeus, the second of a mortal king. In all three traditions, however, they are primarily or usually the "sons of god," that is, of the high god of the sky, and their standard epithets reflect this: the Vedic *Divó nápātā,* the *Dioskouroi* of Homer, and the *Dievo suneliai* of Lithuanian (all of these mean "the sons of god," although the Vedic can also be glossed as "nephews" or "grandsons").

7. *Brothers or lovers of Dawn or the Sun Maiden.* In Vedic the Twins are sometimes equated with, but are usually just likened to, the brothers or lovers of Dawn, or of the Sun Maiden, called *Sūryā* (cognate with the sun in its male aspect, *Sūrya*); but they are also the sons of the obviously related figure of *Saranyū.* In the Greek tradition they are the brothers of the goddess Helena and, in Baltic, of the sun goddess Saulē. When she is a lover, it is of the Twins, and she ascends the sky in their chariot or boat. Their sister-lover, con-

sonant with their own epithet, is referred to by the stock epithet "daughter of god": Vedic *duhitā sūryasya,* and Baltic (Lithuanian) *saulēs dukterys;* and note the etymological sense of "divine splendor" in the Greek term Helena.

8. *The helper function.* In all traditions the Twins are the helpers of man and closer to him than most other divinities: in Vedic they are healers in particular; in Homer, as noted, they appear as saviors, particularly at sea; in Pindar they are "lovers of strangers" *(Third Olympian);* and in the Baltic songs they are generally helpful. In the first two traditions they are signally the patrons of warriors, and in some famous battles the tide was turned by their appearance above the lines.

Aside from the eight or so relatively specific features and functions just sketched, the Twins are also associated with dancing, and they have at least two meanings of a more general order: (1) In all three traditions, but particularly in the Vedic, they patronize or are significantly associated with *fertility, virility,* and the like; in the Greek and Baltic, the focus is on agricultural fertility. (2) At various points, particularly in Vedic texts, the Twins symbolize *cosmic dualism,* a whole set of binary oppositions between light and dark, night and day, life and death, and so forth.

The set of meanings shared by the three systems is relatively full: astral, lunar, aquatic, bird, equine, paternity, brother-lover of the Dawn-Sun, helper, and symbol of fertility and cosmic dualism. This fullness (and complexity) of meanings would by itself justify us in speaking of the three Twin images as cognate, as stemming from the same ancestor. Many of the features are intrinsically linked; for example, the equine and the aquatic have many metaphoric associations (see "the horses of the sea," discussed below in connection with Poseidon). Other associations may be obvious to students of mythology but cannot be set forth here. The three systems also share ambiguities of sex and kinship, the sun being variously masculine and feminine, the Twins being variously brothers and lovers of a female solar figure (Biezais 1966: 22, 127), etc. It is true that twins do appear in some other (i.e., non-Indo-European) mythologies, but they are by no means universal; moreover, the total gestalt of meanings just adduced is really quite specific, and this strengthens the case for their being cognate.

Some interesting etymologies link the Twins with the Dawn Maiden or the Sun Maiden. The name of the Baltic sun goddess, Saulē, may be cognate with that for the Vedic sun goddess and one of the Vedic sun gods: Sūryā and Sūrya. The former of these is of course a perfect cognate of the name for the Greek sun god, Helios (initial *h* in Greek corresponds to Sanskrit *s*, etc.). The name of the Greek sister of the Twins, Helena (and the Helen of the epics), is probably cognate with the Vedic Sanskrit term for their mother, Saranyū. The name for the Greek moon goddess, Selene, may also fit in here, although that seems to lie beyond the bounds of the comparative method.

The attestation for the Twins is solid in all three stocks, ranging from scores of Baltic folk songs to many passages in Homer, Hesiod, Pindar, the Homeric Hymns, and yet other ancient Greek sources and to no less than fifty-four hymns in Vedic Sanskrit; the Vedic Aśvins, in fact, are the fourth most popular figures in the ancient Indic pantheon (Griswold 1971: 255). They even appear in a Hittite text of about 1400 B.C. as *na-ša-at-ti-ia,* which is clearly a cognate of one of their Indic designations, *nấsatya*. Even the acerbic M. Bloomfield concluded that "no rational historian or antiquarian will ignore such parallels" and that "we have the common kernel of a heavenly pair of divinities in intimate relation with a female divinity of the heavens" (1908: 115–17). There is also scattered Germanic and Slavic evidence. The total case is, I think, overwhelming that the Twins are "unquestionably Indo-European" (Ward 1968: 28). Their many connections with Dawn and the Sun Maiden powerfully support the case for the Proto-Indo-European status of the latter and, in turn, for the Indo-European input to the figure of Aphrodite that was eventually synthesized on Greek soil.

The Baltic Sun Maiden

Excellent comparative evidence comes from the languages and folklores of the Baltic stock: Lithuanian, Latvian, and Old Prussian. While some documents stem from the Middle Ages, the great bulk of the evidence comes from the oral traditions of the Baltic peasants that were transcribed during the nineteenth century and are still being transcribed today. These songs and poems would seem to illustrate the strong claim that "the pre-Christian layer [in Baltic folklore] is so ancient that it undoubtedly reaches back to prehistoric times—at least to the Iron Age or in the case of some elements even several millennia deeper" (Gimbutas 1962: 98).

A principal figure in the Baltic pantheon was the goddess Saulē. She journeys through the sky drawn by tireless red horses and in the evening descends into her apple garden or sinks like an apple or a boat below the horizon of the sea. Her daughters *(Saulēs meita)* were her extensions as rays of light or as apple branches. She was served by the morning and evening stars, and, since the latter were also female, it was natural for her love affair to be with the moon, who was male (Mannhardt 1875: 298). The Baltic divinity of fire, incidentally, was also female; she was worshiped on the heights, guarded at sanctuaries by priests, and preserved each night as "the mother of flame."

Indo-Europeanists recognized long ago that Baltic Saulē was close in meaning to the Greek, Italic, and Indic Dawn figure. They also recognized that the form was cognate with the semantically related forms for the Vedic sun god and goddess and with a large set of forms for "sun" in many other stocks: Latin *sol,* Old Irish *suil,* and so forth.[12] It seems reasonable to postulate that the Proto-Indo-Europeans had a sun god with a name derived from **sū-/sāwe-,* as well as a dawn goddess called **áwsōs.* And despite repeated charges of overenthusiasm against the solar hypothesis, it should be noted that many of the studies in question have been backed by solid evidence from folklore. For example, Mannhardt, in his basic study, begins by printing ninety folk songs, of up to fifteen stanzas in length, to which he then refers in the course of his descriptive and historical analysis.

The Vedic Dawn

Ushas (uṣás) is celebrated in twenty-one hymns of the Rig Veda and is mentioned over three hundred times, often in hymns to other divinities; by various criteria she is about fifth or sixth in importance in the pantheon and is the only goddess of importance in an otherwise male-dominated world of fire, sun, drinking of soma, war, sky, and the like.

The Vedic word can mean either dawn or the goddess Dawn, and many of the hymns are powerfully (and poetically) ambiguous in that they refer simultaneously both to the radiant phenomena of nature (and the exalted states it produces) and to the traits and activities of the goddess. It does not follow from this, however, that, as some have argued, she is weakly or slightly characterized or minimally anthropomorphic. She is, on the contrary, vividly and strongly characterized, as I hope the following summary will show.

The hardheaded Bloomfield wrote that the most beautiful hymns in the Rig Veda are addressed to Dawn (1908: 30, 66), and many scholars would probably agree with Macdonnell that Dawn is "the most graceful creation of Vedic poetry" and that "there is no more charming figure in the descriptive religious lyrics of any other literature" (1963: 46; see also the hymn below, p. 193, and Appendix 1). Her "delicacy" and "femininity" are said to stand out. Let us briefly characterize this charming creature, or perhaps I should say concept, taking the precaution of limiting ourselves almost entirely to expressions that occur in the Vedic texts (I have worked mainly from the original and from Geldner 1951; I have also consulted Griffith, despite his faults).

Ushas is herself radiantly beautiful and white or golden in color; "she rises, light and clothed in white, from out of darkness" (1. 123.9-a). Her rays are repeatedly described as (depending on the passage and the translator) red, purple, ruddy, or red-tinted and are said to resemble cows, oxen, or steeds of these colors dispersing from their stalls; she is sometimes called "the mother of cows." She mounts the heavens in a large shining chariot drawn by ruddy beasts. Men rise to greet her from their "pleasant couches."

The rising of Ushas has invited yet other metaphors. She is sometimes referred to as "the sacrificial fee" because it is she who ushers in the sacrificial day. She is said to rise before or with Agni, often with ambiguity as to whether this refers to the god of fire or to the sacrificial and other fires that are lit after dawn. Together with the Twins she removes darkness (often referred to as her sister, Night— the latter bright with stars) and by the same act dispels evil dreams, evil spirits, and the like. Ushas rises or emerges like a girl from her bath; "she is conscious of her body like a beauty; she stands there like a woman bathing to allow herself to be viewed" (5. 80. 5-a). Or she is like a girl being led to her groom by her mother. She discards her attire, displays her form, and, in repeated passages, *reveals her bosom;* "You go like a girl, goddess, proud of your body to the god who desires (covets) you. Smiling, a young wife, you uncover your breasts before him when you shine forth in the east" (1. 123. 10). She smiles, dances, sings with her maid, and "shows sweet things like a singer of new songs"; "she puts on embroidered garments like a dancer; as a cow yields her udder, so she bares her breast" (1. 92. 4-a). Her first rising is like "some chaste woman" who "bends opposite to a man, her forehead downward," whereas at other times she is "like a brotherless girl, she resembles someone who mounts the stage to win prizes" (1. 124. 7-a) (in other words, she is like a girl who, because she lacks brothers to help arrange a marriage, must act boldly on her own behalf). It may be because of her delicacy, on the other hand, that she is not offered the soma (unlike other divinities so denied).

Ushas has yet more general roles. Her rising awakens all creatures, both two-footed and four-footed, to *motion*. She reveals paths and makes them easier to traverse, and she does not miss directions. Like the Twins, she helps and heals human beings and is typically generous to them (*maghōnī* is her main epithet), and so she resembles a wealthy and noble lady. She assures good crops and, above all, virility and fertility in the form of sons—hosts of sons. A more general level for these functions is her birth in law and her protection of the divine order *(ṛta)*. She acts in accordance with the cosmic order, of which she is one of the mainstays and symbols.

Ushas' relations with other gods are uniquely ambiguous. She is *likened* to a lover or bride of Pūshan, of the sun god, of the fire god, of the Twins, and of the others who share in discovering her. But she is also called the mother of the sun and the fire, since she precedes the former in the sky and the kindling of the latter on earth. She is the sister of Bhaga and of the Twins and is repeatedly called the daughter of heaven and of the sun, and she is linked in some ways with the Sun Maiden.

The attractiveness and the erotic tinge of Ushas point in various ways. In one direction, for example, the passage already cited does suggest the boldness or indecorousness of a young woman who has to fend for herself without brothers in a patriarchal society. And the closely related figure of the Sun Maiden, Sūryā, has been described as an "arch-flirt who carries on affairs with the male Sūrya, the Aśvins, and Soma" (Bloomfield 1908: 172). One scholar even went so far as to claim that Ushas was the original divine courtesan. One drawback to this hypothesis is that it rests heavily on the moot gloss of a word for "lascivious" that is used only once *(ódatî)*. In almost all the passages commonly cited about her she is *not equated with* but *is likened to* (Sanskrit *na*, "like") a lover of so-and so; the one exception seems to be in 1. 92. 11, where she shines "with all her lover's splendor." The Vedic poets, in general, were considerably more "delicate" than the more recent students of their lines. The main effect of the suggestive words and passages is to express the diffuse warmth and affection that men feel toward the natural phenomena of dawn and that Vedic man felt toward Ushas.

In many hymns she is referred to in the plural: for example, "the Dawns come on like tribes arrayed for battle" (7. 79. 2-a). This may be a more formal term of address, as the great commentator,

Yaska, thought, or simply one way of viewing her in the company of her maidens. These simultaneous dawns are sometimes called sisters. The sister dawns raise a deeper point of interpretation. As Renou (probably the greatest Vedic scholar) noted some time ago (1957: 6–10), most of the kinship relations that are attributed to Ushas are mentioned only once and are not too meaningful. The exceptions are three. She is consistently and frequently the "daughter of the sky" (and hence, as discussed elsewhere, perfectly cognate with Aphrodite, the "daughter of Zeus," i.e., the sky god). Second, she is often a mother, not only of the sun and fire, but of *all* the gods (1. 119. 19) and is in some very real sense a universal mother. Third, she is a sister par excellence (Dumézil 1973: 323–24). The Vedic term for sister occurs thirteen times, eleven of them for Ushas, and once for a sister of Ushas. She is closely linked as a sister to night and to other dawns. This multiplicity of her roles—as lover, daughter, mother, sister—makes her resemble the Ishtar figures and the Aphrodite to whom we turn in the next major section below.

The deepest ambiguities of the Ushas image involve time, life, and death; "the dividing line between past and future is, according to the Vedic poet, not sunset but dawn" (Griswold 1971: 252). On the other hand, her recurrence is inevitable. She is always young, continuously reborn, and in this sense immortal. She brings the light of each day, and the powers of that light, to man. On the other hand, she also dies every day and shortens and wastes away life, "like a skilled hunter cutting birds into pieces" (1. 92. 10-b), and the soul of the dead man *returns to Dawn*. Thus she symbolizes both youth and old age. Some of these ambiguities are captured in the passages where the present dawn is linked to those of the past and the future: "First of the dawns coming without end, she goes off after the herd of dawns departing" (1. 113. 8-a). In a complex sense, "the immortality of Ushas is made up of the twin processes of dying (implied) and of being born again at dawn" (Griswold 1971: 252). The full signification of Ushas combines cosmic order with cosmic ambiguity.[13]

Greek and Latin Dawn

Indisputably cognate in both meaning and form with the Sanskrit Ushas are the Greek Eos *(ēōs)* and the Latin Aurora. They may look dissimilar to the nonspecialist, but the apparent differences reflect highly regular historical linguistic rules. The *a* in Ushas, for example, is the regular outcome in Sanskrit of Proto-Indo-European *o;* the Greek form illustrates the loss of *s* between vowels in that language, whereas in Latin it goes to *r* under the same conditions. All three forms are thus the regular descendants of an ancestral **áwsōs*. The full philological details are given below in Appendix 5; I would emphasize that the strength of this etymology guarantees the Proto-Indo-European status of "dawn" (and "Dawn"). Let us turn now to the cultural aspects of the Greek Eos (paying relatively little attention to Aurora).

The Greek Eos was the daughter of the solar Titan, Hyperion, and of the Titaness Theia, the "far-shining, from whom all light proceeded." Her siblings were the moon goddess, Selene, and the sun god, Helios (although in Pindar she is also called the *daughter* of Helios). She is often coupled and named with the sun in early Greek poetry and seems centrally ensconced in the solar sector of the pantheon.

Dawn's relations to her husband, Tithonus, are of deep symbolic importance. According to a widespread opinion his name may be derived from that for the Titans (Frisk 1970: 904). At an earlier stage in myth he may have been the sun god, who then was replaced by Helios and reduced to mortal status. In Homer he is still called "lordly" (e.g., *Od.* 5. 1) and is ranked with gods and heroes. In the *Iliad* he is the brother of Priam and so symbolizes Dawn's link with the Trojan East. He was seduced by Dawn and at first lived happily with her on the edge of the world and gave her two sons. One of them, Memnon, had his armor made for him by Hephaestus before coming from the East to help the Trojans, and he eventually slew one of Nestor's sons before being slain himself by Achilles (as described in the *Aethiopis,* eighth century). By the time of the Homeric Hymns, of the seventh and sixth centuries, the originally lordly and at least partially solar Tithonus has degenerated into a relatively pathetic character because of an error on the part of Dawn, who asked Zeus for immortality for him but not for eternal youth. He has become helpless in his limbs, and his cricket-like voice is heard chirping in the golden room where he is kept locked up. The texts vary as to whether the lustful Dawn actually still sleeps with him. She has, as we shall see, "a comparatively well-marked personality" (Rose 1959: 35).

Dawn's other amours are just as suggestive and problematical. According to one myth she was Ares' mistress and so aroused the jealousies of Aphrodite, who then cursed her with perpetual infatuation for someone. But this is a relatively late myth of the second century B.C. (Apollodorus 1. 27).

Through an affair with another god, Dawn created the four winds and the stars, specifically the Morning Star, or "Dawn-Bringer," as related in Hesiod (*Theog.* 378–82); here, then, she is the mythic, symbolic mother of Aphrodite.

Dawn is rapacious in her way. Homer reports that she "snatched away" a mortal called Cleitus because of his beauty, so that he might live with her among the immortals (*Od.* 15. 250–51); here and elsewhere, incidentally, Dawn is the active, pursuing figure, and the Greek *harpazō,* appearing in the active voice, is the verb normally used for sexual abduction by a man and also for seizing property. The image of "snatching up, away" and the related ones of hiding, holding on to, and the like, recur in various stories of Dawn-descended figures like Calypso and Aphrodite (Nagy also discovered this; he gives a paradigm and philological details in 1973: 156).

In another, very early, Hesiodic myth Eos takes up with a mortal called Cephalus and bears him "a splendid son, a man like the gods," whom, when he was still "in the tender flower of glorious youth," Aphrodite snatches up and makes the keeper of her shrines by night (*Theog.* 986–91). In a later version of this same tale Artemis intervenes and sends Cephalus' wife back to compete with Dawn. In yet another, later, myth, finally, Dawn bears this man two sons. The main point is that in these variants, most of which are early, Dawn is clearly in competition with Aphrodite and, to a lesser extent, with Artemis. A minor point, of psychological interest, is that *kephalē* means "head" in Greek, so that this story of Cephalus (Kephalos), like many others about Dawn, has implications of castration.

Dawn's major affair was with Orion, the gigantic hunter and handsomest man of all time (*Od.* 11. 311). Before meeting Dawn he had been blinded by a jealous husband but had then had his sight restored when he was guided by Hephaestus (Aphrodite's husband) toward the East until the rays of the sun (Dawn's brother) shone directly into the empty sockets (here and elsewhere sight and male sexuality are closely linked symbols). After this he is seized by Dawn, but the gods begrudge him to her and he is eventually slain by Artemis with her "gentle arrows"—an unusual detail because, as the *Oxford Classical Dictionary* points out, she "regularly kills women, not men." Then he is cast up into the sky to become the great constellation that bears his name. Note that even here it is the Bear (one of Artemis' main symbols) who keeps constant watch over him (*Il.* 18. 487–88).

The *Verstirnung* (becoming-a-star) of Orion significantly enlarges the astral nature of Dawn. Another link to nature occurs in the related myth in which Orion pursues seven sisters, the daughters of Atlas, who, in astral terms, are the Pleiades (Pindar *Second Nemean* 16). In yet another version Orion is slain by a scorpion, itself an astral symbol borrowed from Babylon, and there may be some connection here with the story of Gilgamesh and his relations to the lascivious Ishtar and his brief sojourn among the "scorpion people." Clearly, the myth of Orion is complexly reticulated with early culture history and with astral phenomena of which the early Greeks were probably aware (granted the paucity of evidence on just what their astronomy was). The myth of Orion's becoming a constellation after his affair with Dawn is ancient even in Homer and is, in fact, the earliest astral myth of the Greeks; according to the *Oxford Classical Dictionary,* it is "an unprecedentedly early star myth."

The last major dimension of Dawn involves her epithets as these refer to her typical acts and her appearance. She is the Early-Born (*Theog.* 381). She is heralded by the Morning Star, who, in the *Iliad* (23. 226), is her son. She then rises in a chariot drawn by two horses. Her abode and dancing area are Aeaea, which is also the island of Circe (one of the "allomorphs" of Aphrodite). In early texts she is referred to as rosy-fingered, of course, but also as rosy-armed (*Homeric Hymns* 31 and 6), and as saffron-robed and golden-sandaled in Sappho, and in Homer as well-throned and bright or brilliant (e.g., *Od.* 4. 188). Now it has been argued that these epithets are natural for the phenomenon of dawn, and it is true that the very last of those mentioned, a particular word for "bright," is otherwise used only of objects. To balance these naturalistic implications I would point out that "rosy-armed" and "saffron-robed" are used *only* of Dawn in Homer. And while she does resemble the other goddesses in being fair-tressed and golden-throned (*Od.* 15. 250), she is never described with Aphrodite's epithet of "golden," although this would seem most "natural." In other words, the way several of her epithets are culturally specific makes them valuable for comparative purposes; "cognates" of this sort are useful, among other things, in the degree to which they are culturally specific as against being predictable in universalistic or "naturalistic" terms.

Dawn's position in myth differs markedly from her position in cult. On the one hand, she had few local cults and no special ritual. On the other, she has a definite if minor place in Homeric and post-Homeric myth; the frequency with which she is invoked in the epics, as when a hero waits for "rosy-fingered dawn," seems to hark back to an earlier time when she was of far greater importance. The scattered but widespread references to Dawn in Homer have the appearance of formulaic relics from a time when this figure was more prominent in the mythology.

Let us now pull together the main strands of the Dawn image and suggest how they relate to our larger problem. We have noted in her profile a considerable number of epithets that are probably very archaic, such as "saffron-robed," and a complexly astral nature tied in with several star myths, notably that of Orion. Salient was a series of affairs with gods and also with mortals, whom she "seizes" and who often die violently; her kidnappings may, according to the *Oxford Classical Dictionary,* themselves be "a euphemism for sudden death." Her violence may have motivated the otherwise baffling statement that, "For some unknown reason, she is imagined as very amorous" (ibid., s.v. Eos). The deaths of her lovers are reminiscent of those of Ishtar's paramours in the Gilgamesh Epic and of the latent perils of Aphrodite.

Dawn and Aphrodite

Dawn's associations with other divinities are also highly revealing and call for comparative generalizations. At one time or another she is associated with over a half-dozen gods and goddesses, notably Artemis, who slays Dawn's lover and helps a woman against her. But her main connection is with Aphrodite. Aphrodite's husband, Hephaestus, arms Dawn's son and helps her lover-to-be, Orion, to regain his sight (symbolically, his sexuality). The two goddesses compete for the same men, and the relation of Dawn to her husband, Tithonus, and their son, Memnon, parallels in many ways the relation between Aphrodite and Anchises and *their* son, Aeneas—for example, in the rapacious attitude of the goddess toward her lover, and the latter's eastern origins. And, just like Aphrodite, Dawn arises daily from the arms of a much older man about whose sexuality there is considerable ambiguity; the lame master goldsmith, Hephaestus, in his glowing, golden smithy symbolically parallels the senile Tithonus in his golden room, singing the way a cricket does near the hearth and its coals (the legs of the cricket may even parallel the bellows of the smith). These last analogies are not explicit in the texts but seem realistic to me. Finally, Dawn and Aphrodite are both insular and astral. The multiplicity and complexity of the many connections between the two goddesses are significant.

To the patterns just stated we can add, as a sort of supplement, the more or less related conclusions that were arrived at independently by Boedeker (1974: 68–79) regarding Eos, the primordial model, and her various descendants, such as Aphrodite and Thetis. Let us review some of Boedeker's main points.

First, these goddesses are attracted by the physical beauty of a mortal lover (or lovers), which is described.

Second, they seize, restrain, or at least seduce these lovers.

Third, their own shining beauty is depicted, often in scenes of dressing and undressing, and among their brilliant garments particular interest attaches to the robe or *pharos*—a word of Mycenaean pedigree that is certainly related historically to the night-dispelling "web" of the Indic Ushas (incidentally, this web imagery must be connected with the weaving and loom symbolism of Helen, Penelope, and Greek women generally).

Fourth, Eos and Aphrodite journey across the sky, and all members of the set are associated somehow with paths or roads; for example, Circe helps Odysseus on his way.

Fifth, the aging of the mortal lover presents a problem for the goddess, not only the obvious one of the lascivious Eos, but also those revealed in the complaints of Thetis. In any case, these Dawn and Dawn-descended figures are themselves the cause of the passage of the days, and so of aging.

Sixth, the fate of the mortal lover is not "predictable" (ibid., p. 78); it ranges from conditioned immortality to death. This makes the Greek and Indic, that is, Indo-European, mortal lovers differ fundamentally from those of the Near Eastern Great Goddesses, for whose lovers three elements are predictable and critical: violent death, ritual mourning, and rebirth (and all three of these elements clearly connect symbolically with the annual agricultural cycle).

Last, and most comprehensively, the Greek models present remarkable structural analogies (or homologies), which I have already discussed, and which I summarize here in paradigm form. In these triads the corners contain, respectively, (1) a beautiful mother/lover/wife, (2) an aging, mortal lover/husband, and (3) a beloved son.

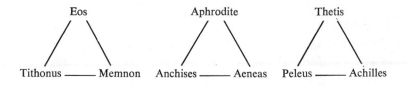

Eos   Aphrodite   Thetis

Tithonus —— Memnon   Anchises —— Aeneas   Peleus —— Achilles

There is a substantial basis for the contention that Eos, Aphrodite, and Thetis all symbolize maternal love for a son (Memnon, Aeneas, Achilles) and the desire to protect one's son against dangerous mortal enemies (Achilles, Diomedes, Agamemnon). These Greek structures are of course closely paralleled in the Indic texts in ways that are more fully specified elsewhere. As Boedeker astutely concludes, "it sometimes seems that in Indo-European religion the Dawn Goddess had a general maternal function" (1974: 83). We note with respect the author's scholarly circumspection ("sometimes," "seems," "general") regarding what is a rather strong case. I will recur at several points below to this "general maternal function" but would emphasize, for now, that Boedeker's study establishes valuable points of emphasis.

A second, supplementary point has emerged in the recent literature. In 1973, Georges Dumézil, the dean of Indo-Europeanist mythologists, brought out the third volume of his magnum opus on myth and epic, much of which is devoted to a Latin mythic structure that is unquestionably cognate to the one developed in this book. If we abstract from the wealth of ritual and historical detail which his book contains, we can summarize the essentials of his discovery as follows. First, Dumézil pulls together the evidence for the Latin Aurora, goddess of dawn, spring, and fertility, whose annual festival fell in June, before the summer solstice. To this Aurora complex Dumézil then relates that of the Mater Matuta, the "Mother of Early Morning," whose rituals took place about the same time of year, that is, June 11. These rituals were acted out by Roman matrons and had two principal components; first, these women, or "good mothers," were represented as a set of sisters or as the children of sisters. Second, these ritual "sisters" at dawn drove a slave woman out of the Mater Matuta temple with lashing and excoriation; the slave clearly symbolized night. The third part of Dumézil's imaginative web weaves together Aurora and Mater Matuta in the history of several decisive victories by the great general Camillus in the early fourth century B.C.; among other things, these victories were preceded by prayers to Mater Matuta at dawn, and the author feels that the historical evidence for the relation between the two goddesses is good (e.g., it is explicit in Lucretius). Fourth, from this complex, Aurora–Mater Matuta, it is a short step to the Indic structures and the patterns in Vedic Sanskrit that I have dealt with above —to Ushas the goddess of dawn, the mother of the sun and indeed of all the gods, and the sister par excellence in a set of sisters who dispel (or expel) the night and are associated with cattle, feeding, suckling, and so forth (Dumézil 1973: 322–30). Fifth, and here I go beyond Dumézil, the Latin and Indic evidence supports the reconstruction of a Proto-Indo-European goddess of dawn who is at once maternal, sororal, and erotic. It is fascinating, incidentally, and consonant with the avoidance-of-Aphrodite problem that I stated at the outset, that Dumézil never connects his far-flung hypothesis to Aphrodite and the other Greek evidence. I would note, also, that while he is extremely reluctant to be linked in the minds of his readers with the "poetic, reconstructivist, naturalistic" connotations of the solar theory (1973: 195), he is in fact masterfully refashioning part of one of its cornerstones. I cannot personally vouch for his theory but feel that it should be summarized here because of its obvious relevance to our problem.

A final point about Proto-Indo-European is the idea of close kinship between a male figure such as Hephaestus (or Achilles) and a female water goddess such as Aphrodite (or Thetis, who, in another myth, cares for Hephaestus for nine years after he has been hurled from Olympus). In early Germanic mythology we find a parallel in the male smith, Volund, and the swan maidens. In early Indic myth there is the "son of water," a virile fire god surrounded by swirling water maidens. Or the sex may be reversed, as among the Balts, to yield a female solar figure and a male aquatic one. In diverse ways, then, the heavily erotic fire-in-water theme has many variations and ramifications in Indo-European (Dumézil 1973: 21–39; O'Flaherty 1973).

My study of the meaning of Aphrodite, while focused heavily on the main figure of Aphrodite herself, must take into account, not only such forbears as the Indo-European *awsos* and sister figures such as Eos, but a number of other female supernaturals that are historically and/or structurally related. These fall into several groups, with no very clear boundaries between them. First is the epic Helen of Troy, a descended or "faded" variant in so many ways that it is hard to draw a sharp line between her and the goddess

Helena, who was worshiped in Laconia, or between her and the mythic Aphrodite. Second, Thetis, the sea goddess and mother of the solar hero Achilles, is probably a regional variant, as is Penelope. Third comes a set of variously beautiful, seductive, and sometimes dangerous goddesses who roughly fit the Aphrodite description— Calypso, Circe, Ino, and so forth.

This panoply of Aphroditoids probably reflects both directions of a continuing pan-Hellenic process, which I deal with elsewhere, in which local sea and love goddesses develop into or fuse with "Aphrodite" and, on the other hand, Aphrodite "descends" into one or another local or temporal variant. The reader should be warned that the issue of "variants," "faded goddesses," and "allomorphs" is a subject of controversy among scholars. My own feeling is that a rigid taxonomy of any kind is going to preclude a great deal of valid insight. On the one hand, we can be sure that the epic Helen is a "faded Aphrodite," and, given the associational nature of myth (Lowie 1972), that Circe is in some psychologically valid sense a "structural variant" or "allomorph" of Aphrodite. But beyond such reasonable certainties I find it preferable to operate by the case and with close attention to context.

In addition to the variations on Aphrodite there is in Greek myth a typologically extraordinary number of female supernaturals: the Furies, the Fates, the Medusa or Gorgon, the Naiads, the Seasons, and so forth. All are connected with Aphrodite at some point; for example, in one myth the Furies are her sisters, in some regions there was an Aphrodite-Gorgo, the Seasons attend her in many versions, and so forth. An interesting monograph could easily be written on this larger context of female figures (and see Faber's article, to which I return below).

Proto-Indo-European *áwsōs, "dawn, Dawn"*

We have considered the meanings in the myths that support what is a well-grounded theory (rather than a hypothesis) of a Proto-Indo-European dawn goddess. The more strictly linguistic evidence that is set forth in Appendix 5 may be skipped over by many readers, who should not, however, fail to note that the word itself, *awsos,* is attested in no less than seven of the twelve main Indo-European stocks that are normally used in reconstruction and that, in five of these stocks, the reference of the term is *to the goddess as well as to the natural phenomenon.* As elsewhere, I will use *awsos* as a shorthand for *áwsōs.*

Let us summarize the evidence for an Indo-European precedent for the Greek Aphrodite. I have delineated the Vedic dawn goddess, Ushas, and her Greek counterparts and have indicated some of what they share: red, rosy colors, bathing in and emergence from water, cosmetics and golden ornaments, display of the body, particularly the breast, smiling, singing, dancing with and being attended by young maidens, multiple lovers and (at least the suggestion of) erotic affairs, the mixing or combining of multiple roles in sex and kinship (including maternal ones), patronage of paths and routes, motion, the sources of fertility and creation, control over living creatures, and association with the cosmic ambiguities of light and darkness, life and death. The Vedic Ushas is more developed than the Greek Eos, and her eroticism is more delicate; but the two do resemble each other in many ways, and both are clearly akin to Aphrodite. All are cognate in meaning with the Proto-Baltic Sun Maiden (and in name as well when it comes to Ushas/Eos). These figures are reticulated closely with one of the most definite figures that we can reconstruct for Proto-Indo-European mythology: the Divine Twins. The Proto-Indo-European name for dawn/Dawn, *awsos,* is accepted without dispute among even conservative Indo-Europeanists. My main conclusion, therefore, is that this *awsos* was a fairly complex, adequately characterized, and important divinity in the ancestral pantheon—that she was, indisputably and, indeed, centrally, Proto-Indo-European.

This is the time to state the historical hypothesis which, I hope, my argument has converted into a theory. Starting with the Proto-Indo-European form *awso*s and the meanings of dawn/Dawn, we come down to an early Greek or "pre-Greek" stage for the several centuries before and after the turn of the second millennium B.C. (roughly, 2200 to 1700 B.C.). At some point in this early period the Dawn figure bifurcates, leaving, on the one hand, the Homeric and Hesiodic Eos, with considerable natural and personal detail, and frequent mention in ritual-formulaic contexts.

A neat analysis of this bifurcation has been provided by Nagy (1973: 162–63). It involves the epithet "child of god," which can be reconstructed for Proto-Indo-European. In Vedic Sanskrit its reflex is used *only* of Ushas, the Vedic dawn goddess. In early Greek, on the other hand, it is *never* used of Eos but *is* used fairly often for some other goddesses, notably Aphrodite, where it is in competition with the equimetrical "smile-loving" (although the latter is also used merely ornamentally in general contexts). Moreover, the epithet "child of god" (i.e., of Zeus) is used of Aphrodite at crucial points in Homer to underscore her status, just as it is used of the "faded Aphrodite," Helen, in *her* interaction with the true Aphrodite. Clearly, what happened during the bifurcation of the mythic figures was a corresponding bifurcation in the epic language, with the epithet "child of Zeus" being reserved to Aphrodite, while "rosy-fingered" and other epithets were limited to Eos (and are never used of Aphrodite).

One critical impetus for the bifurcation was probably the extensive and intensive cultural contact with the Phoenicians and their images of Astarte and Asherah. The Greek Aphrodite eventually fuses the features of the early Greek Eos with many of those of Astarte. My hypothesis (theory?) is summarized below:

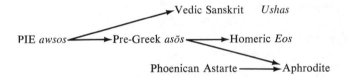

By another hypothesis the name (and the figure) of Aphrodite can be derived directly from Proto-Indo-European ("foam-traveler," as analyzed in Appendix 6). This gives us a different stemma:

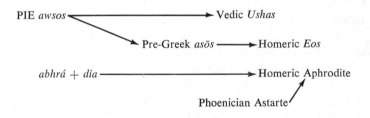

CONCLUSIONS AND SOME SPECULATIONS

Let me now summarize my historical hypotheses regarding the precedents and antecedents for the Aphrodite of Homer and his near contemporaries. I have posited four (or six) sources: Old European, Sumerian and Semitic, Proto-Indo-European and pre-Greek, and Minoan and Mycenaean.

These sources obviously vary in the status of the evidence they provide and in their relations to one another: some Mycenaean patterns come from Old Europe, as do Minoan ones from Egypt, and one cannot draw a sharp line between Proto-Indo-European and pre-Greek or between Sumerian and Semitic. Still, the sources are isolable to some extent, and none can be translated into any other nor can any be excluded. These considerations bear in particular on the perennially popular "Oriental theory," dealt with earlier in this chapter. This extreme position—that the origins of Aphrodite are exclusively Near Eastern—is rendered invalid not only by all the data on the PIE Dawn but by the differences in the texts between the Oriental goddesses and the Homeric (and, even more, the Sapphic) Aphrodite. More generally, the exclusion of one or more of these sources is counterproductive in that it leads one to ignore obviously relevant evidence, as Nilsson does when he claims that the only Indo-European input into the Mycenaean-Minoan religion was the *name* of Zeus.

What, then, was the differential historical and symbolic input of these sources into the eventual Aphrodite?

First in time is the archeologically attested religion and religious pantheon of the Old European civilization (7000–3500 B.C.), with its plethora of female representations, some or most of them religious in meaning. These representations are of two main types: (1) a maternal image, often associated with a child, and (2) a non-maternal figure, often birdlike or somehow symbolizing a bird goddess, and sometimes androgynous. Both female types carry on down into the Greek Neolithic, and the second of them would seem to be an antecedent for the eventual Aphrodite. At a more general level, the basic fact is the *unbroken continuity on Greek soil* from about 7000 B.C. onward of artistic and religious representations of women, representations that far exceed those of men in both their number and their variations. There was a primordial depth on Greek soil of two basic archetypes to which I return toward the end of this book: the maternal "Demeter" archetype and the Aphrodite archetype of eros. Both of these female types symbolize human and cosmic fertility and two main variants of female love: the love of a woman for a daughter and the love of a woman for a male lover.

The second major component is the "Oriental" one of, in the first instance, the goddess Inanna, the dominant divinity of the Sumerians (roughly 3000–2100 B.C.). Inanna emerges as a fully developed patroness of sensuous love and of war, prosperity, and wealth, and she has a host of minor functions. But she is never maternal, and this fact marks a sharp, categorial, cognitive break that is highly significant within the overall context of this analysis. She closely resembles the subsequent Ishtar, into whom she blends, except that the latter becomes more martial in some areas, such as northern Assyria. In the Phoenician area, the one most related to our problem, there are actually three named goddesses during the second millennium, but they become fused later into one all-inclusive figure of carnal love, war, and scores of other functions, including navigation and maternal love. All of these Near Eastern goddesses, from the Sumerian Inanna to the Phoenician Astarte, are astral. Since there unquestionably was much trade contact and cultural exchange between the Phoenicians and Greeks, both the Mycenaeans and those of Homer's time (roughly 1400–1150 and the eighth century B.C.), one can reasonably assume considerable cross-fertilization of religious imagery, and the specifics of Ishtar and Aphrodite *make this assumption virtually mandatory*. Certain aspects of the early Aphrodite become defined more clearly, for example some details of her sensuousness. An extreme position against *any* diffusion from Phoenicia or Mesopotamia seems unrealistic.

This brings us to the third component, the nearest to Aphrodite in space and time: the archeologically attested Mycenaean and Minoan religions of Crete. Minoan civilization was itself highly synthetic from its start in the third millennium, with major elements coming from Old Europe and from Egypt (Childe 1958: 19), but it soon developed a highly individual profile that made it, during the second millennium, perhaps the main center of high culture in the Mediterranean. In the religion of these creative people, goddesses were prominent, particularly a Great Mother and a Mistress of Wild Things, and some of the evidence for them, and for a "dove goddess," can be taken as contributory to the eventual Aphrodite. Women also predominate in the representations of ritual. There is considerable androgyny in the symbolism; this is evident in representations of the human form but mainly in the two key symbols, the ax and the crescent. Androgyny here probably stands for the union of opposite sexes.

Minoan civilization cannot be equated with that of Mycenae, Pylos, and other centers on the Greek mainland, but it *certainly contributed a Minoan stratum to this pre-Homeric system*. In Late Helladic times (roughly 1300–1150 B.C.) in centers such as Mycenae the Greeks achieved much of their synthesis of Old European, Minoan, Indo-European, and Phoenician constituents and created out of these diverse ingredients the essentials of the Olympian religion. Dominant in it were the "queens of heaven"—Hera, Athena, Artemis, and Aphrodite—and also many lesser female divinities, many of them attendant on or otherwise connected with Aphrodite: the Nereids, the Hours, the Graces.

THE ORIGINS OF APHRODITE—A SYNCRETIC-CYBERNETIC
MODEL

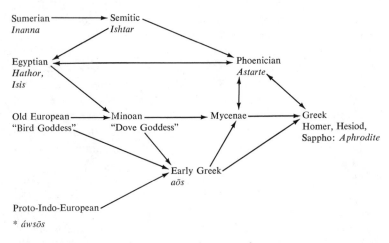

The fourth major component comes from the Proto-Indo-European culture of southern Russia and the Danubian plain that has been reconstructed for about the close of the fourth millennium. On the basis of excellent early Indic (Rig Vedic) and early Greek evidence, with considerable support from Baltic, we can reconstruct a PIE dawn goddess, *awsos,* with many specific meanings that to some degree correspond to other terms and idioms that can also be recaptured. Outstanding among these features and terms are her physical appearance, her multiple relations with other divinities, particularly the Divine Twins, and her more general signification of fertility and cosmic dualism. PIE *awsos* is probably not late (i.e., it is not limited to the "Graeco-Sanskrit level"). She is unquestionably *part of the Proto-Indo-European pantheon,* just as much as the early sky god, **dyews.* PIE *awsos* continues to evolve in pre-Greek in the latter part of the third and the first part of the second millennium, still as a goddess of dawn. As Boedeker puts it (1974: 10), "Greek epic itself is heir to a pre-Greek Indo-European poetic tradition."[14]

A residual speculation remains. While few would dispute contact and borrowing between the Phoenicians and the Mycenaeans and, later, the eighth-century Greeks, the evidence on the Sumerian Inanna and, to a lesser extent, on the early Akkadian Ishtar does raise a secondary and far more problematical issue of culture contact and diffusion, for there are many rather specific resemblances between the Sumerian Inanna and the PIE *awsos*. I grant that *awsos* is not martial and that the eroticism of Inanna is relatively carnal, but I am also struck by features that they *do* share, such as display of the body, erotic beauty, multiple kinship statuses, power over mortals and gods, and several kinds of ambiguity. The overlap in time, moreover, is almost complete between the flourishing of Sumer during the third millennium and the period of the "migrations" of the Indo-Europeans that ended with the entry of the pre-Greeks into northern Greece between 2000 and 1900 B.C. (and of the early Indics into India one or two centuries later). From the middle of the third millennium until about the middle of the second millennium B.C., early Greeks, Iranians, and Indics were often the neighbors or, briefly, conquerors of peoples in Syria and northern Sumer; I have mentioned, above, the kingdom of the (Iranian) Mitanni in northern Syria in the middle of the second millennium. These probabilities of contact make more likely some diffusion involving the early Indo-European dawn goddesses and the Sumerian Inanna and her descendants. As Kirk puts it: "Indo-Iranian mythology and religion themselves seem to have been affected by Mesopotamian ideas during the second millennium B.C., before the separation of the Indian and Iranian strands and the penetration of the Aryans into the Indian peninsula" (1975: 209). His dating of the "separation" is incorrect, but his case for Mesopotamian influences in the Rig Veda is sound.

It seems reasonable that in a relatively late phase some of the Indo-Europeans borrowed and adapted variants or at least characteristics of the Inanna or Ishtar figure. It is *just* as conceivable that the bards who sang for these Indo-European aristocracies (Meillet 1964: 382) had the more sophisticated poetry and so transmitted one of their relatively mature conceptions, that of the dawn goddess, to the pantheons of the Bronze Age agriculturalists and townsmen of Sumer and Syria. Contrary to the usual attitudes,

I *do* think that speculations of this sort are desirable—as long as they are clearly labeled as such.

There remains a theoretical point about the growth of the Aphrodite figure. In brief, at any given time a cultural or semiotic system is both breaking down and becoming internally differentiated and, on the other hand, is growing together and internally synthesizing itself. We need to think in terms of such a "homeostatic model." As a token of this model we have to assume that continuous regional variation contributed to the Aphrodites of Cyprus, Sparta, and so forth. On the other hand, some pan-Hellenic idea already existed in Mycenaean cult and literature and evolved with normal continuity through the Greek Dark Ages (1150–800 B.C.). New pan-Hellenic syntheses emerged during the eighth and seventh centuries, most notably in the hands of Homer, the most gifted exemplar of the Greek genius for religious imagery. These syntheses drew on both the general Greek and the local models: "the Korai of Cyprus, Cythera, Corinth, Eryx and many other places were felt to be one and the same and became absorbed in the great figure of Aphrodite" (Murray 1925: 88); this figure was comparable to Hermes or Apollo in complexity and greater in power and of more universal significance. Aphrodite is at once supremely Greek and also uniquely interesting in world religion and the comparative study of religion. But simultaneous with these new syntheses (and consonant with our homeostatic model) we must assume that diversification continued; a valuable index of the latter is the unusually large number of locally divergent epithets—I counted twenty in Farnell's main chapter on Aphrodite. Further conclusions about the pan-Hellenic Aphrodite and local variants will come when we know more about the psychology of mythic differentiation and "amalgamation," as Boas put it almost a century ago (1891, in Boas 1940).

3

The Meaning of Aphrodite:
A. The Texts

THE "TEXTUAL PROBLEM"

Let us shift to a different track, one that brings to a more concrete level many of the themes that have emerged from prehistory and history and sets the stage for the synchronic and cultural analysis that is to follow. I refer to the appearances of Aphrodite in the Greek texts.

These textual occurrences raise the more general issue of the role of texts in the study of myth. One great tradition, that of the classicist, the Orientalist, the philologist, gives central importance to the text and takes for granted a scrupulous attention to such matters as lexical and grammatical questions, variant editions, and the histories of the texts. In sharp contrast, the anthropological functionalist and, more recently, the sociolinguist argue that the text as such is meaningless when detached from the environments of social organization, or the practical activities and moral values of the community in which they function as a charter (Malinowski 1954: 100). In practice this means the study of where, when, how, and why myths are told and the analysis of their "functions" in allaying the fear of death, validating status differences between clans, and so forth (Kluckhohn 1942).

Field work in rural Greece, particularly among subgroups such as the Sarakatsani shepherds, would provide valuable if highly inferential insights into the values of Homeric society; by an even less direct route, the attitudes of contemporary Greek peasants toward the Virgin Mary might bear in some way on our understanding of the classical Demeter. However, the myth of Aphrodite was extirpated from Greek soil, particularly as a result of Christian ideology. More generally, the functionalist insistence on a "living context" can be carried too far, for the aesthetic-symbolic interest of some myths clearly outweighs their practical or pragmatic functions.

If the reader will grant that the mythic information in Homer's texts is worth studying even without "the myth-maker at one's elbow"—and I think it would be absurd to deny this—then a careful review of the texts and their implicit meanings becomes integral to the present inquiry, particularly since the number of passages that focus on Aphrodite is relatively small. If, moreover, the reader will grant my additional claim that the texts bear directly on our human problems today, then a review of the texts, together with a psychological commentary, becomes indispensable. On this basis, let us turn to the two main appearances of Aphrodite in Homer. We shall preface this, however, by her main appearance in Hesiod.

APHRODITE IN THE GREEK TEXTS

Hesiod's *Works and Days*

Hesiod, of Boeotian peasant background, was a near contemporary of Homer (he flourished toward the end of the eighth and the beginning of the seventh century). Although his poems about the annual cycle and the birth of the gods are of less universal interest than the *Iliad* and the *Odyssey,* the ancient Greeks unanimously grouped him with Homer as one of the geniuses of the epic style.

Near the beginning of his great poem *Works and Days,* to provide a sort of mythic context he describes how Zeus, as a punishment for Prometheus' theft of fire, orders the other gods to create a beautiful woman, "an evil in which all men shall take pleasure, embracing their own destruction" (lines 57–58). Hephaestus is to model the image out of clay, Athena to endow it with skills; Aphrodite shall cover the creature's head with golden grace and imbue her with a cruel power to stimulate the desire and longings that exhaust the body (in the sequel it is Aphrodite's representatives—the Graces, Persuasion, and the Seasons—who actually adorn her with gold and flowers). Hermes, to continue, shall put into her the "mind of a hussy, a treacherous nature" (Lattimore 1970: 67–68); another translator has "a shameless mind" (Evelyn-White 1967: 7), but the Greek is literally "dog's [i.e., bitch's] mind." He also puts in lies, wheedling words, and a wily (or deceitful) nature. This bitch-minded and seductive young thing is Pandora, who releases the myriad evils or troubles *(lugra)* that beset mankind.

Hesiod's distrust and anxiety about women may well have been typical of Greek peasants, but it was partly personal, and his concern with physical virginity differentiates him from Homer, Sappho, and other early writers. Once he warns us, "Do not let a woman, with mantled bottom, beguile you, sweetly purring her wheedling words; she is after your barn! Whosoever trusts a woman trusts deceivers" (*Works and Days* 373–75). At one point he does give a fairly warm picture of a virgin: cold wind "does not blow through the soft young skin of a young maiden who keeps her place inside the house beside her loving mother, not yet knowing the works of golden Aphrodite. Washing her smooth skin and anointing it well with oil, she lies down in an inner room within the house on a winter's day" (519–24). But in general he sees (nonvirginal) woman as threatening man's physical and ritual integrity and, to some degree, as potentially shaming and defiling. The analogy between this conception and the role of Helen and Briseis in the *Iliad* is strong indeed.

Hesiod's *Theogony*

In Homer, Aphrodite is the daughter of Dione and Zeus, but in the *Theogony* of Hesiod, who is as authoritative, the myth goes that Earth, one of the original beings, first bears Heaven, to be her equal. Later she lies with him and bears Ocean and eleven other supernaturals and, last of all, Cronus "the wily, the youngest and most terrible of her children." She also bears the Cyclopes and three one-hundred-armed sons, whom Heaven hated above all and hid in a secret part of Earth, making her groan and feel straitened. Earth made a flint sickle and asked her sons to help in punishing their father, but only Cronus took her up: "Mother, I undertake to do this deed, for I do not revere our father of evil name, for he first thought of doing shameful things." When Father Heaven came the next time, full of desire, spreading himself over the Earth, Cronus stretched forth his left hand and with the sickle in his right lopped off his father's members and cast them away. The drops of blood grew into the Erinyes, evil and punitive figures, and into the giants and the ashwood nymphs. But the members, thrown into the boisterous sea, were swept over the main for a long time, and a white foam spread around them from the immortal flesh, and in it there grew a maiden. She first came ashore at Cythera, an island off Laconia, and then at sea-girt Cyprus as an awe-inspiring and beautiful goddess, "and grass grew up beneath her shapely feet." And with her went Eros and Himeros, the geniuses of love and longing. She was honored at the assembly of the gods, and among men her portion was "maidenly whisperings and smiles and deceits, sweet delight, and love, and graciousness." So goes the Hesiodic myth.[1]

The Sixth Homeric Hymn

A second early appearance in Greek poetry is the Sixth Homeric Hymn. It was probably composed to be sung at a contest (according to Allen et al. 1936) at a date that is uncertain but probably early, that is, about the seventh century.

Revered, golden-crowned, and beautiful Aphrodite
is whom I shall sing,
whose dominion is the walled cities
of all sea-set Cyprus,
where the water force of the western wind, breathing
bore her over the waves of the much-resounding sea
in soft foam.

And the Hours in their golden diadems
received her with joy,
clothed her in ambrosial garments,
and placed a well-wrought crown, beautiful and golden,
on her immortal head
and flowers of copper and precious gold
in the pierced lobes of her ears.

They adorned her delicate neck and silver-white breasts
with necklaces
such as the golden-diademed Hours themselves wear
when they go to the lovely dance
of the gods in the house of their father.

When they had placed all this adornment
on her flesh
they led her to the immortals,
who, seeing, welcomed her
and gave her their hands;

and each of them prayed
that he might lead her home
to be his wedded wife,
marveling at the form
of the Cytherean, crowned in violets.

Hail, you of the quick-darting eyelids,
sweet-smiling,
grant that I may win this contest
and order my song,
and I will remember you in another.

I have synthesized this translation from the previous attempts by C. Boer and Hugh G. Evelyn-White, making numerous additions of my own in the process.

Homer: *Iliad* 3. 369–446

The first main appearance of Aphrodite in the *Iliad*—and this is one of the most important of our texts—occurs in Book Three, lines 369–446. In this part of the story the two armies have agreed under solemn oath to let the war be resolved through a duel between Menelaus and Paris, the two individuals around whom it all centers. Menelaus, after missing with his spear and then shattering his sword, has finally seized Paris by his horned helmet and spun him about; he is now dragging him away into the camp of the Achaeans. Paris' "soft neck" is being strangled by the "much-embroidered" strap of his own helmet (note these suggestions of effeminateness; the second adjective also occurs in Homer as an epithet of Aphrodite's girdle!). But Aphrodite "sharply perceives" this predicament, breaks the helmet strap, and, snatching up her favorite and enveloping him in a cloud of mist, she sets him down in his fragrant chamber in Troy. She then goes to Helen, who is standing with a group of Trojan women on the high wall, observing the war. Aphrodite, appearing in the guise of an old wool-comber of whom Helen had been very fond ten years ago, back in Lacedaemon, tells her that Paris is calling for her in his chamber and, "shining in his raiment and his own beauty," looks, not like a man returned from battle, but like one going to or coming from a dance (since dancing seems to have been mainly a woman's art in this culture, Paris is being contrasted with the more warlike men). Helen recognizes the beautiful neck, the voluptuous breasts, and the flashing eyes of the goddess. This is one of many places in Homer where a divine disguise is ineffectual. Here the image of the old crone, with its associations of death (and of the social status of an aged female matchmaker) is superimposed on the lush sensuousness of a young woman in a masterful concretization of the love-and-death meaning of Aphrodite. This scene, incidentally, illustrates the sophisticated double exposure or overlay technique that is not infrequent in Homer, although it has been neglected by Homerists. Here we actually have a triple exposure, since Helen herself is a "faded" (subsequent, descended) epic version of Aphrodite; obviously, Homer's sense for this was purely intuitive, that of an artist.

Helen then mocks and rebukes Aphrodite for wanting to carry

her off to other countries, where she assuredly has yet other lovers lined up for her. Aphrodite, she says, is a trick-planning person. Let *her* go and "suffer for him forever and look after him" until he makes her his wedded wife or slave girl. Helen concludes (lines 410–12), "There [to Paris' chamber] I will not go; it would be too shameful, serving his bed. All the Trojan women would mock me hereafter, me with endless sorrows in my heart *(thumos)*." This scene is remarkable for the irreverence shown to a god by a mortal, and it is reminiscent, not only of Diomedes' irreverence, but of the passage in the Gilgamesh Epic where Gilgamesh mocks Ishtar about her many lovers and their unhappy fates.

Aphrodite naturally grows angry and threatens to forsake Helen ("I will hate you as much as now I terribly love you") and also to devise "wretched hatred" between the Trojans and the Greeks. Note that she will isolate Helen in the middle, between the two sides; Homer here suggests both her interstitiality or "liminality" and the subjective nature of her danger—topics that I will explore at some length below. Helen is struck by fear and goes back to her husband, led by her spirit, Aphrodite, and enveloped in a robe (not a veil, the symbol of chastity). She is not accompanied by attendants, as would befit a chaste wife of her status.

When they enter Paris' house, the maids turn to their work and Aphrodite seats Helen, even setting a chair for her (a bit of role inversion that greatly bothered the Alexandrian scholars). Homer insists on a further contrast between the two women by using Aphrodite's standard epithet "laughter-loving" (with the *double-entendre* for which I argue in Appendix 6) while, on the other hand, calling Helen, who is a mortal, "the daughter of aegis-bearing Zeus." Just a few lines earlier he had called her the same thing right after her own allusions to Aphrodite's wanton ways. This counterpoint is given yet more depth in terms of our view that Helen herself is not only a faded Aphrodite in a diachronic sense but is also one of the main variants of Aphrodite within the synchronic system of the eighth and seventh centuries.

The bitterness of Helen's words about herself, here and elsewhere, and her hard words to Aphrodite and to Paris, plus his usage to her, all contribute nuances to the total meaning of this scene. Recall that Aphrodite had appeared to Helen disguised as a trusted old woman—the typical age and sex for a matchmaker or go-between. This is connected with something deeper that Homer is suggesting to us, namely, that, although subsequent Greek and other

European literature and art has assumed or asserted that Helen was seduced or had even gone of her own free will, all that Homer ever implies is that she was carried off by force. This scene, then, may be taken by us to *reenact the original rape of Helen* (I am indebted to J. Redfield for this point). And it brilliantly condenses and conveys the complex mental state of Helen, who, as Priam says, is *not* guilty *(aitiē)* yet who is the occasion or immediate cause of the dishonor of Menelaus and his kindred and, eventually, of the dishonor and destruction of Paris, Priam, and all of Troy. In this scene, finally, Aphrodite "projects" impulses and attitudes that create conflicts for Helen and that deepen the plot of the epic as a whole. One of these deeper suggestions is that the love goddess herself is susceptible to internal conflict when different types of the grand passion lead to mutually exclusive actions; in this scene, then, love is not simple.

Iliad 5. 297–448

Aphrodite's main epiphany in the *Iliad* comes in Book Five, lines 297–448. Her son, Aeneas, has been seriously wounded when a pointed rock propelled by Diomedes smashes the socket of his hipbone. Aphrodite rushes in and shields him with her white arms and white robe; as Homer says, she pours herself around him. Diomedes, knowing her to be without warcraft, swings his pitiless bronze and rends her wrist; the ichor flows. Aphrodite gives a shriek and lets her son fall. He is caught up in a dark mist and saved by Apollo. Diomedes calls to Aphrodite (lines 348–51):

Give way, daughter of Zeus, to war and combat at close quarters,
or is it not enough that you deceive cowardly women?
Yet, if you wander into war, why then, I guess,
You will shudder at war even when you learn of it from another.

Aphrodite is led away by Iris and borrows her brother Ares' gold-reined chariot. The two goddesses ascend to Olympus, where Aphrodite tells her mother, Dione, how she was wounded "as I was carrying my own beloved son out of the fighting." She is comforted by Dione, who tells her how several other gods have been made to suffer by mortals and that Diomedes, who was driven on by Athena anyway, will soon make a widow of his wife. Athena, sitting nearby, mocks Aphrodite: maybe she was torn by a golden pin as she prevailed upon some Achaean woman to follow after the Trojans? (an obvious allusion to the fact that Aphrodite *did* cause a woman,

Helen, to follow her and hence deserves to suffer). Zeus admonishes Aphrodite (lines 428–30):

> Not to you, my child, have been given the works of war;
> you, rather, should attend to the charming works of marriage.
> All *those* things are the concern of Athena and fleet Ares.

Meanwhile, back at the front, Diomedes finally falls back after being repulsed three times by Apollo as he tries to break through and attack Aeneas. Apollo then spirits Aeneas away to a temple, where he is healed by Artemis and her mother, Leto.[2]

This last passage has aroused widely divergent reactions. One is that the wounding of Aphrodite is "light-hearted" and "humorous," since she was "just nicked" and then actually dropped her son; some commentators even call her "ludicrous." Another, closely related, set of reactions is that this passage illustrates the notion that Homer's gods serve to provide comic relief (Calhoun 1937: 18–19). Yet another interpretation is that this is "a last gurgle" of the warlike Ishtar, from whom Aphrodite allegedly evolved, and is also evidence of her maternal feelings (which are also clear in the Fifth Homeric Hymn, to be discussed below).

Yet another interpretation, to which I subscribe, is suggested by the fact that in Homer the gods mock and laugh at each other, whereas a human never laughs at an immortal. Here, in Book Five of the *Iliad,* the gods mock Aphrodite, and in Book Eight of the *Odyssey* and the Fifth Homeric Hymn, they try to humiliate her in order to mock her. I think this should be taken, not at face value, but as further documentation of the deeper fact that Aphrodite is the most potent goddess. The author of the hymn asserts both that she is the most potent and that that is why Zeus wants to humiliate her. Such symbolic role inversion is closely paralleled by what we know about the rituals of Demeter (of which more below).

Odyssey 8. 266–369

In the *Odyssey* Aphrodite's main appearance is in Book Eight, in a lay sung by the bard Demodocus (lines 266–369). He tells how Aphrodite first "mingled in love" with Ares, who gave her many gifts, until the Sun spied her and reported to her husband, whose bed and wedlock she had shamed and defiled. Hephaestus angrily fashions bonds that are unbreakable, "not to be loosened," yet are fine as a spider's thread, so that not even a god can see them. He spreads a snare with them, hanging them from the bedposts and the roofbeam, and makes as if to depart for Lemnos, his favorite territory. Ares has been watching for this departure and enters the house, eager for the love of the fair-crowned one, with whom he quickly comes to terms.

Clasping her hand, he says, "Come, love, let us to bed and make love, couched together, for Hephaestus is no longer at home but seems to have gone away to Lemnos to visit the Sintians of savage speech." And a welcome thing it seems to her to lie with him. As they lie down, however, the wondrous snare immobilizes them. Hephaestus, alerted by the Sun, returns. Seized by wild anger at the sight, he cries out terribly to the gods. He complains that his parents made Ares handsome and nimble but him lame and misshapen. His parents are to blame, and now Aphrodite has dishonored him forever. He adds that, while the two lovers may not want to lie there in perpetuity, the bonds will hold them until her father gives back the bride-price that he had paid for the "bitch-eyed maiden; for his daughter is fair but does not restrain her passion." This interesting point brings the whole affair down to the mortal level, with the gods interacting in terms of a human social order.

The gods then gather at the threshhold of the bronze house, but the goddesses remain away "because of shame" *(aidōs)*. Aphrodite's behavior would scandalize the variously asexual queens, in part because it breaks the taboo against being seen *in flagrante delicto*. Also implied, I think, is the popular social context of Homer's audiences: in the Greek village and the regional groupings of the aristocracy such fornication would be forbidden to women—as would their laughing about it with men in public (I am indebted to William Wyatt for this point). Probably significant is the fact that the gods openly mock Ares and Hephaestus much more than Aphrodite. I find this ambiguous: it may symbolize her shame, or her freedom from it.

The male gods laugh "unquenchably" at Hephaestus' craft but not, be it noted, at his having been cuckolded. Nor is anyone bothered that the three main figures are half-siblings. They comment that the slow and lame has caught the swiftest and concur that Ares will have to pay the *moichagria,* the fine, or *moichos,* that is due from an adulterer. There follows an amusing exchange in which Hermes, in response to a question by Apollo, says that he would gladly lie forever beside the golden Aphrodite, even if he were bound with three times as many toils and if all the gods and goddesses were looking on. But Poseidon does not laugh with the others and requests the release of Ares, promising to pay the bride-price if he runs away: "I myself will pay you this" (using the verb *tinō* that is closely related in sound and meaning to the verb for [dis]honor, *atimazō*, with which Hephaestus began the scene). So the bonds are loosened. Ares goes off to Thrace and the smile-loving Aphrodite back to Cyprus, to Paphos, where the Graces wash and anoint her and dress her in lovely raiment. The affair ends, and the transition is indeed abrupt; as Calhoun observes (1937: 11), "in three lines we pass from a scene that might have shocked the good wife of Bath [hardly: Friedrich] to the august serenity of the earth's most potent goddess."

The scene in Book Eight of the *Odyssey* used to upset the ancient commentators, some of whom rejected the entire passage on moral grounds. Many scholars during the last part of the nineteenth and the first half of this century described it as "scandalous, ridiculous, indecent, immoral," and what not, and this sort of reaction is far from dead among younger scholars today (I have heard or read them saying "ridiculous, ludicrous"). Others feel that it exemplifies a special style within the *Odyssey* as a whole: "the love affair of Ares and Aphrodite in the eighth Odyssey [represents] sophisticated Ionian developments belonging to the latest stages of the true oral tradition" (Kirk 1975: 174). Whatever the worth of these considerations, *Odyssey* 8. 266–369 raises serious questions about the symbolism of the relation between Aphrodite and Hephaestus.

First, Aphrodite differs from the other queens of heaven in the frequent description of her ornaments, which are mainly of gold. The goddess of love is married to the smith of the gods, who can fashion the golden ornaments in which she delights (although it is not clear that he makes all of them). This relatively superficial side of their relationship must be added to the deeper symbolism of cuckoldry and castration.

Hephaestus himself suggests profound contradictions. He is unloved by his mother (he was lamed by her when she threw him from Olympus), is cuckolded by Aphrodite, and is somehow generally despised (he provokes the gods' "unquenchable laughter"); but to these obvious variations on the themes of impotence and castration must be counterposed his marvelous skill and physical power (as Ernestine Friedl pointed out to me, smiths in early society are normally strong, virile men who, because of some accident, cannot hunt, plow, and so forth). And Hephaestus' smithy suggests a symbolism that only the most inhibited imagination could deny: his bellows as testicles, his hammer as a phallus, the gold he works as semen, and the fire of his great forge as the lust of sex (a symbolism found in many parts of the world, for example among the Bambara of Africa).

The ambiguities of Hephaestus are part of the ambiguities in his relation to Aphrodite. In the major myths, each has only one parent, and of the opposite sex. This creates the chiasmus

The marriage of Aphrodite and Hephaestus is itself an inversion of the usual union between a sky god and an earth goddess. Here a god who has been cast down from above and who works in the gloom with a forge is wed to a goddess who emerges from below and lives above in the sunlight, in the company of high-flying birds (this is paralleled by the Old Norse myths of love between a blacksmith and a bird goddess). Moreover, it is Aphrodite who is dominant. Another inversion is manifest in the way Hephaestus is victimized by Aphrodite in one of her more destructive roles; this reminds us, by a simple commutation, of his positive role in fashioning another variant on the Aphrodite theme: Pandora, the source of all evils and diseases. These many relations illustrate my general position on the ambiguity of practically all symbolism in myth.

The Fifth Homeric Hymn

Our next main source is the Fifth Homeric Hymn, to Aphrodite (the germ of which already occurs in *Iliad* 2. 819–21). The poem has been compared by many to the lay of Demodocus in the *Odyssey,* with the difference that here "her passion has been imposed on her by Zeus. Her position is not unlike that of the epic Helen. . . . The adventure is treated with frankness but without loss of dignity" (Allen et al. 1936: 349). To this I would agree; and to the idea that she feels shame at this point I would add that the same is true of Book Eight of the *Odyssey* (as noted above).

Various scholars and commentators have complained about the length of this hymn or of its poetics. It strikes me, on the contrary, as brilliant and unitary, composed in a sensuous language that contains an unusual amount of sound texture, including unusual frequencies of internal rhyme and resonance. As the commentators conclude, "the [internal] unity of the hymn is so obvious that it has suffered comparatively little from criticism" (e.g., of the Analytical sort). Most germane to our project is the fact that the poem shares much with the hymn to Demeter and is closer to it in language than to any other, just as both are closer to the *Odyssey* than to the other Homeric Hymns. It "can hardly be dated later than 700 B.C.," that is, it is essentially contemporary with Homer, and the author may have been Aeolian, specifically Lesbian (Allen et al. 1936: 349–51). My own hypothesis is that it was composed by an innovative Lesbian poet who synthesized the formal epic style (dactylic hexameter, etc.) with certain elements of a local lyric style, possibly under the influence of another Greek or contiguous Indo-European lyric or choral tradition. I should note, on the other hand, that the early date just mentioned contrasts with the fact that certain features impress some scholars and translators as Hellenistic.[3]

The hymn begins with a description of the power of Aphrodite over the world of animals, mortals, and the gods. Only the three virgins, Artemis, Athena, and Hestia, are immune to her. She even causes Zeus to mingle in love with mortal women. To counter her power to do this (and to mock her victim after the fact), Zeus casts a "sweet desire" into Aphrodite to make her join with a mortal, the "godlike Anchises," of whom she then becomes terribly enamored. But first she repairs to her sanctuary in Cyprus to be washed and anointed with oil and perfumed with ambrosia and dressed and decorated with gold by the Graces. She then flies to Mount Ida, near Troy, a great center for the worship of Aphrodite; there were many shrines on its rocky slopes. Animals fawn on her, but she casts a love spell and they go off, playing in pairs (this scene seems to echo the scene with Circe in the *Odyssey*). She finds Anchises alone, playing thrillingly on his lyre. (The shepherd's hut and the rest are part of the liminal or marginal locale, outside the usual realm of houses and fields, where unusual events can be expected.) Aphrodite stands before him "in the form and size of a young virgin" in a robe that was "brighter than a fire-flash, and she had on spiral ringlets, and bright ornaments, and necklaces around her delicate neck that were very beautiful and lovely and golden and finely wrought, shining like the moon on her delicate breasts, and astonishing." Love gripped Anchises, who said that she must be a goddess or one of the Graces or a mountain nymph, that he would build her a temple, and that she should in turn make his progeny flourish and his age great. (His response clearly parallels that of Odysseus when he meets Nausicaa—whom he surely did not regard as a goddess—and both responses would seem to illustrate the code of courtship and amatory flattery.) Aphrodite answers that she is the daughter of the king of nearby Phrygia, speaks Trojan because of her Trojan nurse, and has been caught up from her dancing round and whisked away to Mount Ida by Hermes, who has told her she would be Anchises' lawful wife, bearing him "splendid babies." She begs to be presented to his family "as a virgin (unbroken) and unexperienced in love," and that her own family be informed, so that the proper dowry of gold and garments can be provided, as well as a desirable wedding feast. She throws "sweet desire" into Anchises. (Note that the idiom here is the same one used of Zeus, with its implication of acting on an object, as contrasted with the usual Aphrodite action of entering into someone and so arousing passion within them.) Anchises is seized by love and declares that nothing can stop them from making love now, even if they have to go to Hades as a result. Aphrodite follows, her eyes lowered, to Anchises' couch of bear and lion skins, and "first he took the bright ornaments from her body, brooches and spiral ringlets and flower-like necklaces. He loosened her beautiful clothes and her girdle and put them on a silver chair . . . and slept, a mortal, with an immortal goddess, not knowing what he did." He eventually falls asleep. Awakened in the late afternoon by Aphrodite, he finds her before him in undisguised and divine beauty, "and her head touched the well-hewn rooftree. Beauty shone from her cheeks." Anchises is terrified and, turning away, asks that he not be made impotent. She reassures him and tells the story of Ganymede, who was granted immortality because of his beauty; but she tells also of Dawn, who forgot to request youth for her lover, Tithonus, along with eternal life. (Here Aphrodite explicitly parallels herself to the figure who, as I argued above, is certainly her close cognate in the origins of Greek myth.) "I would not want you to be among the immortals like that, and live forever." Yet there is no suggestion—as there would be if another queen of heaven were involved—of her slaying Anchises for having slept with her, or of having him slain, or of his being slain through the jealousy of another divinity. Her main concern is for their child, whom she promises to have brought up well by the ambrosia-eating nymphs. (The model of being raised by the nymphs may be of Phrygian origin.) This son of theirs, the future Aeneas, will be returned in his fifth year and will rule among the Trojans. But her second and almost equal concern is about having slept with a mortal; she fears mockery from her fellow Olympians. Thus she enjoins Anchises to declare to all that the child's mother was a "flower-like nymph," for otherwise he will be struck down by one of Zeus's thunderbolts. (There is a special irony here, since it was Zeus who got her involved with Anchises in the first place and would thus be well aware of her visit and its outcome.)

Some scholars with a psychoanalytic orientation have cited this passage as evidence of an overdeveloped castration complex or some more diffuse sense of male inadequacy in ancient Greece. To this I would counter that Anchises' reaction is normal and predictable in light of the patterns and attitudes of almost all cultures: to wake up from a deep sleep after having made love and find the woman transformed into a goddess, standing with her head to the ceiling and her eyes flashing like fire or gold, should awaken primeval fears in any man, and also culturally specific fears of death, blinding, castration, and the like. So this vague generalization is off the mark. In other contexts, however, the variants or descendants of Aphrodite do explicitly threaten castration. In the *Odyssey,* for example, Circe would have "unmanned" Odysseus but for the warning and the talisman of Hermes (*Od.* 10. 301, 341). This and other specific myths, many of them already referred to above, symbolize anxieties of the Greek male about castration by a sexually aggressive woman.

A second mythic input has been suggested by Rose. The scene of the Fifth Hymn is set in the Troad, near Phrygia (both in what is now northwestern Turkey), and Aphrodite herself claims to be Phrygian. This Phrygia was a great kingdom, centered on Gordium, that flourished between 800 and 600 B.C., during which time the hymn was composed. A principal myth of the area, centered in the Celtic region of Galatia, involved the following sequence: an androgynous figure castrates itself, an almond tree arises from the genitals, a goddess Nana eats one of the almonds, is fertilized, and gives birth to Attis, who grows into a handsome Adonis-type figure; he has an affair with Cybele, a Great Goddess, who combines maternal and sensuous components, but he then castrates himself beneath a pine tree, and his blood, staining the violet, gives it its color. The Attis cult was brought to Rome in 204 B.C. and also spread through Syria. The priests, or Galli, were all men who had emasculated themselves during a frenzy in the annual festivals of Cybele. In this important myth of Phrygia, then, the theme of castration is salient, and some influence of this myth on Aphrodite, and possibly on the Aeolic author(ess) of Hymn Five, may be postulated.

APHRODITE IN LATER TIMES

These texts—the passages from Hesiod's *Works and Days* and his *Theogony,* the two Homeric Hymns to Aphrodite, and the three passages from Homer—constitute the bulk of our evidence from the early period, aside from Sappho and a number of brief, scattered references (many of which will be cited in later discussion). It seems reasonable to assume that the passages in Homer and Hesiod draw upon a significant portion of the traditions that had been evolving since before Mycenaean times, although by no means all of them.

The cultural-semantic analysis in the next chapter sometimes draws on but does not heavily or systematically take into account the rich Attic and Hellenistic information—for example, Aphrodite's early affair with a cockle shell, her absorption of the Ariadne cult, the Callipygia ("beautiful buttocks") image, her role as a patroness of ordinary prostitutes, and the entire Hermaphrodite complex.

Certainly the most important of these post-Homeric components is Adonis. In most variants of the myth, his mother, because of her neglect of Aphrodite, is compelled by the latter's curse to conceive an incestuous passion for her own father, the king of Assyria (or Cyprus). She manages to make love with him for nine nights during the feast of the Thesmophoria (which emphasizes mother-daughter ties) but is discovered and pursued by her outraged partner until she is transmuted into a myrrh tree, from which, nine months later, Adonis emerges. He is loved by Aphrodite and entrusted to Persephone (queen of the underworld), who then refuses to give him back. Zeus eventually resolves the conflict by decreeing that Adonis shall live above ground a third of the year, below it a second third, and wherever he will for the remainder (naturally, this means eight months with Aphrodite). Later he is killed while hunting, either by Artemis, who is angry, or by a jealous Ares. His blood colors the anemone, whereas Aphrodite's blood, from a cut sustained while running to his aid, reddens the rose.

Recently Detienne has greatly enriched classical and anthropological studies by a thoroughgoing structuralist analysis of the myths of Adonis and, more comprehensively, of what he calls "the mythology of perfume" (mainly as it flourished after the fifth century

in Greece and Rome). He has sorted out and explicated the constituent symbolic systems: the perfumes of Arabia; the key birds,
such as the vulture, the wryneck (*iunx*), the eagle, and the "super-
eagle," the phoenix; the role of perfume, incense, and so forth in
joining gods and men, the high and the low, the near and the far,
sun and earth; and the related myths of Myrrh, Minta (the concubine of Hades), and Phaon (the boatman who attracted Sappho).
He has analyzed the symbolism of the festivals of "the gardens of
Adonis," staged mainly during the dog days of July on the roofs of
courtesans' houses, where, in shallow pots, the plants flourished
and died in a week, and has opposed this to the complementary
structures of Demeter, Eleusis, the Thesmophoriae, the Lemnian
women, and others. His interpretation as a whole is based on the
categorical opposition between (1) wet, rotten, cool, and low as
against (2) dry, perfumed, hot, and high. Equally central is the
motif of Adonis as sexually "overpowerful" but not productive or
procreative. I must limit myself here to a list of some ideas that
may suggest the fascination of these later systems and Detienne's
lucid treatment of them. However, I will reintroduce some of the
elements at a crucial place in chapter 9.

Adonis' annual comings and goings obviously symbolize the sea-
sonal vegetative cycle, and in many parts of the eastern Mediterranean his death was mourned annually in city-wide rites; this was
the explicit view, not only of Frazer, but of many of "the natives."
Most scholars and, again, many ancient authors accept the (fairly
unquestionable) parallelism between Adonis and Aphrodite, Osiris
and Isis of Egypt, Astarte and Tammuz of the Semites, and, finally,
the Sumerian Inanna and Dumuzi. Not only do we have a regional
structure of great geographical extent and time depth, but the Greek
variant specifically resembles that of the Sumerians, as in the detail
that Adonis died in a field of lettuce.

By the most widely accepted chronology (shared, for example,
by Wilamowitz and Frazer), the myth and rites of Adonis spread
to the Greeks after the middle of the seventh century—first to
Cyprus, then to other centers influenced by the Phoenicians, and
eventually to the whole Greek world. Yet it seems incredible to me
that many Greeks of the eighth century and even much earlier (e.g.,
during the Mycenaean-Sidonian interaction) would have been
totally ignorant of this generally eastern Mediterranean and Near
Eastern mythology. The striking absence of Adonis from Homer
and Hesiod surely reflects, not a total or even general Greek igno-
rance, but an ideologically, religiously motivated omission.

The temporal limits defined above are not intended to deny the great value of the historical study of the Aphrodite image of later times. Her cult flourished in the Roman world, and Venus-type figures continued through the Middle Ages, with many ancillary variations, such as the *incubus-succubus* one. And there are echoes in James Joyce's Molly Bloom and many other works of this century.

The imagery and cult of Aphrodite and Hermaphrodite were prominent in the Attic and Hellenistic periods, but under Christianity, and above all Byzantine Orthodoxy, she was purged from Greek soil. Studies of local cults and of stories and shrines of the nineteenth and twentieth centuries have revealed numerous survivals of the usual sort, Apollo being translated into Elijah, Hermes into Michael, and so forth. But almost no trace has been left of Aphrodite. Most writers would probably concur that "Aphrodite, not styled by her name but as 'the Mother of Eros,' has had only a vague and shadowy existence in Christian times, and now she has vanished" (Fermor 1958: 182). The reliable Seltman, however, reports a real exception in the place where we would most expect it: Cyprus, where "she still lives on, at least in name. In more than one Cypriot village church the Paphian has been merged in the Virgin Mary, who is supplicated there under the title of Panghia Aphroditessa" (1956: 99).

4

The Meaning of Aphrodite:
B. The Structure

This second of my two chapters titled "The Meaning of Aphrodite" rests on the assumption that myth has a cognitive and semantic organization rooted in the life of the emotions and that this organization and its roots can to some extent be dealt with in terms of complex dimensions that interlock along many planes and angles.

I present below a systematic comparison that I think reflects the distinctively Greek mythic breakup of "the feminine" into contrasting features and functions. Of course this breakup is only implicit in the texts, and what I have done is to infer and make explicit the contrasts between Aphrodite and the three other queens of heaven: Hera, Athena, and Artemis. My contention is that the four goddesses make a set that can be well defined by eighteen semantic dimensions or features, such as "locality," "martiality," and "subjectivity."

In substantive content none of the dimensions is actually specific or unique to the queens of heaven. Take, for example, the dimension "locality"; other things in the Greek universe obviously were local, and others, to take a second dimension, were associated with birds. But all the dimensions in question are weighted in a special way when they enter into a definition of the queens of heaven; for example, the virginity or nonvirginity of these goddesses differs qualitatively from the same feature among humans. The dimensions not only define the queenly set uniquely, as I will show below, but lead to a characterization of each of them that is intuitively adequate.

"Intuitively adequate" in at least two senses. First, the structure that I have inferred contains (although it goes beyond) approximately the same information to be found in the standard inventories and humanistic essays, among which I have found the following particularly helpful: the synthetic works of Kerényi, Otto, and Rose and the contributions to the Pauly-Wissowa encyclopedia and the *Oxford Classical Dictionary*. I do not, however, claim to fully represent or agree with any of them.

Second, the eighteen basic dimensions to be set forth probably correspond to the knowledge or "feel" for Aphrodite in the mind of the eighth- and seventh-century Greek appreciator of Homer. I do not mean that they correspond in terms of analytic abstractions and prehistoric data, of course; but such an idealized hearer, when presented with the symbol "Aphrodite," would surely know its main associations with Cythera, apples, and so forth. The oral literature of the early Greek poets could not have been understood without such knowledge.

The "naturalness" of my reconstructed meanings can be brought home by a reduced or simplified statement. In brief, Aphrodite's place is islands and mountains; she is associated with fruits and flowers, such as apples and roses, and with birds, such as the swan; she is the most golden and the most beautiful of the goddesses and the one most connected with the sun and sunlight, but she is not connected to the moon; according to one story she was born from water, according to another, from Zeus and Dione; she patronizes love within marriage and outside marriage, and either emotional bond can cause much trouble; she is friendly, nearby, mobile, erotic, and sometimes intimate with gods or mortals; she was never a virgin; she is attended by the Graces, the Seasons, and other nymphs; she is wily and guileful and wise about love and combines wild animal desire with artfulness and cultivation; she sometimes helps in war but is not warlike; she controls human and animal fertility and causes states of mind, such as longing and jealousy. Shortly after Homer, Venus (again) becomes her star. I hope the reader will keep this simple set in the back of his or her mind while going through the sometimes complex analysis below.

DIMENSION 1: LOCATION (ISLANDS AND MOUNTAIN PEAKS)

In the first place, all the queens, while pan-Hellenic, are also intensely localized through their association with particular places, as Athena was with Athens and Hera was with the Argolid and the island of Samos. Artemis' centers were also two. The island of Delos, her birthplace, was hard and rocky (which seems congruous with certain features of her personality). Her second main center was Ephesus, in what is now western Turkey (her temple was one of the Seven Wonders of the World).

Similarly, the cult of Aphrodite, as noted in my introduction, was spread from Sicily to Asia Minor (e.g., Mount Ida), and from Thebes to Sicyon and Laconia. Her cult was located in two kinds of places. Foremost were the *islands:* Cythera, where she first came ashore, followed by Cyprus, her permanent abode, and also Crete, an early center of her worship. The variants of Aphrodite are also generally insular: Circe, Calypso, Penelope.[1]

Islands are interstitial between land and water. I would infer that Aphrodite's insularity symbolized her liminality (a concept to which I have already referred). Her islands are not compared to the star Venus in my texts, but the metaphor is obvious and is used in later Greek and other (e.g., Persian) poetic systems. Her role in cult as a goddess of water and navigation (Farnell 1897: 636) certainly derived in part from Asherah's patronage of sailors and navigation among the Phoenicians. Insularity, on the other hand, is not evident in Aphrodite's Indo-European, Sumerian, or Semitic antecedents.

Aphrodite's second type of locus, as I have already noted, was *mountains,* notably Mount Ida, the Acrocorinth at Corinth, and Mount Eryx in Sicily. These centers of her cult were often located so as to emphasize wild nature and horn-shaped crags. Speaking of the one at Tyndaris, Scully writes, "The scale of the view thus becomes strange and giddy; the high, solid rock of the temple, the constantly shifting ebb and flow below. Once again it would appear to have been the unexpected violence of contrasting states of being juxtaposed which caused the site to be seen by the Greeks as expressive of a Helen-Aphrodite" (1962: 97). (I shall later discuss the mountain site as a symbol of liminality.) Historically, of course, the early Greek preference for such places may reflect Phoenician (and other Semitic) customs regarding "sacred mountains" (see Gordon 1966: 20), although there are also Indo-European (e.g., Germanic) parallels. We must also consider that the island and mountain symbols, although they came to overlap, have different origins and significantly different meanings.

DIMENSION 2: FRUITS AND FLOWERS

A second feature, concrete but indispensable, is that of *fruits* and *flowers.* Neither Artemis nor Athena seems very involved with these, although Athena does create the olive tree. In the Homeric Hymn to Demeter both fruits and flowers are associated with Persephone and her bevy of nymphs and nereids who are gathering crocuses, hyacinths, and other flowers, but this does not make these goddesses essentially floral. In the same vein, Hera's seduction of Zeus on a bed of flowers (*Il.* 14. 348–49) is a feature of the erotic setting rather than a personal attribute. On the other hand, it is true that Hera is often worshiped with flowers in early cult and that she is occasionally and ambivalently associated with the pomegranate (a fertility symbol here, presumably).

As contrasted with the first three queens, Aphrodite is diagnostically floral, even in Homer; for example, she uses rose-sweet, ambrosial oils to protect Hector's body from disfigurement at the hands of Achilles (*Il.* 23. 185–87). A somewhat later poet, Stasinus of Cyprus, author of the *Cyprian Lays* of the seventh century, wrote, "She put on the garments which the Graces and the Seasons had made for her and had dyed in spring flowers such as the Seasons bear, in crocus and hyacinth and the bloom of the rose, in beautiful flowers and sweet nectar, the ambrosial calyces, the flowers of the narcissus and the lily. In such fragrant garments is Aphrodite clothed at all seasons" (Evelyn-White 1967: 499). In yet other, later texts she is "celebrated as the lady of spring blossoms, especially roses in bloom" (Otto 1954: 94–95). Other, definitely aphrodisiac flowers and fruits are the myrtle, lily, poppy, pomegranate, and apple (or quince). In Attic and, even more, in Hellenistic times we see a shift from the more "natural" beauty and aroma of flowers to aromatic herbs and (imported) perfumes; the scent of myrrh, cinnamon, fennel, and the like become quintessential to this more urban and artificial goddess (Detienne 1972). In plastic art (but not in Homer) she is almost stereotypically represented holding a lily. Fruits and flowers work at diverse levels: fruit suggests progeny, flowers the generative organs, and both suggest sweetness, fragrance, bright colors, and eros and procreation in general.

Aphrodite's fruits and flowers also have widespread historical and comparative implications. The apple was the main symbol of the Baltic Sun Maiden, the pomegranate and lily of the Ishtars, and the rose of the Indo-European Dawn. Fruits and flowers also link Aphrodite, the goddess of sensuous love, with Demeter, the goddess of maternal love. The poppy is shared by them, just as the pomegranate is shared by Aphrodite and Persephone (see below). And the "fruits" of Aphrodite parallel the cultivated grains of Demeter (the Greek *karpos* is used for both). Two great classes of flora are paired with two aspects of love in woman.

DIMENSION 3: BIRDS

A third concrete feature is that of *birds* (or animals). Artemis is
linked with the quail, a ground fowl that has always been a favorite
target for hunters, but this association is, it must be admitted, relatively minor compared to her relation with many animals—the hare,
stag, wolf, boar, lion, and, above all, bear and deer. Hera is associated in post-Homeric texts with the cuckoo, a harbinger of rain;
Zeus, for example, first arouses her feelings by taking the form of
a cuckoo, then ravishes her. There may be a parallelism between
Hera's ambiguous maternity and the fact that cuckoos lay their eggs
in other birds' nests.

Athena is more strongly ornithic, not only through her owl but
also the heron, sparrow, vulture, and sea eagle; consonant with her
character, two of these are predatory. In Book Ten of the *Iliad*
(lines 271–82) she sends forth a heron to call to Odysseus and
Diomedes. At times she turns herself into a bird at the close of a
conversation in which she has been disguised; in the Odyssey
(3. 370) she transforms herself into a sea eagle after talking with
Telemachus.

Most people have assumed that the term mediating between
Athena and the owl is wisdom, but the more likely connection is
simply one of locale; as Nilsson has pointed out, the little owls in
question nest in the Acropolis of Athens and the rocky slopes nearby. It is often true that the relation between a goddess's trait and
an ornithic or other natural feature is often slippery or secondary.
Is the bird (or other creature) a symbol because of the given trait,
or was the pairing made on other grounds and the feature, such as
wisdom, then set up by a sort of folk analysis? In the present case
(if Nilsson is right) we have a beautiful example of a part-whole
(metonymic) relation—the owl as part of the Acropolis—evolving
into a fixed or conventional metaphorical one, with the owl and
Athena sharing the component of wisdom. Often, and possibly in
this case, a symbol is simultaneously metonymic and metaphoric.

Aphrodite is as ornithic as Athena. She is often paired with the
dove, which appears on her head, at her elbows, or in her hand. The
pattern may stem from the Semitic Ishtars; it was well established by
Mycenaean times, is mentioned in Homer, and becomes ubiquitous
in Attic and Hellenistic representations. In these various sources the
dove may be taken to connote peace, affection, and sensitivity,
partly because the distinctive behavior of these birds suggests ob-

vious human parallels that have been drawn by individuals and societies of very different backgrounds. In other words, certain obvious features of a goddess of love are paired with the equally obvious billing and cooing of the dove in an excellent case of natural symbolism, a case of the sort that flies in the face of those who argue that mythic imagery never has direct relations to "the real world."

Aphrodite is also shown with, or even borne by, waterfowl: the duck, swan, or goose. A significant minority of her representations in the Louvre includes one or more of these birds. Of them, the goose and swan fly high and so, like the eagle, are associated with the high realm of Olympus. Pindar, in the *Fourth Pythian,* says that Aphrodite "sent down from Olympus the bright wryneck . . . the passionate bird." This wryneck is central in the later mythology of perfume and Adonis: "the wryneck has only one function: to unite the lover with his mistress or the mistress with her lover" (Detienne 1972: 162). Obviously, more study is needed of the Greek view of geese and swans as erotic (and also of the Greek view of beautiful courtesans as toads). And the same holds for the bird of Aphrodite that is not aquatic: in Sappho her chariot is drawn by sparrows ("sparrows were notorious for their wantonness and fecundity," and their flesh and eggs were eaten for aphrodisiac effects [Page 1955: 7–8]; perhaps related is *Iliad* 2. 311).

None of Aphrodite's ornithomorphs is predatory. Her ducks, geese, and swans lack Sumero-Semitic antecedents and probably derive in part from the Old European water-bird goddesses described above and from the swan symbolism of the early Indo-Europeans. Her swans appear to be cognate with those of the Rig Veda and the early Slavic and Germanic peoples and with "the wealth of swans" in early Celtic myth; swans with chains of gold or silver about their necks are also important in early Old Irish literature as a form taken by goddesses (Ross 1967: 236; see also note 14 to chapter 2 on the early Irish Morrigan figures). On the other hand, as already noted, swan maidens are very widespread in the myths of the world outside Europe; indeed, goddesses tend to have ornithomorphs.

DIMENSION 4: GOLDENNESS

Fourth, all the queens are in some way golden. Demeter is typically "of the golden sword" (i.e., ear of grain). Hera is golden-sandaled and golden-throned (the latter epithet is also used of Dawn). Arte-

mis, although primarily associated with silver and the moon, is
golden-reined, golden-bowed, golden-throned, and with golden arrows. Even Athena, the least golden of the queens, sometimes has
golden sandals (e.g., in Book One of the *Odyssey*). But in all these
cases the word "gold" occurs in a compound, as Boedeker has also
noted (1974: 22).

Of the queens, only Aphrodite is intrinsically golden. She is the
most golden, and "golden" is her most frequent epithet. The two
adjectives *chruseos* and *chruseios* are used of her alone, and often so:
they are *her* epithets (Calhoun 1937: 23). Since the second of
them is otherwise normally used for the metal or something studded
with it, the transfer to Aphrodite has very special connotations. She
is only rarely associated with other metals or even colors (in Pindar's
Ninth Pythian, for example, she has "silver feet").

Gold is a master symbol in Homer. Its centrality in many passages
(e.g., the gold of Egypt in the Shield of Achilles) reflects strong
feelings about the actual metal and the objects of goldsmithing;
these are reflected too in Pindar's famous "but gold, like a gleaming
fire / by night, outshines all pride of wealth beside" *(First Olympian)*. Such feelings about gold go back to the gold-oriented Mycenaeans and were certainly shared in the contemporary imperial
centers of Egypt, Babylon, and Anatolia and by the gold-trading
and gold-working Phoenicians (*chrus-* is actually a Semitic root).
Ultimately the auric symbolism is shared by the Sumerian Inanna
and her golden ornaments and by the yellow, tawny, and golden
dawn goddess of the Proto-Indo-Europeans; in this latter case it is
connected with the worship of sun and fire. Even as late as Homer
there is a clear and obvious link between the quintessential goldenness of Aphrodite and her solar character.

Aphrodite's goldenness has other, less metallic meanings. By what
seems to be an ancient pattern, "golden" is associated with "beautiful" in a way that may be unfamiliar to some readers. This closeness
of meaning has already been suggested by some of the Greek data
cited above and is apparent in many passages in which Aphrodite
adorns herself or is so adorned (for example, in the passage of the
Homeric Hymn in which Anchises wonders at the splendor of her
ornaments). The Greek gold/beauty association is strongly paralleled in Russian, where the word for "beautiful" consists of the word
for "red" plus an intensifying prefix *(pre-krasnyi)* and the connection between the two meanings is felt to this day. In Chinese and
the Tarascan Indian language there is a similar link between beauty

and red, or (blue-)green. In other words, in some systems one or two colors are felt to be particularly beautiful.[2]

The purely chromatic meaning remains to be established. "Gold" was probably yellow or reddish-yellow in some contexts and at this level is probably akin to the tawny color of Dawn in Indic myth. But Gladstone argued that goldenness "always belongs to light rather than color" (1858: 482); if so, this would, incidentally, relate it to the solar-astral feature. At a deeper level there is an association between gold, honey, speech, and sexual fluids, as we find in Slavic (especially gold/honey) and Indic (gold/semen). As for gold/speech, the entire phrase "speech sweeter than honey" is, like that for "undying fame (glory, reputation)," one of the relatively complex syntactic units that we can reconstruct with complete confidence for Proto-Indo-European because of point-for-point correspondences between the strings of words in Greek, Celtic (Old Irish), Anatolian, and yet other languages (see Schmidt 1967 for a rigorous treatment of these and other syntagmata). Gold and its semantic cognates in speech, honey, and semen therefore symbolize the yet deeper Aphrodite values of procreation, verbal creation, and so forth. There are more strands to this skein, but I think that what I have drawn out so far should suggest the richness and complexity of the supposedly "simple" epithet "golden."

DIMENSION 5: SUN, MOON, AND STARS

A fifth dimension consists of the linked features of the *sun* and *moon* and the *stars*. Artemis and Hera are strongly lunar, the former typically moving in the moonlit midnight air, the latter often depicted with a lunar crescent. Their symbolism has rich antecedents in Old European civilization, and there is of course the more general psychological association between the moon and menstruation, virginity, and the female principle in general. Athena, although sometimes depicted with the moon, is, like Apollo, a creature of clarity and open sunlight.

It is Aphrodite who more than any other goddess is unambiguously solar in many passages, and this solarity is naturally connected with her goldenness. Note that she seduces Anchises by daylight. There is a deep-lying opposition or contrast between her sunlit sexuality and Artemis' furtive and moonlit anxiety and hostility as regards carnal love. On the historical side, the fact that Aphrodite is the most solar and the least lunar of the goddesses reflects her Indo-European origins and may relate her to a "masculine principle." On the other hand, it entails an ambiguity vis-à-vis the Ishtars, who, like her, are generally not lunar, with the signal exception of the variant she most resembles, the Phoenician Astarte.

This brings us to the astral feature. Its changes through time pose special problems. I have already stated that Inanna and the Ishtars were saliently astral, in terms of stars in general and Venus in particular. I have also noted above that the Proto-Indo-European Dawn and her Greek descendant, Eos, were both closely connected with the Divine Twins, who in Vedic, late Greek, and Latin texts are associated, or even identified, with the Morning and Evening Star (Rose 1959: 231); other myths make Dawn the mother of the Morning Star.

The Aphrodite of our eighth-century texts, on the other hand, is *not* astral. The simplest and perhaps soundest explanation is that after the hypothesized split of the pre-Greek Dawn figure, Eos remained astral, whereas, for a while at least, Aphrodite evolved in a different direction. It is also conceivable that Homer and Hesiod reflect a religiously motivated deastralization of some sort. Subsequently, during the late seventh century, the astral feature, together with Adonis and other components, spread through the Greek world and became part of the Aphrodite complex. The "Heavenly Aphrodite" of classical times and the Roman Venus were both astral.

DIMENSION 6: WATER

A sixth dimension is association with *water,* especially aquatic birth. Hera and Athena are not generally aquatic, although the former, according to one myth, annually renewed her virginity in a spring near Nauplia. Athena, though sometimes depicted as a sea goddess with a snake, is not especially aquatic. Artemis and Aphrodite, on the other hand, both originate in an aquatic milieu, and in parallel ways. In both cases there is a real or intended concupiscence between supernaturals, followed by opposition or conflict—conflict between Kronos and Uranus in Aphrodite's case, between Hera and Leto in that of Artemis. And, for both these goddesses, islands, as already noted, are crucial symbols.

Aphrodite's association with water and her birth from whirling foam may be Near Eastern or go back to Old European (see note 1 to chap. 3); a tortoise is sometimes carved beneath her feet (Farnell 1897: 674). Her patronage of navigation is probably ancient—

derived from, or at least influenced by, the early Phoenician (Sidonian) Asherah. The navigational feature does seem to be symbolized in such Aphrodite-like figures as Ino, Calypso, Circe, and Nausicaa, who guide Odysseus, the seafarer (the name Nausicaa is a compound meaning "guide of ships"; she is also partly like Artemis). And it is clear that Aphrodite does emerge as a goddess of the serene sea in classical times; on Cyprus she was consulted at Paphos about voyages and was worshiped by seamen (in a cult linked with that of the Divine Twins; see the Thirty-third Homeric Hymn). She was also sometimes associated in ritual with Poseidon. But the fact remains that in Homer she is not a goddess of navigation, nor is the ocean important (she is not even born in the sea). Since navigation is linked symbolically with astrality, her loss of both astral and aquatic features in Homer must be significant and specially motivated.

DIMENSION 7: ORIGIN FROM ZEUS

A seventh dimension is *origin from Zeus* (the descendant of the Proto-Indo-European sky god). Athena is the most directly descended, since she sprang full-grown from his head, after a blow from Hephaestus (but only after Zeus had swallowed her pregnant mother, Metis [*Theogony* 891]; births not resulting from copulation could be fruitfully analyzed as a set). Artemis' birth, together with that of her twin brother, Apollo, results from the time when Zeus, in the form of a swan, seduced Leto. This sexual violence is later converted into Artemis' own hostility toward men and is consistent with her relation to her mother—as when she helps her brother slay the giant who tried to rape Leto, or when she slays another male for attacking her mother, or when she slays all of Niobe's children because Niobe boasted that her own fecundity was superior to Leto's. These three—Athena, Apollo, and Artemis—are children of Zeus, whereas Hera was sired by Kronos and so is Zeus's sister as well as his last legitimate spouse.

There are several variants of Aphrodite's birth. Two appear in the texts cited above (pp. 57, 58, 66) but should be discussed at this time. In Homer, my main source, she is born from Dione, the fourth of Zeus's eight wives. Dione is a Titan; not much is known about her except that she is affectionate toward Aphrodite in the *Iliad*. Her name is cognate with that of Zeus, both being variant descendants of the PIE *dyewos*. All of this seems congruous with the birth, from the same PIE sky god and his consort, of the main

Indo-European antecedent of Aphrodite, namely, the PIE dawn goddess. The ancient associations of Aphrodite, not only with Dione but with Themis, Hebe, and the Graces, all argue for the significance of her Indo-European origins, and the way in which Homer adheres to the Dione genealogy reflects his archaizing tendency to draw on Indo-European rather than Near Eastern sources. The Dione variant remained well known and widely accepted throughout classical times, including Roman times, when it became politically charged by Caesar's claim to be descended from Aeneas (Aphrodite's son). According to a third, and also important, version, that of Hesiod and the Sixth Homeric Hymn, she emerged from the severed genitals of Uranus and is thereby one generation *above* Zeus and mythically in the oldest stratum of the Olympians. The many variants of the birth of Aphrodite reflect the diversity of her origins in Semitic, Indo-European, and even Old European myth and the problem of assigning to her a place in the pantheon.

They also reflect her psychological complexity. Her birth from genitals is obviously connected with her sexual-sensuous functions and contrasts symmetrically with Athena's birth from Zeus's head and her patronage of wisdom. Both of these appearances or emergences (rather than literal births) symbolize genetically the intimate relation of each goddess with her father and, by extension, with males generally. By one type of definition you are what you come from. Both, thus, are strongly identified with their father, and each, in her way, symbolizes the denial of the mother.

DIMENSION 8: KINSHIP

As fundamental psychologically as the astral feature is the feature of *kinship*. As some mythologists have quite soundly argued, Greek myth is strongly concerned with kinship and with "tensions in the family" (Kirk 1975: 226). It seems realistic and legitimate to assume that the familial structure depicted in Greek myth corresponds in a number of systematic ways to the structure of the Greek family; it thus symbolizes certain conflicts and suggests interpretations. I am going to assume that each of the queens has a status and role in the Olympian family that corresponds to some analogue in the nuclear and extended families of Homeric times (without making claims about other myth systems).

In the first place, both Athena and Artemis symbolize sisters, albeit of very different kinds. Artemis projects onto the screen of myth some of the attitudes of the young unmarried sister (or daughter) who dances with other young girls and leads "the life of many an unmarried daughter among the gay and feudal families pictured by Homer" (Seltman 1956: 126). But she also symbolizes to an exaggerated degree certain anxieties about married life, including its sexual side, that follow relocation to an unfamiliar and possibly distant family. I think it may be assumed that among the eighth- and seventh-century aristocracies the girl normally and usually went to live with her husband and that the latter was seldom a neighbor. As part of her complex of feelings, Artemis is distinguished by her intense identification with her mother; as noted above, she slays individuals for even claiming to be more fertile than Leto. The way that she slays women—in childbirth, or because of their sexuality, or simply out of possessiveness or for their lack of devotion to her— indicates that she symbolized yet more general aspects of female psychology.

Athena is also a daughter of Zeus, and, as noted, her birth from his head does imply a profound identification with him. But in many other ways she is a sister figure, and of a particular type. She is the understanding, sympathetic, and supportive woman with whom there is no thought of sexual involvement. We could, I think, argue this sororal status on purely psychological grounds, but it is also corroborated nicely by the actual genealogies of Achilles, Odysseus, Diomedes, and Heracles, all of whom are descended from Zeus and so are her brothers or cousins or distant nephews in some vague but significant sense. I have in mind the so-called classificatory kinship statuses, which refer not only to primary relatives, such as "brother," but also to more distant ones (subsumed under that same rubric in terms of specific dimensions, such as patrilineal descent). The actual genealogical connections between Athena and several of the major heroes considerably reduces the division between the mortal and the immortal that is so basic in Homeric religion.

Hera, on the other hand, is in some ideal sense the wife. Utimately, she is descended from a supreme maternal figure of Old Europe and the Early Helladic. Her marriage with Zeus is probably an adaptation from an earlier, pre-Hellenic myth of sacred marriage with an annually dying god of fertility, but this is speculative. It is just as arguable that her primary function originally was that of *wife* and that fertility and other features were later added to her. In any case, her name is probably simply the feminine form of "hero." By the time of Homer she is still primarily the wife and the patroness of marriage; in Pindar's *Tenth Nemean* she is "lady of marriage." In the plastic arts she seems to represent a stabilizer of the family order, "the Queenly Bride, diademed, a veil over her head, discreetly draped, with a scepter in her hand" (Seltman 1956: 35). These and other functions, such as her patronage of childbirth, seem, as noted, logically and historically derived from her status as wife. Hera is fully realized or completed *(teleia)* only through marriage (Kerényi 1975: 98).

The image of Hera as the matriarch in an extended patrilocal and patriarchal household becomes salient in Homer to the point of quite overriding her maternal one—to say nothing of her motherliness. Homer, in fact, never depicts her as a loving mother, a motherly woman; on the contrary, when she is vexed by Hephaestus' ugliness, she casts him headlong from the heights of Olympus (*Il.* 18. 395–96). But note that Hephaestus himself stands for the failure of her marriage, through his birth by parthenogenesis (Hesiod *Theog.* 927–28) and the deformity which keeps him from being the fulfilling son. In Homer and elsewhere Hera's negative sides reflect her anger, resentment, and frustration as a wife; a gruesome condensation of this is found in the image of her, hung by Zeus by a golden thong around her wrists, with anvils at her ankles. She emerges as an icon of diverse conflicts: of resentment against one's children as well as pride of motherhood, of majestic and mature beauty combined with nagging jealousy toward a philandering husband, and of homicidal vindictiveness toward his lovers.[3]

Contrasting with the two structural sisters and the matriarchal Hera is the golden Aphrodite, particularly because of the multiplicity and contradictory nature of her roles. In an important way, mentioned frequently in Homer and Sappho and widespread in cult, she was the patroness of marital love, of the arts of love in legitimate wedlock. As Zeus says to her at one point in the *Iliad,* "You should attend to the charming works of marriage" (5. 429). And Hesiod, a bit later in time, speaks of the unmarried girl as "not yet knowing the works of golden Aphrodite" or, as Lattimore has it, "not initiated in the mysteries of Aphrodite" (*Works and Days* 521). Of later, classical times, Detienne writes (1972: 120), "Protectress of marriage, at the side of Hera and Demeter, the same power represents on the religious level that part of sexual desire and amorous pleasure *(aphrodisia)* without which the union of man and woman in marriage cannot find fulfillment." Farnell, focusing on her role in cult, writes that she "appropriates the functions [of marriage].

. . . Aphrodite of the bridal chamber [is] the goddess who joins in matrimony" (1897: 656). Aphrodite thus patronizes *the loving and passionate wife* in a way that crucially complements Hera (and Demeter)—a point that has been critically neglected. Such a positive image of the physically passionate wife is also neglected in world religions and similar normative systems. I will return to this below.

Many of the myths and expressions about Aphrodite's sexuality, on the other hand, make her the symbol of the unfaithful or otherwise *dangerously passionate wife or mistress*—as in the story about her adulterous affair with Ares. This is one meaning of the abduction of Helen of Troy. Aphrodite stands for any young female relative in a man's household, whether a wife, sister, or daughter, and for the attendant liaisons and other compromises and complications. She maps and illustrates some of the most bitter and tragic (and highly structured) conflicts in Greek literature. This role as an erring female relative reminds one of the Semitic Ishtars and, to a lesser extent, the Vedic Ushas. Other texts document her strong maternal side, particularly as expressed in her relation to Aeneas. To sum up, Aphrodite stands at various times for the passionate legitimate wife, the dangerously passionate and wayward female relative (e.g., wife or daughter), the sister, and the loving mother.

DIMENSION 9: FRIENDLINESS AND INTIMACY

The twin dimensions of *friendliness* and *intimacy* are close to those of kinship, which I have just discussed. Hera, to begin, does patronize some mortals (e.g., Achilles, *Il.* 1. 195), but always for her own ends and often with unhealthy consequences. In Homer she is vindictive some of the time, as in the famous passage in Book Four of the *Iliad* describing her lust to have Troy sacked. The matriarchal head of the Olympian family, she is not close to Zeus and is sometimes in conflict with him. Artemis, in turn, is vindictive, watchful, and wary and is friend to no epic hero; Homer calls her "a lioness unto women," and I have noted that she not infrequently slays them. Both Athena and Aphrodite, on the other hand, are often affectionate and helpful to various persons. The former befriends Diomedes and helps him in his combat against Ares; above all, she closely follows and advises Odysseus: their friendship and affinity constitute one of the richest themes in Homer (Stanford 1968: chap. 3).[4]

Aphrodite is also friendly, but her friendliness has different implications. She is friendly to Anchises, her lover, and to her son, Aeneas, to Helen, her alter ego, and to Helen's lover, Paris; in these and other cases her friendliness is interpenetrated with sensuousness. At one level she comes closer to being benign and tender than any of the other queens of heaven, and this has to be emphasized when evaluating her. But at another level there are ambivalences and black valences, which will be taken up shortly.

DIMENSION 10: VIRGINITY

The dimension of intimacy is inversely linked with that of *virginity,* and both are strongly associated with kinship. Athena and Artemis are, as noted, rigidly virginal in attitude as well as body (granted that they do not have "bodies" in the human sense). In any case, they stand aligned with Hestia (goddess of the hearth) as the only three beings in the universe who are impregnable to Aphrodite's charms. Artemis' virginity is both a cause and an effect of her distance and inaccessibility. That she can symbolize chastity as well as virginity is exploited by Homer in the *Odyssey* when Helen, now happily reunited with Menelaus, emerges publicly for the first time "like Artemis of the golden arrows" (4. 122). Athena's virginity is, as already remarked, indispensable to her role as a sexless, sororal, manlike friend of epic heroes. These virgin goddesses' strong antipathies to sex are attested by the myths of their slaying would-be suitors or violently cleansing themselves of pollution; witness Actaeon, who, after accidentally seeing Artemis naked, was turned into a stag to be rent asunder by his own hounds, or how Athena guides the spear of Diomedes home into the flank of the swashbuckling Ares (*Il.* 5. 857), the god who, I argue, incarnates pollution through sex and war.

The "virginity" of these two goddesses is partly independent of their being called *parthenos.* In Homeric Greek this word usually means a young, sexually inexperienced woman and does not seem to have definitely implied physical virginity. The more general meaning is simply "young woman," whether a nubile virgin or a concubine with children; the derived noun, *parthenios,* for example, refers to the "son of an unwed girl" (*Il.* 16. 180).

Hera is a mother and the patroness of mothers and childbirth and, in Homer, the mother of Eileithyia, the goddess of childbirth. But she seems to symbolize virginity in other contexts, as in the post-Homeric myth of her annual renewal of her virginity in the spring near Nauplia, or the myths of her twice giving birth by parthenogenesis (the offspring are the lame Hephaestus and the monstrous Typhon). In Pindar's *Sixth Olympian* she is "Hera of maidenhood," and her vindictiveness toward various males may be part of this syndrome (for example, her "boundless anger" toward her stepson, Heracles [Hesiod *Theogony* 315]). From another point of view, of course, her aversion to Zeus is, to say the least, well motivated. In sum, all three of these goddesses are virgins in some degree, and in each case their association with the crescent-shaped moon may symbolize cruelty or at least hardness of heart. All three patronize female activities: Athena the woman's domestic arts; Artemis the dance, other maidenly rituals, and childbirth; Hera, also childbirth, and motherhood (but not motherliness), and wifehood (but not the arts of love in marriage).

Aphrodite is obviously not virginal, but this "obviousness" actually masks a number of less obvious issues about which we know very little. No myth, for example, deals with her virginity or its loss, nor is she ever abducted or raped or the subject of an attempt of this sort; presumably she is so powerful sexually that to rape her would be implicitly contradictory. Aphrodite does rank with Hera in being not virginal, but we must recall Hera's semivirginity (annually renewed) and her lack of "love" for man. At one point she seduces Zeus because she wants to keep him from noticing what is going on below, on the field of Troy—her "love" thus being the means to an end. Aphrodite, on the other hand, seduces men or has a liaison with a god because of gifts or flattery, to be sure (*Od.* 8. 269), but also because she feels "sweet desire" or a terrible longing. She herself experiences the passion she arouses in others.

Aphrodite is what many today would call "sexually generous," being intimate with several gods: Ares, Hermes, Hephaestus, and Poseidon (to whom, by one myth, she bore a daughter). She has mortal lovers in many lands, as Helen unambiguously suggests in a passage that, as already noted, is remarkable for the sarcastic mockery of a divinity by a mortal or semi-mortal (*Il.* 3. 399–409); she also proposes that Aphrodite, since she is so impressed by Paris' qualities, opt to become his wife or slave. Helen's own sexual history (e.g., her earlier affair with Theseus, as reported in the *Cypria*) lends these lines an effective irony. The generous carnal affections of Aphrodite and her lack of virginity, and lack of anxieties or ambivalence about sex, make her unique among the queens of heaven. I will return later to her "love" and to the widely held opinion that one should not use this term when translating or interpreting Homer.

DIMENSION 11: ATTENDANT NYMPHS AND MAIDENS

An eleventh dimension is that of *attendant nymphs* and *maidens* or other females. Athena, consonant with her martiality, is not so attended, nor is the majestic Hera. Artemis and Aphrodite often are. The former is seen in the wilds with nymphs, but the argument that she is the *most* attended is not supported by our texts. On the other hand, she *is* typically celebrated by unwed maidens, who dance in her honor at weddings and similar rituals (in some cases dressed as bears). Female attendants, incidentally, like the veil, are a basic symbol of chastity; compare Penelope, veiled and attended in Ithaca, with the unattended Helen on the walls of Troy.

Aphrodite is surrounded, not by such bevies of unnamed nymphs and mortal maids, but by specific named minor goddesses. She is attended by the Hours or Seasons, as in the Sixth Homeric Hymn, and these are the daughters of Themis, the pre-Olympian goddess of the principle of order in nature. In both Homer and later texts she is also anointed by the Graces; in the Fifth Homeric Hymn, for example, before going off to seduce Anchises, she retreats to Cyprus, "and then the Graces bathed her with heavenly oil." The Graces are often associated with poetic creativity, as in Pindar's great invocation in the *Fourteenth Olympian*. They and Aphrodite inspire the poet. In post-Homeric texts Aphrodite appears with the Moirae and the golden Nereids. Her having these minor goddesses as attendants is mainly an inheritance from Indo-European; the Graces and the Hours, in particular, can be posited for Proto-Indo-European with some confidence. They are sometimes depicted as dancing and are definitely associated with dancing places and ring dances, which in turn are probably cognate with Slavic ones and descended from Proto-Indo-European cult. Finally, Boedeker has shown (1974: 51, 59–60) that this archaic dance complex is itself associated with dawn.

DIMENSION 12: BEAUTY

Twelfth, all of the queens of heaven are *beautiful,* since the Greeks, unlike the Babylonians and others, did not tolerate ugliness in a major goddess. This invariant category of beauty sets off the queens from mortal women. Their beauty has diverse aspects: Artemis is the tallest, Athena the stateliest, and Hera has the whitest skin. Hera's sensuous appeal, obscured by other features in later sources, is given its full worth in Book Fourteen of the *Iliad*. But even Hera calls on Aphrodite for the finishing touches, and of the four queens it is Aphrodite who is the *most* beautiful; the standard adjective for beautiful, *kalē,* belongs to her almost as much as "golden" does. The most eloquent way to extol a woman's beauty is to compare her to Aphrodite, as happens to Helen's only child, Hermione (*Od.* 4. 14) or the captive concubine whose seizure by Agamemnon catalyzes Achilles' wrath in the *Iliad*. That same Achilles, at his most lyrical, exclaims that he will not wed a daughter of Agamemnon "though she vie in beauty with the golden Aphrodite" (*Il*. 9. 389; see also Friedrich and Redfield 1978). But note that Persephone is also called beautiful, even "very beautiful" *(perikallēs).* "Most beautiful" *(kallistē)* is used intermittently in Homer of Dawn, Athena, and other goddesses.

Homer usually describes such beauty by speaking of it indirectly, in terms of its effects—as when two cricket-voiced elders on the walls of Troy speak of Helen. When it comes to Aphrodite, on the other hand, the physical details are often described directly. We are told of her flashing eyes, her soft skin, her smile and golden ornaments. The beauty of her breasts made Menelaus drop his sword on catching sight of them during the sack of Troy (according to Lesches, a seventh-century poet [Evelyn-White 1967: 519]). This emphasis is of great significance for the sort of psychological interpretation in chapter 9 below. Explicitness about physical details is further elaborated in Homer's description of faded Aphrodites like Penelope, who is beautified by Athena and made a marvel to the Achaeans by use of the ambrosial balm of Aphrodite (*Od.* 18. 193–94).

DIMENSION 13: INTELLIGENCE

The thirteenth dimension, that of *intelligence,* has two main aspects. One of these is the relation of intelligence to culturally conditioned concepts of biological and psychological dispositions. As one feminist reader has pointed out to me, there is a sense in which three of the queens are positively characterized by their sexuality: Hera the mother, Artemis the virgin, Aphrodite the lover. And each has an intelligence that is correspondingly "intuitive" in the conventional (and some would say "sexist") sense. Thus, Hera is sometimes guileful and has a wise intuitive understanding for relations in a large family and the philandering of one's husband.

Artemis, neither guileful nor intellectual, possesses an intuitive knowledge of wild nature. Aphrodite has intuition for sexual matters and amatory relations—a complex type of intelligence. Athena, with her "masculine" intellect is also the least marked for feminine sexuality; many people—Walter Otto, for example—feel that she basically *is* male, and her physical stance and inevitable helmet do indeed suggest this.

A second aspect of intelligence involves qualities and quantities within a simple paradigm defined by inheritance from Zeus. Athena's *mētis* is mainly, as already noted, a combination of rationality with astuteness, political sagacity, and practical skills; in Hesiod, for example, the carpenter is her "apprentice" (*Works and Days* 430). Later her key term becomes *sophia,* in the sense of "wisdom," including the philosopher's. Apollo is, already in Homer, the patron of such "higher" levels of intelligence as self-knowledge and the measure and harmony expressed in music. Aphrodite, while charged with the nonrational forces of procreation, is also the mistress of deceits, wiles, persuasion, and other arts for amorous ends between man and woman. The mental powers ascribed to Aphrodite and Athena are in a sense combined in a fourth offspring of Zeus, Hermes, who commands magic, thieves' cunning, business and technological acumen, and the skillfulness of the messenger and negotiator, most of which require the ability to act between boundaries. All four types of mentality—those of Athena, Aphrodite, Apollo, and Hermes—stem from Zeus, so that this aspect of intelligence intersects with our seventh dimension ("origin from Zeus") and the one to follow ("nature versus culture").

DIMENSION 14: NATURE VERSUS CULTURE

Types of intelligence—Athena's intelligence in particular—lead to the next feature, *nature versus culture.* Athena exemplifies the value of *mētis,* which is exemplified all the way from Kronos, who is *ankulomētis,* to Prometheus and Zeus, each a *mētietēs,* to Athena, who is *mētioessa,* to Odysseus, the *polumētis* hero. In Athena's case *mētis* implies arts and crafts (including women's domestic ones), masculine skills, such as shipbuilding and carpentry, and, more generally, all manner of skill, persuasiveness, and courteous or appropriate deceit in conversation or public debate or other types of verbal exchange. This idea of skill in word and deed was one of the most integral values in the civilization of the ancient Greeks, who contrasted themselves with both barbarian peoples and wild nature by virtue of possessing it. Artemis, on the other hand, is the goddess of unsullied nature, of wild, untamed animals and wild, uncultivated fields and fruits. She is symbolized, above all, by wild animals—the bear, the stag, and the doe, whom she may incarnate or slay with arrows. All these pristine and untended things are associated with her virginity, aloofness, and fierceness and what we today would call her "alienation." Her wildness and purity also justify the frequent use for her of the epithet "holy" (*hagnē*). The clear dyadic opposition between the Artemis of *nature* and the Athena of (Greek) *culture* or civilization raises the more general question of how the meaning of Aphrodite includes the two poles of this opposition and mediates between them (discussed at length in chapter 6).

DIMENSION 15: ABSTRACT FEATURES, E.G., MOBILITY

The fifteenth dimension is really a congeries of relatively abstract properties: proximity, light, mobility, direction of movement, and color.

Let us begin with *proximity*. Hera and Artemis keep their distance from heroes (the apparent exception of Hippolytus proves the rule, since Artemis patronizes him—even, in one myth, brings him back to life—precisely *because* he keeps his distance.) On the other hand, Athena gets physically close to her friends, beside them or behind them, even touching them, but this proximity is combined with a fierce chastity. Aphrodite also gets near those she longs for or befriends, but, whether helping or simply conversing with a god or a mortal, she is, in many cases at least, a potential lover. This feature of proximity is closely bound to that of friendship and intimacy.

The interplay between proximity and *light* yields an interesting paradigm. Artemis belongs with Apollo in terms of distance but with Hermes in terms of night, whereas Aphrodite belongs with Apollo in terms of daylight but with Hermes in terms of proximity. The set can be diagramed as in the accompanying table. The four divinities make up a perfect set because all intersections of the

	Proximate (Nondistant)	Diurnal (Nonnocturnal)
Artemis	—	—
Aphrodite	+	+
Apollo	—	+
Hermes	+	—

features are realized. Aphrodite and Hermes were linked ritually at a number of cult centers and seem closer to each other in overall gestalt than either is to any other deity. In post-Homeric times, on the other hand, it is Dionysus who increasingly resembles Aphrodite. Like Ares, he shares with her the ability to enter into a person until that person is possessed by him. This raises the question of *aphro-ditē* as a psychological state, as contrasted with the goddess Aphrodite.

A third abstract feature is *mobility*. First, what are the types of mobility? Athena, in visual art and sometimes in the texts, may simply stand, her mere presence sufficing; much of the time, of course, she is in motion—before the ranks, guiding a hero, traveling great distances. Hera is perhaps most characteristically seated on her throne in regal immobility; she is preeminently Hera of the golden throne. Artemis is typically in motion, darting and flitting. Aphrodite is similarly active, though to a lesser degree and over less space. Mobility may be linked with age and sexuality: Hera, the senior matron, contrasts with the two goddesses who are youngest and most charged sexually—Artemis negatively, Aphrodite positively. The two most charged are highly mobile.

A fourth abstract feature, closely related to mobility, is *direction of movement* and its chromatic implications (*color*). Although highly speculative, I think my idea is worth a brief statement. Athena, when she moves, as I hinted above, tends to advance—into battle, toward victory, or to the hero she is helping. This active forwardness may be associated with the "advancing, attracting, or penetrating quality of red" by the theory of "chromatic aberration" that is "commonly known to phenomenologists, as well as aestheticians and psychologists" (Sahlins 1976: 5). I do not know whether Athena was actually associated with red in, for example, the painting of statuary.

Artemis seems to move off and away much of the time, in flight from men and gatherings, and she is the most distant of the goddesses. She suggests the color blue and its values, according to the same theory, of receding and withdrawing. Blue is a quality of night, moonlit mountains, and the like. She is never referred to as blue in Homer, however, because of the peculiar fact that his language (like pre-Conquest Tarascan and some other languages) apparently lacked a term for this part of the spectrum (Gladstone 1858).

When we turn to Aphrodite, we find her advancing, assertive, active, as when she is bringing Paris and Helen together or when she or Eos, her alter ego, seduces or snatches men up. But she also withdraws—herself from battle, her favorites from battle, Helen from Sparta, and her own affection from those who incur her wrath. The emotions she inspires are ambiguously negative: longing or yearning for a person absent or unreached. Her typical pose in statuary is slightly bowed, with one knee bent in an attitude of receptivity that was largely a creation of Praxiteles (psychological criteria influenced the sculptor's solutions as much as the "formal" ones Clark deals with [1956: 77, 86]). Aphrodite patronizes both unfulfilled and fulfilled, both illicit and/or marital, love—a synthesis of positive and negative values that is like her synthesis of nature and culture. The combination of active-advancing and passive-retreating would seem to correspond to the perceptual ambiguity of her diagnostic color: golden (i.e., yellow, tawny, and so forth)— granted that, as already stated, the exact chromatic value cannot be ascertained.

The interrelated features of proximity, light, mobility, direction of movement, and color are so complex that I have included only mobility in the chart on page 102, below.

Dimension 16: Fertility

The sixteenth dimension is *fertility*. All of the queens of heaven, including Athena, derive in part from prehistoric goddesses of fertility. Hera patronizes the growth of the family. Even Artemis, while virginal and aloof, has suzerainty over wild things and is a patroness of animals and children. The representations of her at the great cult center of Ephesus had from eleven to forty-four "udder-like protuberances" (I think the phrase is Seltman's); these relate to the archaic sow and cow icons of the Mother goddess. And we recall that Artemis punished Niobe for claiming to rival Leto's fecundity. The early Artemis was probably a patroness of human fertility, closely connected with the Mother goddesses.

But of the four queens, it is Aphrodite who most centrally symbolizes growth, fertility, and procreation. In this she is also the heiress of Inanna and *awsos*. The early, Hesiodic, myth of her birth from the sky god's genitalia in a swirl of foamy water is a metaphor of this basic power. By the time of Homer she is "the goddess of nature in bloom, and is associated with the Graces, the kindly and beneficent spirits of growth. With them she dances, by them she is bathed and anointed, and they work the clothing she wears" (Otto

1954: 94; *Odyssey* 18. 194; 8. 364; *Iliad* 5. 338). But more importantly than "bloom," she stands for the individual urge or in-
stinct in animal and man to join with another, to procreate. In man,
of course, these impulses are linked to values of family, name, and
so forth. Aphrodite also symbolizes the *collective* desire for fertility.
She has no rival as a divinity of procreation and, as the Fifth Homeric
Hymn says, her power to arouse and control these passions extends
over all creatures in the universe except the three virginal immortals:
Artemis, Athena, and Hestia (the myths of Hippolytus, Smyrna,
and other mortals who resisted her call are post-Homeric and, as
noted, are "exceptions that prove the rule").

In Homer physical procreation is already linked to other kinds
of creativity, and later this inclusive idea became more intellectual-
ized. The early poet-philosopher Empedocles (fl. 440 B.C.) makes
Eros the creative, cohesive force pervading the universe. In the
fourth century, in Plato's *Phaedrus,* Socrates brackets his discussion
of love with (1) a reference to Sappho's poetry and an invocation
to the Muses and (2) an encomium of the fourth and highest form
of madness: of Eros and of Aphrodite. Similarly, in the *Symposium*
he draws some obvious connections between biological, genealogical, and intellectual-artistic creativity as these were transmitted to
him by the seeress Diotima of Mantinea. It can hardly be over-
emphasized that in these immortal dialogues Socrates-Plato unambiguously implies that it is females—Aphrodite, Sappho, Diotima—
to whom one goes for the truthful vision of love.

In Euripides, Aphrodite stood for the cosmic generative force;
as he says at the beginning of *Hippolytus*: "Wide o'er man my realm
extends, and proud the name that I, the goddess Cypris, bear, both
in heaven's courts and 'mongst all those who dwell within the limits
of the sea and the bounds of Atlas, beholding the sun's light; those
that respect my power I advance to honor, but bring to ruin all who
vaunt themselves at me" (Oates and O'Neil 1938: 1:763). In
later cult she continues to incarnate the power of love and the forces
of procreation (Farnell 1897: 669). It is Aphrodite's hegemony
over, not just love life, but fertility and creativity that accounts for
her enormous popularity in the classical and Hellenistic worlds
(evident in the remarkable invocation to Venus by Lucretius [first
century B.C.]).[5] In the great collections of the Louvre, mentioned in
chapter 1, there are more figurines of Aphrodite than of all the other
goddesses taken together (granted that the instincts of the French
collectors may have skewed the sample!).

I have been emphasizing fertility and procreation (and descending to classical sources) because these deeper forces may be obscured by some of the less vital features that I have detailed above and, perhaps even more, because they have so often been neglected by specialists in Greek religion. They also get lost in the reduction of Aphrodite to a "good-for-nothing," "a female Tom Jones" or a "Lady with a Penis." These and other simple-minded epithets from the scholars illustrate Lévi-Strauss's contention that modern intellectuals still classify like savages much of the time (1967b: chapter 9—his polemic against Sartre). Fertility and procreation in the large sense are the substantive basis for Aphrodite's power and, as such, are as significant as sexuality and liminality.

DIMENSION 17: WAR

A seventeenth dimension, *war,* yields a fairly clear dichotomy between Athena and Hera as against Artemis and Aphrodite. Most warlike is Athena, she of the tumult, the battle cry, of epiphanies before ranked troops, shaking her aegis and lance (the butterfly-shaped battle shield is her archaic and perhaps quintessential symbol). She would appear to have been assigned one of the two major functions of the love-and-war goddesses of the Near East, although it is also arguable that she developed without much foreign input. Hera, also devoted to warcraft, tends to enter directly into battle, to take sides actively, and to plan eagerly for the destruction of cities. As Homer's Zeus puts it: "If you entered the gates and the great walls and were to devour Priam and the sons of Priam raw, and the other Trojans too, then maybe you might heal your ire" (*Il.* 4. 34–36).

Of the two nonmartial goddesses, Artemis is almost as ineffectual in war as Aphrodite, as we see in Book Twenty-one of the *Iliad* (esp. lines 415–96), when her arrows are broken and she is thrashed with her bow. Her role as huntress and slayer might strike some as a transformation from a martial one, and indeed hunting and war are metaphors of each other in Homer, as in the many similes. But I would say that Artemis' hunting is more probably an aspect of her supervision over the life and death of wild animals; she fosters their young but also slays in the hunt, just as she helps women in labor yet sometimes slays them too. What Artemis does share with Hera and Athena is a feature that crosscuts martiality: all three inflict pain and death in a direct or "objective" sense, and this suggests a deep opposition to Aphrodite.

The linked features of war and slaying often bespeak a quality of character. Hera, Athena, and Artemis are all intermittently ruthless, hardhearted, remorseless, implacable—characteristics that Homer labels with epithets and illustrates with actions. Such hardheartedness is predictable under certain circumstances—Hera's toward Troy or toward a paramour of Zeus (e.g., Leda, whose parturition she tries to block); Athena's toward enemies in battle or the foes of her protégés (e.g., the suitors of Penelope, Odysseus' foes); and Artemis toward any man who sees her naked or is the lover of a devotée and toward various categories of women (e.g., Ariadne and her two sisters, whom Artemis slays [*Od.* 11. 324]). Since this hardheartedness is always present, at least potentially, we may call it an invariant trait of character of these three goddesses.

At first blush Aphrodite might also seem martial, at least to some extent. One of her main lovers was Ares, the war god, with whom she had the well-publicized affair in the *Odyssey* and with whom she appears twice in battle in the *Iliad* (books 5 and 21); in the second of these appearances she tries to help the wounded Ares and is called a "dog-fly" by Hera (21. 420–22). Some of her traits can be interpreted as metaphors of war within the synchronic Homeric system or as reflexes of an earlier martial version. In Sappho, also, the perils of Aphrodite are sometimes compared with those of war. In several parts of Greece, notably Sparta and Corinth, there was a local cult of a warrior Aphrodite.

But let us look at the other side of this image. First, though she is linked to Ares, the linkage is through antithesis or opposition, and this, by implication, reduces her martiality; the fact that she seduces Ares was sometimes taken to mean that love is stronger than war (granted, this is post-Homeric). She is ranged with the Trojans because of her Eastern affinities and the fact that one of their leaders is her son, but she is a feeble combatant, carrying no weapon and scared of fighting. In Homer and Sappho she is mainly associated with courtship, children, flowers, the arts of love, and the like; the amorous dove is one of her birds. Much of this symbolism may come from the Indo-European Dawn, and it differs greatly from the bloody Ishtars. A finer point is that, although the line between love and war is sometimes thin or even broken, the comparisons in the case of Aphrodite are *outward,* from love *to* war, whereas in the Sumerian, Babylonian, and Canaanite figures the direction is inward, from war to love; the poem by Enheduanna, for example, is overtly about war and violence, although at times it may possibly be a metaphor of "love." These facts about the direction of metaphorization seem to lend further confirmation to the relatively peaceful and amatory nature of Aphrodite.

DIMENSION 18: SUBJECTIVITY

Let us look at Aphrodite from a related perspective and so enter upon the discussion of an eighteenth dimension, *subjectivity*. In Homer, Sappho, and others Aphrodite is perceived as the root cause of strong passions, above all of longing and love but also of hate, rivalry, and jealousy. Not an Artemis, she does not shoot people down with arrows, nor is she a Hera, bloodthirstily planning the sack of a city or the torments of a male victim. What she does do is create states of mind that may become the causes of murder, interfamily feuds, the sack of cities, and wars between nations. And she *is* like Artemis in that it is women whom she most often dooms. "She wrests them out of a life of security and restraint and causes them distress by a blind and often criminal devotion to a strange man" (Otto 1954: 98). This is why Homer, and Sappho even more, describes her, like the other queens, as remorseless, implacable, and cruel—but cruel in the special sense that she causes "cruel longing" and "cares that exhaust the limbs."

The critical thing about her hardheartedness—what sets it off from that of the other goddesses—is its *subjectivity*. This is already explicit in Homer and Hesiod (see, e.g., *Works and Days* 66), and it is greatly elaborated in Sappho. This subjectivity is connected with the ambiguity, already noted above, between the goddess, Aphrodite, and the psychological state, *aphroditē,* particularly when Aphrodite/*aphroditē* "enters into" a person (Seltman 1956: 79–80). The distinction between what is subjective and what is objective cannot be pushed too far, of course, for what might be thought descriptions of some overt act by her are often (if not always) metaphors for an underlying psychological phenomenon. But this is true of the other goddesses. What differentiates the subjectivity of Aphrodite is that she creates states in others, that is, her subjectivity has a causative, factive value. In this way the references to physical danger from her are primarily rather than secondarily metaphorical (e.g., the "rending arrows" in Pindar's *Fourth Pythian*). Good examples of Aphrodite's subjective workings are her making Dawn perpetually infatuated, as already noted, and the famous case of Stesichorus: angry with him for forgetting to sacrifice to her, she made his daughters marry two and three times and then desert their husbands. The subjective nature of Aphrodite's workings is unique to her and explains in part why the poets and dramatists, including Homer, felt her to be the most potent goddess. It also goes a long way toward explaining why the meaning of Aphrodite is of so much more general, universal, and singularly contemporary significance than that of the other goddesses.[6]

The subjective perils of Aphrodite that make her unique also contribute to the ambivalence of her meanings and the ambiguity of her "gifts," and there is little question but that Homer and his audiences felt her in this way. The ambiguity comes out in the dyadic relations between Aphrodite figures and their lovers: in Aphrodite's initiative in seducing Anchises and the fear of castration which she subsequently inspires in him; in Calypso's relations to Odysseus, with whom she makes love but then imprisons against his will; in Circe's relations with Odysseus, whom she first would have unmanned but then treats as a lover; in Aphrodite's relations to Paris, with its disastrous consequences for his honor and his whole people; in Penelope's relation to the suitors, to whom she would seem to have given more implicit encouragement than is recognized and who end heaped up in their gore. The ever-present, potential danger of Aphrodite's attentions comes out most clearly in the crucial scene in *Iliad* 3. 383–420, where she is rebuked by Helen, her human alter ego, and then speaks out in terrifying words. Her love is sometimes near to hate, just as the consequences of her love are sometimes fatal. Yet, even in this passage from the *Iliad,* her threats are not of direct or physical chastisement but of the withdrawal of her affection and "the devising of hatred."

The foregoing discussion can be summarized to some extent by the following schema:

	Hera	Athena	Artemis	Aphrodite
Martial	+	+		
Objectively cruel	+	+	+	
Potentially hardhearted	+	+	+	+
Subjectively cruel				+

Some of these points are concatenated in the key emotional symbol of "desire, longing," one of the main "works" of Aphrodite. In

Homer the noun form *himeros* by itself refers mainly to sexual desire, usually in the here-and-now—as when Paris desires Helen in Book Three of the *Iliad* and recalls their first dalliance, or when Zeus feels a desire for Hera in Book Fourteen (after she has bewitched him with Aphrodite's magic), or in the Homeric Hymn to Aphrodite where he casts a "sweet desire" for Anchises into Aphrodite's heart. *Himeros* can also be used for the desire for food or the desire to see one's parents (and probably for the desire for other objects). It is associated with the usual word for love and sexual relations (*philotēs*), and with the general domain of the language of love-making and courtship (*oaristus*). It is associated with ring dances and dancing places, "where desire is aroused" (Boedeker 1974: 51). In Hesiod the personified Himeros joins Eros to conduct the newborn Aphrodite to Olympus. Longing and desire are, if anything, even more central in Sappho (as is shown in the next chapter). And, three centuries after Homer, the protagonists in Plato's *Symposium* fully agree that longing is the chief element in love. The comic genius of Aristophanes (one of the participants in the dialogue) then generates (or revitalizes) a wondrous myth to explain "the intense yearning which each of them [the lovers] has for the other, [which] does not appear to be the desire of lovers' intercourse but of something else, which the soul desires but cannot tell." The critical initial move by Socrates, when his turn comes to talk, is: "May I ask you, further, whether love is the love *of something*?" (italics mine). But let us come back to the *himeros* of Homer.

Besides its sexual meaning in Homer, *himeros* occurs almost as frequently in the Homeric formula "the desire to weep," particularly the desire to weep for a person who is missing or dead or is met again after a long separation. The Achaeans feel this for Achilles, Telemachus and Penelope for Odysseus; and Odysseus feels it when he is clasped in the welcoming arms of Penelope. This desire to weep is close in meaning to that of *pothē*, also glossed as "longing, yearning" and used for someone who is dead or missing: Achilles yearns for Patroclus, the Trojans for Hector, and so forth. *Himeros* is also associated with shame in several passages.

These patterns for the noun are confirmed by an inspection of the adjective (*himeroeis*) and the verb (*himeirō*). In seven occurrences these forms refer to longing or to the desirability and loveliness of a person, as when Hera wonders how she might beguile Zeus to desire to lie by her side (*Il.* 14. 163); in three of the seven the reference is specifically carnal, that is, to the flesh or body. Five other references are to song or dance, and four more involve death or some analogous situation, such as the "longing sobbing" of Odysseus' men after they have been transmuted from pigs back into men (*Od.* 10. 398). (Incidentally, *himeros* and its congeners have a good Sanskrit cognate in *smárati,* "to remember, bethink.") The lexicology of the early Greek words, in any case, points to one powerful underlying emotion that we variously gloss as "yearning, longing, desire."

The positive, mainly sexual value of the simple, unqualified form *himeros* and the negative values of the variously modified ones, as found in Homer, seem to me to be congruous with the more general contrast that I have been developing between love and death. The two ideas of sexual desire and of longing for someone dead or gone, either of which can be concrete or abstract in value, fit perfectly with the basic paradigm of the love-and-death values of Aphrodite.

CONCLUDING REMARKS

This concludes my comparison of the queens of heaven. To my knowledge, no precedent analysis has appeared in anthropology, the classics, or elsewhere. While it is to some extent inspired by linguistics and current semiotics, it deals with *cultural* values in primarily cultural terms. More centrally, it tries to recreate and take the point of view of an eighth- or seventh-century Greek. The central question is: What did Aphrodite mean to an appreciative and informed Greek in Homer's audience? What sort of structure of perceptions and ideas did he bring to a hearing? My approach is thus essentially a phenomenological one, and it is with the results of such a phenomenological approach that I have been trying to connect the system of prehistoric antecedents and, later on, the perspectives of a contemporary psychology.

What forms do the eighteen features I have presented take in combination? Persons interested in formal analysis will observe that the categories do not fall into a hierarchy of progressively less and less inclusive units; in other words, although some "shallow taxonomies" are given en route, my overall conclusions do not take the form of a taxonomy. The results, rather, appear in the form of a complex intersection. At one level, a simple one, they appear in two-dimensional array (see the chart on p. 102, below): the four queens appear across the top, the dimensions down the left-hand side, and a scoring, in terms of plus, minus, and so forth, appears in the body of the chart. But even this is a drastic heuristic device because the features, or dimensions, differ in power, scope, and logical nature (there is, for example, the difference between continuous and discrete dimensions). Moreover, the different parts of the system are variously interconnected. To take some simple cases, the second dimension, "fruits and flowers," includes the apple, which stands for "fertility" (dimension 16), and the myrtle, which stands for "death" (part of 18). Or "water" (6), through its main subfeature, is linked with fertility and "subjectivity" but, through the subfeature "navigation," is linked with trade and, in this sense, is partly opposed to "war" (17). Similarly, the terms to be defined, that is, the goddesses, are differentially interrelated. On the one hand, the dimensions shared by Aphrodite and some other goddesses are reflected in local cults, in the later Greek world, to Aphrodite-Athena, Aphrodite-Persephone, and Aphrodite-Hera (as discussed in Farnell 1897: e.g., 696); on the other hand, the irreconcilable nature of the opposition between Aphrodite and Artemis seems reflected by the absence of syncretism "on the ground" of cult. At a more interesting level, about which I can only hypothesize, the meanings of the dimensions constitute a multidimensional network of some sort—like a Calder mobile with many pieces, each with many parts, and each interconnected with the other by an electronic communications system. Moreover, the network is open: there are probably other interesting dimensions, and there can be, in theory, no limit to their number.

Another important conclusion emerges. While some dimensions appear to be binary, many others are, even more clearly, continuous, and all of them can be so interpreted. In such terms Aphrodite is, for example, the least lunar, the least virginal, the least specific in her kinship role. In positive terms, she is the most floral, the most insular, the most solar, the most aquatic, the most intimate with humans, the most attended by nymphs (the Graces and so forth), and the most (i.e., the only one who is) subjective in her workings, in the sense that her power consists mainly in inspiring compelling subjective states. She is also the most golden, the most beautiful, and the most charged with fertility and the powers of creation. In short, she is the most potent of the goddesses—the most intensely characterized or "highly marked" of all the queens of heaven.

Some dimensions in the accompanying chart clearly possess degrees of intensity. These degrees are indicated by a number, with 1 indicating the greatest intensity. Other features seem basically binary and are thus marked plus or minus (a double plus indicates especially strong marking or, to be less precise, characterization). In other cases the actual symbolization is written in (e.g., "olive"). When there is little or no evidence, the slot is left blank; but where there is substantial evidence on both sides, the slot contains both plus and minus signs. Items enclosed in parentheses are of relatively minor importance.

THE EIGHTEEN DIMENSIONS

		HERA	ATHENA	ARTEMIS	APHRODITE
1.	Location	Argos	Athens	Delos; Greece and Asia Minor	Cythera, Cyprus, Crete
2.	Fruits and flowers	Flowers in cult; pomegranate	Olive		Rose, poppy, lily, apple
3.	Birds	(Cuckoo)	Owl; other birds on special occasions	(Quail)	Dove, swan goose
4.	Goldenness	2		3	1+
5.	Moon	2	3	1	−
	Sun	−	2	−	1+
6.	Water (e.g., aquatic birth)	Minor	Minor	+	++
7.	Origin from Zeus	−	++	+	+, −
8.	Kinship	Wife, mother	Older sister	Unmarried younger sister	Wife, mother, mistress, errant female relative
9.	Friendliness and intimacy	Minor	+	−	++
10.	Virginity	+, −	+	+	−
11.	Attendant nymphs and maidens	−	−	+	+
12.	Beauty	+	+	+	++
13.	Intelligence	+	++		+
14.	Nature versus culture		− +	+ −	+ +
15.	Mobility			+	+
16.	Fertility	(+)			++
17.	War	+	++	−	Metaphorically
18.	Subjectivity	−	−	−	+

Aphrodite is also the most extreme in another, more comprehensive sense that pulls together much of the foregoing discussion. While two of the other queens are to some extent mannish or masculine in terms of such conventionally male arts as war (Athena) and hunting (Artemis), Aphrodite never is. Hence she is the most "feminine," in the conventional sense of ancient Greek and modern American culture (senses that today would be [implicitly] sexist).

There are of course some exceptions to this claim about the intensity of her characterization: Artemis is, after all, the most mobile, and Athena is the most intelligent and martial. "Intensity of characterization" is itself a matter of degree, for Artemis, the second most intense, is in many ways dialectically opposed to Aphrodite. It has been suggested to me that my conclusions about intensity, and my selection of the features themselves, may have been skewed by a special interest in Aphrodite. To this I would answer that the facts I have used come from dozens of sources. Moreover, nonaphrodisiac features, such as martiality and wisdom, have not been avoided. It is a matter of intellectual history that *intensity of characterization* emerges rather naturally from a review of the basic texts and the secondary sources. The independence of the discovery lends more weight to my analysis, in the next chapter, of the Sapphic treatment of subjectivity.

The cultural and semantic analysis in this chapter is connected with my antecedent analysis of origins in a number of vital ways. All of the eighteen dimensions can be traced back in part to at least one of the main sources: Old European, Sumero-Semitic, Minoan, Mycenaean, and Proto-Indo-European. Most of the earlier imagery that I discussed—of bird goddesses, Inanna's sensuousness, the water nymphs—is of the sort that can be perpetuated for centuries and even millennia in folklore and oral literature, even though the individual constituent units may be reordered, recombined, or transformed in the most diverse and indeed infinite ways (Boas 1916, in Boas 1940: 404–5). The fact that in many cases it is impossible to demonstrate conclusively the precise nature of the connections between specific antecedents and the form they later took in the early Greek synthesis does not deprive relatively informed hypotheses of their interest. Finally, apart from demonstrated and positive facts about such strictly historical interconnections, an explicit linking of prehistoric symbols with their likely, conceivable, or possible later manifestations increases the significance of Greek mythology for a substantial part of the audience for whom I am writing—not a trivial reason for trying to integrate archaeological and semantic analyses.[7]

5

Homer, Sappho, and Aphrodite

INTRODUCTION

From the mainly Homeric context of the preceding chapters I now turn to Sappho and her signal contributions to the meaning of Aphrodite. I am acutely aware of the differences between the two poets but will argue that attention to the often neglected similarities between them can afford us insight into the general problem to which this book is dedicated.

Since what follows is fairly discursive and often moves by association, I will begin by identifying several lines of thought that the reader can bear in mind as I move along. The Greek framework of myth and poetry is first sketched; this is followed by some high points in the Homeric view of Aphrodite and its relation to Sappho. I then move on to the main points in Sappho's life and personal relations and the various aspects of her subjectivity and art that support my general contention that she was a Lesbian in several senses and a religious seeress who invented love. The form of my argument involves a series of dimensions and their interaction in a multidimensional network, but the content of my argument is that Sappho created a vision of love that, even on the basis of the fragmentary evidence, must be ranked with those of Solomon, Socrates-Plato, Tolstoy, Martin Buber, and other persons of great stature.

My initial framework for this discussion is that in early Greece, particularly in the seventh century, there were myth and poetry in two major senses. First, there were the regional variants—of Ionia, Aeolia, and so forth—and the even more local ones of an island like Chios or a city like Mytilene. Second, I think we can also assume a system that was pan-Hellenic to a significant degree. It comprised the major divinities, such as Aphrodite, and their genealogies; the epic tales—of the voyage of the Argonauts, the abduction of Helen, the siege of Troy; and a great body of other myths, fables, sagas, and folklore. Many mythic images and even lines of poetry were known throughout the Greek-speaking world, in considerable if varying detail (without such shared knowledge, much early Greek poetry would have been quite unintelligible). A body of oral literature, much of it cast in the traditional formulas of Mycenaean and even earlier times, came down through the Dark Ages (circa 1100–800 B.C.) and was diffused and shared throughout the Greek-speaking world.

The Homeric Background

This framework is vital to our understanding of the relation between Homer and Sappho. It is vital, too, to realize that poets, especially the most brilliant and popular, were highly mobile, that they recited and competed in many places and exchanged ideas and technical skills wherever they went. We can assume this of Sappho and Pindar, and it is vividly depicted in "The Contest between Homer and Hesiod." We know that the monumental composer of the *Iliad* and the *Odyssey* drew on these local and pan-Hellenic materials.

My position on the unity of the Homeric poems is connected with a second one, regarding the complexity and multilayeredness of Homer's view of myth and of the figure of Aphrodite in particular (for the contrary contention that Homer is "single-layered," see Auerbach's *Mimesis*). To begin, there is no *one* Homeric vision of the goddess but several, some harmoniously integrated, some implying contradictions or dynamic tension. One of these visions consists mainly of folkloristic and storytale elements. A second suggests an irreverence that irritated later commentators. In Homer Aphrodite comes out very scathed—as when she is wounded by the contemptuous Diomedes or is told derisively by Zeus to stick to her "works." The point of her entrapment in the *Odyssey* is to shame her before the gods. The superficial aspects of this tale have made her seem comic or silly to some readers, but I would argue that it is "single-layered" on the reader's part to take this mockery of Aphrodite literally when what we actually have is the sort of status inversion so typical of myth: Zeus, potentate of the divine family, wants to mock and humiliate Aphrodite precisely because she is the world's most potent goddess, the goddess of love and growth.

Several components in the Homeric view of Aphrodite need to be mentioned. Her association with the arts and desires of love remains primary, but there is no explicit association with courtesanship. The martial component has been practically removed, in contrast to the local residues of it in Sparta, and, of course, in contrast to the curses and subjective dangers of the goddess, which are present in the Homeric poems. Last, in Homer's (and Sappho's) myth, Aphrodite is born from the union of the sky god Zeus and his female counterpart Dione. In these and other ways Homer and his bardic peers revitalized the Indo-European components in the syncretic tradition they had inherited and so in their way contributed to Sappho's eventual vision.

Homer's vision of Aphrodite is profoundly if implicitly philosophical, since it raises issues such as the ones we have introduced: the relation between nature and culture, and the problems of fertility, creativity, and procreation, of love and death. Homer was the architect of a new religious synthesis, some of it a reform in the direction of abstraction, some of it a distortion or skewing of the earlier system (to this I return in chapter 7). From the seventh century down through classical and Roman times and, in a sense, to this day, Homer has been seen as a divinely inspired person with unique insight into religious truth; Socrates' attitude at numerous points in the dialogues epitomizes this.

GRACE (*charis*)

One narrow but important bridge between Homer and Sappho is the symbol of "grace" (*charis*), a distinctively Greek (and Mediterranean) cluster of meanings that, with less modification than one might expect, has lasted down to the present time (and lacks close analogues in English, Russian, etc.). Of the meanings that are synthesized by "grace," the first is personal beauty, loveliness, and handsomeness (such as Athena sheds on her favorites [*Od.* 23. 162]). "Grace" also applies to deeds and words, as in the speeches of Odysseus (*Od.* 8. 175). It includes gratification through pleasure and beauty, as when talking of a newly wedded wife (*Il.* 11. 243), and, closely related to this, the sense of thanks for services and favors or the rendering of favors to others. Grace is reticulated with metaphysical harmony and is projected imagistically through Aphrodite's main attendants, the Graces, those kindly spirits of harmonious growth; their mythic roots, as I have noted, go far back into the past (see Appendix 2 for an etymological hypothesis). The symbol of grace lacked many of the moral values that it has acquired from the Hebrew, Aramaic, and Koine Greek of the Bible, but it brought

other aesthetic, practical, and metaphysical ones together in a way
that, as noted, bridges some of the space between Homer and
Sappho.

SAPPHO'S APHRODITE

As we turn from Homer to Sappho, we find that her Aphrodite is
similar in many ways, that is, she is deceitful, mocking, fun-loving,
and fond of children, sunlight, flowers, fine raiment, and beautiful
things—and she is beautiful (only the last three features, incidentally, are predictable from the idea or archetype "love goddess").
In both poets she is the patroness, of course, of the desires and arts
of love, and these are part of the cultivated, civilized life. Super-
ficially, then, she still looks like the goddess of love and sex who
had already been in the eastern Mediterranean area for a long time.

The meaning of Aphrodite in Sappho's poetry can be viewed in
terms of a general semantic framework that I have worked out elsewhere. Sappho's Aphrodite is repeatedly identified as insular (Cyprus, with its city of Paphos, is the island most often mentioned).
She, too, is associated with birds, as instanced by her swan- or
sparrow-drawn chariot (Frag. 1);[1] both birds are symbols of erotic
love and fecundity. She is associated with Sappho's favorite flower,
the rose, and with the Graces, as in "Come here, holy, rose-armed
Graces, daughters of Zeus" (90). A bride in one Sapphic hymn
teems "with rosy (rose-colored) loves, most beautiful ornament of
the Paphian" (147).

Her Aphrodite is associated with the sun (Loebel and Page 65).
And Sappho links herself to the sun in some of her best lines: "I love
the exquisite (refinement), and light and beauty are my lot, and love
of the sun" (118).

Sappho's goddess is often golden, as in "O golden-wreathed
Aphrodite" (9), as are her companions, the Nereids, the Graces,
and the Muses: "But the golden Muses gave me true wealth, and
when I die I shall not be forgotten" (11, see also 129). This goldenness is part of the physical beauty of Aphrodite, and, since gold is
"pure of rust" (109), as Sappho reminds us, it helps to symbolize
her freedom from pollution and from aging and death (the death-
lessness and noncorrosibility are of course closely linked symbolically).

Sappho's Aphrodite is unlike Homer's, however, in relation to
the Phoenician Astarte. Her poetry, for example, contains the first

mention in Greek literature of the lover, Adonis, and also one reference to fields of lettuce—an image that is surely Phoenician and even Sumerian and that, by classical times, had become a master symbol for death and barren love (Detienne 1972). In Sappho, battle is mainly a metaphor for love or is used in amorous contexts; Aphrodite is a "stay in battle." In Homer, finally, the homosexuality that might have been suggested by Astarte (or by much Greek practice) seems to have been excluded by a combination of a taboo in the epic language (Wackernagel 1916: 224–29) and a norm of his native Ionia (see Pausanius' speech in Plato's *Symposium*). Eros, unimportant in Homer, is frequent in Sappho as a "loosener of limbs" and the like, and it seems reasonable to assume that she was aware of Eros' patronage of male homosexuality that was to become prominent by Plato's time (in *Phaedrus,* for example, Aphrodite, the mother of Eros, is a background, generic figure). Sappho's goddess, on the other hand, patronizes love between man and woman and between women.

SAPPHO'S LIFE AND PERSONAL RELATIONS

As will become increasingly clear, Sappho's goddess is a projection of herself, and in various ways: as patroness of love (with its ambiguities), as a strongly poetic figure, and in her traits of character. This fundamentally differentiates her vision from Homer's. It follows that we should look closely at the life of the poet, at its orientations and excitements.

Sappho was born about 630 B.C. in Mytilene, the main city of the beautiful island of Lesbos, "well-wooded, well-cultivated, well-populated" even today (Roche 1966: xi), located within a few hours of the sophisticated city of Sardis, capital of the wealthy kingdom of Lydia on the Anatolian mainland. Lesbos was fully participant in the intensified trade and colonization of the seventh century and was also affected by the troubled factionalism and civil war that was then dividing Greek cities between aristocrats and traders and commoners. Sappho, an aristocrat, was alternately the victim and beneficiary of violent factionalism, but her poetry is almost totally apolitical; in this she is an analogue of Aphrodite among the contentious gods.

Contrasting with her silence on human relations in the public, political sphere is her constant preoccupation with the private, individual relations that sociologists call "primary"—those between friends, relatives, lovers, or small groups of them. In this she feels and expresses the emotions of a woman, often of a very Greek woman, toward human beings in various contexts and stages of life. Sappho's preoccupation with concrete, immediate, human relations differentiates her from the many poets concerned with nature, theological abstractions, politics, and yet other themes and is a central component in her vision.

One of the most primary of these ties is to a small girl, and Sappho loved her only daughter passionately: "Once I saw a delicate little girl gathering wild flowers" (107), and "I have a little girl beautiful in form as golden flowers: Cleïs, beloved, in exchange for her I would not take all Lydia, nor even lovely Lesbos" (130). She named this daughter after her mother, but the latter is mentioned only once; and she rarely mentions a girl's or woman's feelings toward her mother.

Sappho's love for her daughter must, I think, be considered in conjunction with the primary reading of many of her poems about young girls who are unmarried or in the process of getting married (where often a Lesbian reading is secondary if it is relevant at all). This crucial set of poems to daughters and daughter-like girls has, in turn, to be taken together with her erotic work; the meanings of Demeter and Aphrodite, or the complexes of sexuality and maternalism, are partly conjoined in Sappho, who is quite definite about the analogy in at least two fragments (82, 142); the latter runs simply, "I've flown to you like a child to its mother," and the former comes near the end of a strongly erotic Lesbian poem. Perhaps this blending is one reason for the rage she has aroused in some minds for over two thousand years.

Sappho's human concerns were focused primarily on groups of women in Lesbos who devoted themselves to diverse arts. There are two extreme views about these groups, one that they were circles of Lesbians (Page 1955), the other that they constituted "academies" (Wilamowitz 1913); according to a third view, she was to women what Socrates was to men (Maximus of Tyre; Edmonds 1963: 155).

I follow Schadewaldt (1950) and others in holding that there is excellent textual and ceramic evidence from many parts of Greece for the existence of groups of young women who were instructed in dance, music, singing, the care and adornment of the body, and probably the lore and knowledge of sex and motherhood as well. Similar institutions are found in parts of Africa, Australia, and other parts of the primitive and archaic world. Since we have comparative evidence on dancing groups of premarital women from the Slavs and elsewhere, it is not unreasonable to posit the entire complex as Proto-Indo-European. The main function of such groups was and is to prepare girls for wedding and marriage, but the cultural, human, and often very personal bonds formed between the members and their leaders could be expected to continue and grow in later life.

Four important features distinguished these women's groups on Lesbos. First, they were dedicated to the Muses, Aphrodite, and the Graces, in contrast to Lesbian society at large, which worshiped the trinity of Zeus, Hera, and Dionysus (Page 1955: 69). Second, the women of Lesbos were noted, already in the early Greek world, for their pulchritude and their mastery of the traditional feminine arts. Over a hundred years before Sappho, Homer, speaking through Agamemnon, specifies the choicest gift of exchange: "And I will give him seven Lesbian women, skilled in perfect handiwork, whom, when he himself seized well-built Lesbos, I selected, who surpass all the races of women in their beauty" (*Il.* 9. 128–30). I am reminded of the fact known to anthropologists, and indeed any traveled person, that, in a given language and culture area, one city or locale tends to have and cultivate such a reputation for its women (e.g., Villon's Paris).

In the third place, the efflorescence of lyric poetry that began about 700 B.C. was exceptionally intense on Lesbos and included the very early originator, Terpander (who was called to Sparta to teach poetry), and the two poets whom many authorities would rank as the greatest monodic lyricists: Alcaeus and Sappho. As the latter puts it, with pride: "Towering like the singer of Lesbos over those of other lands" (148). This local hypertrophy remains a conundrum for the cultural historian. I think it was connected with the high status of women on the island and the role of poetry in everyday life, particularly the life of the women's groups. Lesbos may have been the most distinguished in what I think was an early pan-Hellenic "woman's culture" of colloquial poetry whose brilliance is hinted at in our evidence; we know, for example, of Erinna, who died at nineteen but is in the Greek Anthology, and of Corinna, the teacher of Pindar.

Fourth, it appears that individuals in these women's groups, especially leaders, competed with and for each other. Much of Sappho's verse is about competitors and about lovers being competed for:

"Andromeda has a fine recompense" (125). She had three main rivals and many serious loves, and some of them are mentioned repeatedly within this competitive amorous context. Such competitiveness is in tune with the personal and political relations between men in much of early Greece.

The quality of Sappho's personal relations with these Lesbian women deserves a few words as a supplement to the more basic discussion of friendship that follows; the qualities are referred or alluded to so often in the fragments as to render line citations otiose here. One such pattern is the directness with which she often expresses her personal feelings, compared, for example, to the often self-conscious or devious poetic styles of today. Yet we must also remember that some poems of hers which seem direct to us may have been intended as *indirect* allusions in the presence of certain audiences. A second of her qualities is her habit of teasing and mocking both friend and foe, either directly or through her divine persona, Aphrodite. Such teasing and mockery is of course the standard form of social control and competition through loss of face in what anthropologists call a "shame culture." A third and related quality is her stress on deceit and the use of ruse, wile, and stratagem, and this was also one of the main features of Aphrodite ("weaver of wiles"; Frags. 1, 134); it was also part of the Greek feeling that women better understand the *jeu d'esprit et du hasard* of amorous matters. A fourth quality, which emerges at times, is her capacity for anger and hostility or even vindictiveness: she boasts that her name will be remembered (11) while that of another woman (probably a rival) will be forgotten in Hades (71); in another fragment (55) she speaks of someone "satiated" with a rival (presumably with the same *double-entendre* we would hear). As the examples imply, these qualities tend to emerge in competitive relations among women, and Sappho is being explicit, expressive—honest, if you will—about the normal emotional reaction to the loss of a loved one to another: jealousy. Yet she can be contrite: "I am not resentful, but have the heart of a little child" (74). The fifth quality is her concern with the values and idioms of friendship and personal attraction, empathy, and sympathy. She is drawn to various people and expresses this vividly and diversely. The qualities I have identified—directness, mockery and teasing, wiliness and deceit, capacity for anger, and strong personal attraction—add up to an emotional texture that differs markedly from much recent poetry, whether neo-Romantic, "cool," or simply anemic. Yet it resembles some poems by Louise Bogan, for example, or Marina Tsvetaeva (e.g., "Attempt at Jealousy").

Many of Sappho's poems deal with the affection, love, passion, tenderness, infatuation, and other feelings of a woman for one of her own sex. Most of the feelings and actions, as observed in a superficial reading of the poems, are fairly innocuous. In fact, some writers claim that no poem or fragment requires a "homoerotic" reading or that the entire image of Sappho and her friends as "practicing Lesbians" is one vast male fabrication of gossip and slander, a male myth of sorts—notably in Ovid, who put the extreme case: "What did the Lesbian Sappho teach but to love girls?" (*Tristia* 2. 365)—Ovid, in whose mythology many hundreds of women are murdered, raped, mutilated, and otherwise metamorphosed. Even Sappho's most physically intense poem, the so-called pathographic Fragment 2 (Saake 1971), does not necessarily imply a physically sexual relationship, although it seems to to most readers, including me:

> O Brocheo, I see you
> and speech fails me,
> the tongue shatters,
> my skin runs with delicate
> flame—my eyes dim;
> I'm hearing things!
> and sweat cascades,
> a trembling clutches
> my whole body,
> paler than grass,
> lacking little to death.
>
> (trans. D. and P. Friedrich)

One can sympathize with the idealists, but it does seem that many poems or fragments are either highly ambiguous or do call for a primary Lesbian reading; and this reading is always diffuse or refined. For example:

> You lay in wait
> behind a laurel tree,
>
> and everything
> was pleasant:
>
> you a woman
> wanderer like me.

> I barely heard you,
> my darling;
>
> you came in your
> trim garments,
>
> and suddenly: beauty
> of your garments.
>
> (trans. W. Barnstone 1976: 91;
> 118A [App.])

It has seemed to many for almost three millennia that some fragments, including some of the most brilliant, conclude or break off in
a way that suggests the erotic. One, Fragment 83, for example, begins, "Honestly I wish I were dead," and depicts the sorrow of a
departing friend and how Sappho consoled her with reminders of
their happy times together. It ends:

> and with much oil of flowers
>   precious and regal
> did you anoint your skin   opposite me
>   and on a soft bed from the hands of female servants
> satisfy your longing [*pothos*]
> and no hill or sacred place
>   was there we did not go
>   groves   sound
>   song

This poem, both the final, preserved lines and the isolated words,
suggests a physical reading, obviously; but note that even here
the poet's perception corresponds to the well-established "proprio-
ceptive" nature of female sexual responsiveness (i.e., response to
general emotions within oneself, over longer time spans, with longer
afterglow). Such a psychology would tend to generate a more diffuse and symbolic poetic representation, and this raises in acute
form the question of canons of criticism and, particularly, of symbolic analysis. If we stick to a literal interpretation, not going beyond
the evidence (whatever that means), we will be left with pseudo-
medical descriptions of somatic states, with reddish moons, and
so forth. If we grant that Sappho is one of the great erotic poets—
and we do so with good reason—then her body becomes an icon for
a myth of the inner life, and her "rosy-fingered moon" (in the
famous Fragment 86) becomes an extraordinary symbol that combines a reddish dusk, a transformation of a setting sun into a rising

moon, an erotic condensation of Lesbian loveplay, and, perhaps, an experiment with a new, woman's, language. An uninhibited symbolic approach to Sappho will lead us into the many interacting planes and levels of which her work is constituted.

Some of the fragments seem unquestionably carnal and erotic—for example, "dripping clout" (131), "I long and I yearn" (23), and an entire encounter poem that ends, "But send away your hand-maidens, and may the gods grant me whatever they have" (46). What struck some scholars as a mystery seems to have been re-solved by the discovery, in a papyrus, of the frankly erotic Frag-ment 99 (Loebel and Page), which was translated as follows by Davenport (1965: 111, cited in Roche 1966: xlv–xv): ". . . slick with slime . . . Polyanaktidas . . . shoots forward . . . playing such music upon these strings/wearing a phallus of leather . . . such a thing as this . . . enviously . . . twirls quivering masterfully . . . and has for odor . . . hollow . . . mysteries, orgies . . . leaving . . . comes . . . companions . . . mysteries . . . sister . . . so . . . wishes . . . displays again Polyanaktidas / this randy madness I joyfully proclaim."

The lush hues of this fragment remind us that almost all of Sap-pho's actual work was destroyed by Christians and that, according to an alternative biography (or myth), there were really two Sapphos, one a poet and one a courtesan, or simply another Lesbian called Sappho, or that Sappho herself was a courtesan. But after noting these speculations, let us also recognize how different this fragment is from the rest of Sappho, not only in its words but in its perception of love in terms of sex objects in an object world—the sort of view that characterizes serious erotic poetry by men and by Lesbians who have taken over that male way of seeing things. It also characterizes pornography done by and for men and suggests the work of some anonymous Egyptian-Greek male working in the meter of Sappho (an early precedent for the recent Sappho article in *Playboy Magazine*).

Sappho deals with other aspects of female psychology. At times she writes about virginity through a metaphor: "Like a pippin reddening on the high tip of the highest branch—the applepickers forgot it, no, they didn't forget but couldn't reach it" (150). At times she is ambiguous, as in, "Do I still long for my virginity?" (159), and at times lighthearted: "Virginity, virginity, leaving me, where would you go?" (164). (The key term, *parthenia,* can denote the social status, the physical state, or the maidenhead itself; the same ambiguity is discussed below, in chapter 8.)

Unlike Homer, Sappho does refer to courtesans, contemptuously so when she vents her anger at Rhodopis, for whom her brother had conceived a notorious infatuation: "with whom you mingled in vagrant love which deems beautiful what may be had for the asking," or, "as for you, black bitch, may you put your evil snout to the ground and go hunting for others." In defense of her brother, I would note that the large sums he spent were used mainly to purchase Rhodopis' freedom from her Egyptian slave-owner. It also seems that Sappho's contempt and hostility are not necessarily motivated by moral indignation at the world's oldest profession (although that would be generally consistent with some aspects of her view of love). Her main motives may have been jealousy of her brother and a practical concern that the family's money was disappearing into one of Egypt's most alluring fleshpots. A high moralistic tone here strikes me as possibly out of character, since it would contradict her worship of Aphrodite.

Sappho has a jaundiced view of middle and old age, as in her "old age makes [a thousand wrinkles] go about my skin, and love is in no hurry to fly to me" (42), or "I pray for long life and health, may I escape wrinkles, my children" (113). In this she is fairly typical of Greek poets. Her dislike of death and the ravaging effects of age are consonant with her view of growth, beauty, and love. Sappho, in sum, deals with various stages in a woman's growth, mentality, and sexuality but mainly with the affections of mature or at least nubile women for each other.

But I disagree with the many who claim that she was interested only in emotional relations between women. She was attached to her brothers and jealous about them, although the way she pilloried the prodigal may indicate that she never had cared for him. She was a friend of the other great poet of Lesbos, Alcaeus, who was a leader in the political faction with which she was aligned and also wrote one of the finest lines ever about her: "Violet-haired, pure, honey-smiling Sappho" (Alcaeus, Frag. 124). She was married to a wealthy businessman from Andros (granted, she never mentions him). Many of her lines, or even whole poems, are about a woman's affection for a man, whether lover, groom, or husband. She must have held in awe, as part of her general identification with the goddess, the story of Adonis and his affair with Aphrodite.

Actually, a substantial portion of Sappho's poems are wedding songs, or epithalamia (a tenth or more, depending on the classifier). In part, this reflects her group's function of preparing girls for marriage, and, congruous with this, the epithalamia themselves differ formally (in line and diction) from the rest of her corpus in ways that make them look like an archaic residue—a special traditional form left over from earlier times. But they do deal with and often extol weddings and marriage and the love between man and woman. (That so many of the epithalamia survived may be due to the relative innocuousness of their theme.)

The epithalamia sing the pleasures of conjugal life, including the carnal ones: "I am overwhelmed through Aphrodite with longing for a tender youth" (135), or, "Your form is grace and your eyes of a honey color, bride, love pours over your face; Aphrodite has honored you exceedingly" (158). Somewhat stronger is: "If my paps could still give suck and my womb were able to bear children, then I would come to another marriage bed with unfaltering feet" (Edmonds 1963: 213; the translation includes Edmonds' conjectural interpolations). One of her longest poems (66) celebrates the marriage of two paragons of civic virtue, Hector and Andromache. (I take exception to Kirk's statement that this poem is a "routine exercise" and "one of Sappho's least successful surviving poems" [1975: 213]—as if there were a failed set to chose from!)

The love that Sappho's Aphrodite controls may be heterosexual or Lesbian; the poet does not draw a sharp line between the two. In one fragment the goddess is equally responsible for Helen's going to Troy and the departure of the poet's friend for Lydia; for Helen's fulfilled love for Paris and for the poet's unrequited longing for her absent friend (Gerber 1976: 111, apparently quoting G. Privitera). Many of Sappho's poems and short fragments are ambiguous about which love is at stake and hence are more significant than if this were clear. There is no evidence that Sappho was a man-hater, and the tendency in some quarters today to make this association is distasteful if not blasphemous (if I may paraphrase the familiar objection to identifying Sappho's Aphrodite with the late Roman Venus); I have in mind, also, the image conceived by a pronouncedly Lesbian contemporary poet of a "stone Aphrodite" grinding up penises in her lap. There is, on the other hand, plenty of evidence that Sappho was more responsive to women than to men.

Sometimes she is just elegantly ambiguous, as in the following:

> Let the depths of my soul be dumb
> for I cannot think up
> a clarion song about Adonis

for Aphrodite who staggers me
with shameful lust
has reduced me to dull silence,

and Persuasion (who maddens one)
from her gold vial
spills tangy nectar on my mind.

(trans. W. Barnstone 1976: 81)

Whether or not Sappho was a practicing Lesbian or just passionately attracted to women is superficial compared to the more basic fact that her love *must include a woman*. Here Lesbian love and heterosexual love are combined to contrast with male homosexuality (about which she says nothing and implies almost nothing, probably because of lack of interest). Her implicit classification differs strongly from the male-dominant heterosexuality of the *Iliad* and the idealization of erotic love between male intellectuals and artists in Plato. It certainly has always had its adherents and practitioners and does so today, but, again, it differs from other views that may be more popular, such as that "gays and squares" are pitted against each other or that radical Lesbians are pitted against the rest of the world; there are other possible positions, of course. The principle or motivation for these popular classifications is mainly moralistic and often intensely politicized, that is, linked with issues of racism, the holding of public office, and the like. The Sapphic grouping, on the other hand, based on the woman as the sine qua non, derived from and was consistent with Sappho's vision of beauty and creativity: creativity and beauty require a female principle as a necessary and a sufficient condition.

SAPPHO'S SUBJECTIVITY

Sappho's poems have to do with personal feelings between people. This subject matter was shaped partly by her elaboration of Aphrodite's diagnostic feature of operating and influencing, not in a direct, material sense, but through the mind and the emotions by causing such psychophysical states as longing, jealousy, and hatred. Her focus on personal feelings and intersubjective bonds, coupled with the vividness of that focus, does much to explain her singular modernity. Unlike any Greek poet except Homer, Sappho is a vital part of today's poetic scene, a major source of inspiration for some of the best poets of our century.

What was the main source of this subjectivity of hers? Many scholars derive it from Archilochus, a mercenary soldier and innovative genius who lived about 680–40 B.C. (or several decades earlier). Snell, for example, says, "She has learnt the lesson from Archilochus," and "Sappho learned from Archilochus how to experience, and to express, her luckless love, which comes near to death" (1960: 56, 53). In the face of this widespread opinion, I would point out that Archilochus, as a lover, was mainly a vaunting male or an embittered hater who, among other things, drove a young woman to suicide through his satires (which, in an extreme shame culture, are tantamount to murder or, at least, to torture). The following fairly represents his "lesson": "Feeble now are the muscles in my mushroom," "And to fall upon her heaving belly, and thrust your groin into her groin, your thighs between her thighs," "His penis is swollen like a donkey from Priene," "What sensuality and fat ankles. O fat whore for hire!" (Barnstone 1976: 30). To contend that Sappho "learned to experience from Archilochus" is bizarre male chauvinism.

A subjectivity far beyond that of Archilochus had already been wonderfully elaborated by Homer, for example in the sustained ambiguity of the interaction between Odysseus and Penelope so masterfully analyzed by Harsh (1950) and Amory (1969). Homer handles a wide range of subjective states through simile, dialogue, and other techniques. His protagonists give voice to fear, anger, sorrow, pain, longing, and affection with a poignancy and eloquence that have inspired poets ever since.

Sappho's debt to the Homeric legacy was probably increased by her personal mobility. We know that, because of political factionalism, she spent a number of years in Sicily as a small girl and again as an adult, that the Greek city-states of Sicily were in artistic ferment, and that one of the main centers of Aphrodite's worship was located there. We also know that Sappho's lyric tradition was extremely ancient and was almost totally oral, like the epic tradition with which it interacted. Sappho, as a famous poet of her time, voyaged to many parts of the Greek-speaking world—to the islands, the mainland, Sicily—and competed at festivals with her songs and hymns. It is inconceivable that a poet of her genius, at the turn of the sixth century, should not have heard most or all of Homer many times; she must have known many thousands of his lines by heart. She was an artistic and linguistic virtuoso (Boas 1914: 482, in Boas 1940) who strove to understand and rival her main predecessor in the creation of song and mythic text.

Sappho's indebtedness to Homer is conclusively shown by the internal evidence of language. The classicists have generally admitted this; indeed, they have written scores of articles on the particulars. An excellent bibliography by Gerber (1976), listing and annotating ninety-five articles about Sappho published between 1967 and 1975, includes a number on her specific ties to Homer (for example, Aphrodite descending, in Sappho's Fragment 1, may have been modeled on her descent and ascent in Book Five of the *Iliad*). Finally, a tenth of the diction in some of her poems (e.g., Frag. 66) is modeled on epic, and the fraction goes higher if we use a "generative" approach that admits analogies as well as direct borrowings (Nagler 1974). But all these assessments are based on the scholarly grounds of metrics, diction, positive theme, and so on; they understate or ignore the relation between the two poets on the psychological and metaphysical level that I am urging. Incidentally, I stress Sappho's debt to Homer not with the goal of establishing her subordination to him but of illustrating a case where a genius of the highest order internalizes and draws on the creativity of his or her main predecessor in order to attain equal heights (though within a smaller range). Legitimate analogies would seem to be Chopin's relation to Bach or Anna Akhmatova's to Pushkin. In these terms, then, I renew my earlier question: What did Sappho add to the meaning of Aphrodite? In particular, what did she add to the subjectivity of Homer's Aphrodite?

To the already sophisticated subjectivity of Homer, Sappho added at least four major things. First, there are, in her poetry, new planes, if not degrees, of intensity. Often this intensity has a feminine ring or reference, as in, "Come here tonight I pray, Gongyla, my rose with your Lydian lyre; my longing hovers about your beauty" (45). Many passages, as in this one (54), express love and yearning with a fresh force that has since become one of the main connotations of the term "Sapphic":

> like a wind
> crashing down
> among oak trees
> love shattered
> my mind.

There is no "positive evidence" whatsoever that "she recollects her emotion in tranquility," as Page would have it (1955: 136); on the contrary, the fragments strongly suggest the fury of creation, both in its inception and during composition, in what Turyn has pinpointed as the nexus between "the moment of perception and the onset of emotion" (cited by Page 1955: 69). This emotion may emerge as an outcry or as a delicate tissue of traditional imagery; it is referred to as "love," Eros, Aphrodite, soul-wind, or mind or heart *(thumos)*. Sappho was the first to map out this complex of sentiment, and no one has ever excelled her. I would agree with Schadewaldt (1950: 8) that she is "the inventor of love" as that term has been used and varied upon by poets ever since and by Everyman in his poetic moments, or as Barnstone, speaking of the poem to Anaktoria, puts it more freshly, "She elevated love to the criterion of value" (1976: 65).

Sappho's second contribution was to put her subjectivity in a special way into the first person of the lyric poet. Lyric forms, particularly the satire, had been widespread for over a century, if not much longer. Ward (1973) has amassed much evidence on satirical verse in Greek, Germanic, Celtic, and other early systems and has inferred that the genre itself was probably Proto-Indo-European. Many of the specific metrics, idioms, and styles had been around for some time. Archilochus, poet of elegies, epodes, and of satires in iambic, comes out of, and fits into, the tradition of these forms and certainly pioneered in the use of the first person. And the themes of longing and affection, spoken in the first person by a woman, had been treated with supreme mastery in Andromache's speech in Book Six of the *Iliad,* in the funeral laments in Book Twenty-four, and in the Homeric Hymn to Demeter (seventh century). Thus in both content and form there were many precedents for Sappho.

Sappho, however, restructured and deepened the first-person mode by combining it with her intense emotionality. Perhaps the best example of her novel semantic and psychological depth is Fragment 2, which I discussed and half-translated above. It begins with the line "He is equal (similar) to the gods" and then depicts Sappho's watching (presumably jealous and Lesbian) the conversation between a handsome man and a woman lover. But beyond this reading, which is obvious and primary only from a certain point of view, there are at least four other main readings that are quite admissible (for example, Sappho may be speaking of herself facing the man; she identifies with the man as a man before the woman; she is not jealous, only responding to her lover, etc.). These alternatives partly reflect the potentials inherent in the speech situation, but the critical thing is that Sappho suggests them to the reader by the power with which she depicts her own emotions. Some subset of these various readings is at work, I think we have to assume, during sensitive rehearings. The complexity or, if you will, the spiritual depth of Sappho's first person is partly created by this kaleidoscopic shifting between readings, during which her first person moves from position to position in the active and latent dyads and triads of the speech situation. Instead of trying to prove that one reading is the correct one, the genuine critical effort, the one perhaps yielding the greatest analytical interest, would be devoted to exploring the hierarchy of these ambiguous alternative readings and the dynamic interactions between them.

Sappho's third contribution was a marvelously personal texture at the delicate "seventh level" of sound that is hard or impossible to capture in translation. She is the sort of poet who makes us aware of the inherent beauty of words and makes people ask which of her words is the most beautiful (one answer was "honey-voiced" [*mellikopōnē,* from Frag. 30]). Of the many specific exemplary passages I could give, I limit myself to the first stanza of Fragment 1 (the full translation into English appears below on page 124).[2]

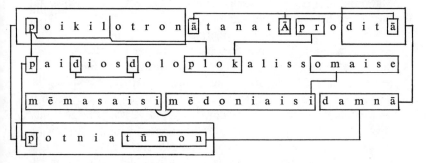

By the device of connecting many of the sounds that alliterate, rhyme, and echo each other, I hope to convey, in the accompanying chart, some idea of the phonic texture that weaves the stanza together. Otherwise, I cannot define Sappho's "seventh level" without entering into details of Greek metrics, wording, and style that are beyond the scope of this book. Her work illustrates the dictum of her student, Osip Mandelstam: "As a stone in a great cathedral, so a word yearns for its place in the poem."

Many have claimed that Sappho's language was completely colloquial and vernacular—that she was a sort of Greek analogue of Robert Burns. But this is unprovable in the absence of independent evidence on spoken, everyday Lesbian. It is probably true that "rarely, if anywhere, in archaic or classical poetry shall we find language so far independent of literary tradition, apparently so close to the speech of everyday life" (Page 1955: 30), but this evaluation holds mainly for the intimate, personal poems; comparatively speaking, Sappho is dependent on more than one tradition. That she often lacks obvious dependence on a tradition, particularly the epic tradition, does not, of course, mean that she is ever "artless" or "purely colloquial."

The generalization that can stand is that her language, on the surface, is *relatively* colloquial and *typically* simple and direct. This quality was combined with extreme elegance and technical virtuosity in the use of complex forms, such as the eleven- and fourteen-syllable "Sapphic lines" that she invented and popularized (she also invented the *pectis,* a kind of harp with which to accompany poetry). To paraphrase Roche, she synthesized the popular immediacy and colloquialism of a Bob Dylan with the technical virtuosity and originality of a Gerard Manley Hopkins, or, if this seems incongruous, the colloquialism of Diane Wakowski and the technique of Marianne Moore. In the same context she could be likened to the Pushkin of *Eugene Onegin* and to Robert Frost.

This third contribution, of poetic form, brings us to yet another contrast between Sappho and Homer. The latter (like Hesiod) took the many thousands of preexisting, prefabricated formulas of the epic's special artistic language and, fitting them together and creating new ones by analogy, constructed his monumental epics, devoted to such traditional themes as honor, wanderings, war, the gods, the character of heroes, agriculture and hunting. Sappho, on the contrary, drawing mainly on the spoken language, wove a more delicate texture of sound. This delicacy of texture is, I feel, a sort of phonic icon of the values of delicacy and refinement in her vision of love.

These values in her language and outlook may in part be symbolized by the Greek words *habros* and *habrosunē,* which we translate as "exquisite, exquisiteness, refined, refinement, delicate," and the like. These words are poetic in the strict sense of occurring almost only in poetry, and lyric poetry at that. Their nonoccurrence in epic may be connected with the sometimes disparaging tone they have in some authors, as when used of things Asiatic or too dainty. They form a little paradigm with dolls, pets, toys, children, girls, women, the (woman's) body, Eros and the Graces, and Sappho was very fond of them, as in her line, "as for me, listen well, my delight is in the exquisite." Sappho's exquisiteness or refinement overlaps her feeling for "grace" *(charis)* that I defined above (which differs somewhat from Homer's). In the matrix of connotations of words like these, the Greek meanings of Aphrodite and the language of love were enlarged and deepened.

SAPPHO AND APHRODITE

The three things Sappho added to the subjectivity of Homer—new intensities, a complex first person, and unique poetic texture—may now be drawn together and added to a fourth that is already partly familiar: her vision of the poet's connection to religious, mythic force. A few other divinities are mentioned, and there is a poem to Hera (40) and perhaps one to Artemis; but it is Aphrodite who is invoked repeatedly, and there are four different names for her in the scores of times she appears (Page 1955: 126–28). She is the theme or central figure in many poems, including many of the greatest. Other early Greek poets, notably Homer and Euripides, wrote hymns or other poetic statements to or about the gods or a god, and Hesiod had an unparalleled vision of their entire genealogy; but Sappho is unique in early Greece for the directness and prominence of her tie to a single divinity: in the sense of presence, immediacy, and reality that she creates for her Aphrodite. In this she ranks with David of the Hebrews, the Spaniard, Saint John of the Cross, and the unknown poet-sages of the Rig Veda, who over three millennia ago sang to Ushas, the goddess of dawn.

Sappho's closeness to Aphrodite and the clarity of her perception of her gave her, as a poet, a deeply religious meaning in the early Greek world, similar to Homer's. She is the seeress who reveals to us, mankind, the personification of growth and beauty and all the rest of Aphrodite's characteristics—her insularity, her goldenness, and her liminality (movement in the interstices between normal structures). Above all, Sappho incarnates the goddess' most fundamental trait: her subjectivity, working through the heart, the synthesis of wild emotion and high sophistication. These aphrodisiac traits are congruous with what I earlier called Sappho's singularly contemporary focus on intersubjective processes and relations. Much of this is condensed in her greatest poem, Fragment 1:

Hymn to Aphrodite

You of the inlaid throne, deathless Aphrodite,
Daughter of Zeus and weaver of wiles, I entreat you,
Oh Queen, don't break me with suffering and sorrow

But come here now if ever before in the past
You heard my cries from afar and marked them
And, leaving your father's golden house,

Yoked your chariot and came. Swift
Beautiful sparrows bore you over the black earth;
Moving thick-feathered wings from heaven through
    the middle sky

They arrived. And you asked
Blessèd one, with a smile on your immortal face,
What ailed me this time, why did I call you again,

And what did I most want for myself in my wild heart.
"Whom shall I persuade this time
Into the harness of your love? Sappho, who's wronging you?

For if she flees, soon she'll be chasing.
She doesn't accept gifts, but she'll be giving,
And loves not but soon shall—whether or no."

Come to me now, too; set me loose from this agony.
Fulfill everything my heart longs for.
Be my comrade.

                (trans. P. Friedrich)

Sappho's relation to "Aphrodite" is characterized by the ambiguity, already noted, between Aphrodite, the personalized, anthropomorphic member of the Olympian pantheon, and *aphroditē,* the complex of attraction, empathy, and passion that we can sometimes gloss as "love." In some cases there is *relatively* little ambiguity: the actual goddess probably does not "enter" Sappho, and the emotional complex does not wear a golden bracelet; but, as I hope the reader is realizing, even these cases can be ambiguous. The characteristic that we can describe as "a god combined with or embodying an emotion" is shared by Ares and Dionysus. Its potential for poetry is realized in Sappho.

Sappho's status as a variant of the goddess was in a way confirmed by the story, or myth, of her death. At least one fragment (99) deals with her power over a younger man:

> . . . but, though loving me,
> win a younger bedmate,
> for I cannot endure
> to cohabit with a youth,
> being the older.

(trans. P. Friedrich)

In her fifties this physically small and slight "nightingale with mis-shapen wings" became hopelessly enamored of a young and hand-some ferryman (to whom Aphrodite, disguised as an old woman, had given an aphrodisiac for ferrying her). When the ferryman lost interest in Sappho, she followed him, until, realizing the desperate-ness of her predicament, she hurled herself to her death from the Leucadian Cliff on an island near Corfu. Now, it was Aphrodite who first leapt from the white cliff, and she did it on the suggestion of Zeus in order to get rid of her passion for Phaethon. The white cliff itself is part of an inebriating metaphorical set that runs from the leap into the sea to "sexual relief," to the boundaries of the sun and consciousness, to the gates of the underworld, and to the dream gates of ivory and horn (Nagy 1973). Sappho herself interrelates the Cyprian, sun, and death:

> In Kypros I am Queen
> and to you a power
> as sun of fire
> is glory to all.
> Even in Hades
> I am with you.

(Loebel and Page, 65; trans.
W. Barnstone 1976: 96)

SAPPHO IN A LARGER CONTEXT

The copious Sapphic scholarship, on which I have drawn widely, falls into several traditions. One, relatively innocuous, consists of ecstatic outbursts. The second consists of technical scholarly arti-cles, and there are more about Sappho than about any other Greek lyric poet except Pindar. How many articles and notes are there about individual fragments, even words? And some of the scholarly evaluations do her justice: "No masculine love poetry among the Greeks even approached the spiritual depth of Sappho's lyrics" (Jaeger 1945: 134). I hasten to add that, to keep this statement out of the "ecstatic outburst" category, we must give "spiritual depth" not a German or English, romantic or idealistic, gloss but a psychological one of subjectivity and a semantic one of complexity and multilayeredness. Some of these scholars and critics would rank Sappho with Pindar and Alcaeus in terms of quality.

There is a third tradition, which overlaps the second. It persists in equating Sappho not only with Alcaeus and Archilochus (which is reasonable, since they are, if not in her class, at least in the next one down) but also with Simonides, Alcman, Stesichorus, and many other lyricists from the seventh to the fifth centuries who got into the Greek Anthology. This evaluation may be a contemporary variant of the one that criticized Sappho for being a poet and by which we lost almost the total corpus of another colloquial woman poet, Corinna (I am referring to what we may assume was a pan-Hellenic tradition of "woman's poetry"—almost all of it lost due to the male-dominant values of the times). The negative attitudes toward Sappho in academia may be reflected in the fact that only one lecture is typically allotted to her in the standard semester on lyric poetry. It may also be reflected by one of the major specialists who, in his authoritative book, speaks of Sappho, or of various passages in her work, in the following terms: "trivial," "conventional," "[lacking] artifice," "not spiritual," "transition not adroitly managed," "placid spirit," "a little fanciful or a little dull," "detached about her emotions." The unfortunate prejudices and often implicitly derogatory criticisms seem to be shared by many, if not most, of the specialists in early Greek poetry (almost all of whom are men), and they seem to be particularly widespread in England and the United States.

Sappho has inspired hostility since shortly after her death. She was pilloried and derided by Aristophanes and some other classical writers. Between the first and fifteenth centuries of our era, notably as a consequence of Christianity, 95 percent of her poems were destroyed, that is, most of the estimated 9,000 lines that had been arranged into seven or nine books by the Alexandrians. Some of this rapine occurred during outbursts of Greek Orthodox fanaticism. Some of it was performed by French and German Crusaders who took part in the infamous Fourth Crusade (financed by Venice), when they sacked Constantinople in 1204. On several occasions her poems were publicly burned by the orders of popes and bishops or by mobs of zealots (Barnstone 1965: xxi–xxii). This compulsion to burn Sappho indicates that her vision threatened the Christian foundations of patriarchy, hypocrisy, and puritanism.

What survived chanced to be illustrative material tucked away in technical works on grammar and style or, weirdly enough, served as the papyrus ingredients of the sort of papier-mâché used for coffin cartons, mummies, and the stuffing of stuffed crocodiles! Her hymn to Aphrodite—perhaps the greatest lyric in Greek—was preserved as part of a syntactic treatise by Dionysius of Halicarnassus as an example of "finished and brilliant composition." Of her five-hundred-odd poems, there survive to this day between six and seven hundred lines. Her work was extirpated from the Greek-speaking world just as ruthlessly and almost as successfully as the image of her persona, Aphrodite.

In contrast to her treatment by Crusaders and popes, Sappho has always enjoyed a special status among poets and poetry lovers, particularly those really familiar with her work. Her fellow citizens regarded her highly as a teacher and a poet. Her poems were known in various degrees by millions of ordinary persons in early times, and their effect is illustrated by one anecdote: "One evening over wine E. sang a song of Sappho's which his uncle liked so much he bade the boy teach it to him, and when one of the company asked in surprise, 'What for?' he replied, 'I want to learn it and die' " (Edmonds 1963: 141). Socrates is typical in calling her "Sappho the beautiful" (at a critical point in the *Phaedrus,* one of the two great dialogues about love). Greeks of the late period, such as Strabo, saw her as a marvel—and this in a male-dominated epoch when women were criticized for competing with men in poetry. Many simply ranked her in the same class as Pindar and Archilochus, but the majority seem to have placed her in a separate category as the greatest of the nine "greats" of lyric poetry or, better, as the "Tenth Muse": "Memory [the mother of the Muses] was astonished when she heard the honey-voiced Sappho, wondering whether mankind possessed a tenth Muse" (Palatine Anthology, in Edmonds 1963: 165) (the Muses, as we recall, were strongly associated with Aphrodite). Among Greek (and, for that matter, Latin) poets Sappho is, as I have already suggested, surpassed only by Homer in her potential relevance to contemporary poetry—its practice, aesthetics, and myth.

The special elevation of Sappho probably resulted, at least in part, from the way she combined the features that I have tried to spell out above: (1) her poems are composed, usually, in simple, direct language; (2) they exhibit formal elegance and elegant form, and "exquisiteness"; (3) they treat of physical passion, often di-

rectly expressed (about love and death); (4) they express a strongly
religious vision.

The few other poets who also may be said to combine these elements include Solomon, Saint John of the Cross, the Mexican woman poet, Sor Juana Inez de la Cruz, and the Russian modern, Anna
Akhmatova. In the United States one thinks immediately of Emily
Dickinson, if you grant, as I would, her physical passion about
death. And in this century there have certainly been, intermittently,
many individual poems—by Hilda Doolittle, Louise Bogan, Sylvia
Plath ("Ariel"), Tess Gallagher, Louise Glück, Olga Broumas
("The Triple Muse"), and others—that have put the Sapphic ingredients together into hard-wrought masterpieces; for the most
part, however, the poets do not have the Sapphic vision of love.
Maybe in coming decades some woman will match or excel Sappho
(as Tolstoy partly succeeded in his self-imposed goal of matching
Homer).

After this digression into the present and future, let me return
to Sappho and Aphrodite. Sappho may be said to have rewritten
the pan-Hellenic meaning of Aphrodite in a number of ways. She
intensifies passionate love in various physical and psychic shades
and blendings. She enriches and deepens the subjectivity of the
goddess and increases our insight into such feelings as yearning,
desolation, jealousy, and rapture. While she is negative about
courtesans, she speaks in her poetry of single as well as multiple
love, conjugal as well as nonconjugal (including Lesbian), and the
love both of a heterosexual lover and of a mother for her child,
specifically, a daughter. Her vision rests on important assumptions
about beauty in things and the possibility of empathy and attraction
between persons as being, in a sense, "all we've got." By a striking
coincidence, since they were separated from each other by almost
two millennia, the world's first woman poet, the Babylonian Enheduanna, sang of Inanna as a goddess of war, and the world's
greatest poet, Sappho of Lesbos, finally recast Aphrodite as a
goddess of little else than love, but of most varieties of that.

6

The Religious Meaning of Aphrodite

What is the religious meaning of Aphrodite? While an insistence on working definitions and issues of classification can become sterile, I think it apt and useful to be explicit here. Let me start with an adaptation and paraphrase of a definition by Clifford Geertz with which I provisionally concur: religion is a system of symbols by which man constructs powerful, pervasive, and perduring moods and motivations by composing comprehensive and profound conceptions of a general order of existence and clothing those conceptions with such factuality and credibility as to make the moods and motivations seem uniquely realistic (Geertz 1966: 4).

Let us now compare this definition with one offered by another anthropological theorist, Edward Sapir, who wrote:

> Religion is man's never-ceasing attempt to discover a road to spiritual serenity across the perplexities and dangers of daily life. Where the need for such serenity is passionately felt, we have religious yearning; where it is absent, religious behavior is no more than socially sanctified form or an aesthetic blend of belief and gesture. . . . There can be neither fear nor humiliation for deeply religious natures, for they have intuitively experienced both of these emotions in advance of the declared hostility of an overwhelming world, coldly indifferent to human desire (1928, in 1951: 347).

A close comparison of the full texts of these two celebrated essayists points to a number of questions and problems regarding the religious meaning of Aphrodite. For example, what is the role of the emotional as against cognitive factors (granted that the line between them is not clear)? Aphrodite involves certain affective domains that are normally slighted in religion. What is the role of a pristine sense of holiness as compared with an intellectual capacity or need to explain? Aphrodite clearly draws most on the mysterious and irrational. To what extent does religion create for its believers a stronger sense of reality, of what Geertz calls the

"really real," as contrasted with an escape from the here and now
into absolute religious values? Here the worship of Aphrodite divides between the heightened perceptions that go with love and,
on the other hand, a transport into aesthetic values that can play
the part of abstract absolutes. To what extent is religion a matter of
"functions"—of enabling man to cope with a sense of helplessness,
despair at death, infatuation, etc.? Or is religion to be seen as a
cultural system in some pure sense, abstracted from biological needs
and material reality? The worship of Aphrodite lends support to
both approaches or points of view; it is functional in a narrowly
functionalist sense and yet, as my fourth chapter shows, entails
a complex cultural code of interacting dimensions. Finally we can
ask: Is religion primarily an individual experience that gets extended
out to group phenomena, such as communal rituals, or is it mainly
a sociocentric reality that is particularized and lived by the individual? Both emphases can be argued for the religion of Aphrodite;
some combination of them would be realistic. In addition to these
suggestive contrasts, the two theorists and many others agree on
certain things: that religion makes the paradoxes of nature more
intelligible and at times even interesting, alluring, or inspiring; that
religions are built of intuitions concerning realms of experience that
are beyond our ken—the uncanny, the awesome, the mysterious;
and that religion critically creates some heightened sense of
"reality."

Let us now deal in turn with three problems of religion and
religiosity: the relation of myth to the sacred, the role of latency
in the power of mythic or religious figures, and, last, the religious
force that is defined or catalyzed or energized by what I have been
calling *liminality*.

MYTH AND THE SACRED

From one interesting and irreverent point of view, the difference
between myth and folktale is a matter of degree and the dichotomy
itself is a folk dichotomy carried over from the nineteenth century.
From another, the dichotomy has some usefulness. Here folktales
are characterized as less serious, more concerned with narrative
interest and wish-fulfillment; the use of generic names for their
characters and similar criteria are also used (Kirk 1975: 37–41).
From yet another widely accepted, even traditional, point of view,
myth is part of folklore in some vague sense, but what sets it off is

its *sacredness*. As Kluckhohn put it: "Granting that there are sometimes both secular and sacred versions of the same tale and that
other difficulties obtrude themselves in particular cases, it still
seems possible to use the connotation of the sacred as that which
differentiates 'myth' from the rest of folklore" (1942: 46). Kluckhohn himself was not too clear about what defines the sacred, nor
have others done much better. Leach, for example (1958: 97),
offers this rough-and-ready schema:

> In anthropological jargon the category opposition between *sacred*
> and *profane* is given a special meaning. Roughly speaking:
>
> *sacred* = abnormal, special, otherworldly, royal, sick, taboo
> *profane* = normal, everyday, of this world, plebeian,
>   permitted, healthy

Others have argued that the sacred is, as already noted, about the
mysterious, the unknown, the terrifying and uncontrollable, just
as religion can "account for, and even celebrate, the perceived
ambiguities, puzzles, and paradoxes of human existence" (Geertz
1966: 23). In yet another formulation the sacred condenses and
symbolizes in a particularly intense way the needs, aspirations, and
values of a given social group (Durkheim 1915). This particularly
includes the Aphrodite values of fertility and procreation, with
which human beings in the great majority of cultures are so terribly
concerned.

LATENCY IN THE POWER OF MYTHIC FIGURES

What is the relation between explicitness and frequency in myth
and the effective power of mythic figures? My analysis above showed
that Aphrodite is the most intensely marked of the goddesses—
which seems consistent with her sensuousness. This structural intensity of hers was not consciously known to Homer, of course,
and has not been recognized to this day, and yet it is congruous
with her workings in the epics and elsewhere. Compare her with
Athena, in particular. The latter does hurry after and hover over her
heroes, but as a sort of efficient cause, whereas Aphrodite, though
she appears relatively seldom, functions as the final or ultimate cause
that motivates much of the action: the key conflicts over Helen,
Briseis, and Penelope, the launching of the thousand ships, the
homecoming of Odysseus. Aphrodite's effect on action is powerful
but indirect, insidious, often unmentioned, and sometimes even

latent in the epics; this, *together with* her intense marking and power, enhances her mystery.

This brings us to the multiple ways that Aphrodite operates in the interstices between structures, what Turner and others have been calling the "liminal" (from Latin *limen,* "threshold"), or, more specifically, "the betwixt and between." These currently voguish terms and the exciting theory to which they refer call for a somewhat extended discussion.

LIMINALITY

By "liminal" I refer, in the first place, to rites or other acts and to images and ideas; the fact that I am primarily concerned with images mainly reflects my materials. On the other hand, since marital love-making itself may be ritualized, the myths of Aphrodite can be seen as related to marital behavior in early Greece, and it is important to keep this in mind, even though we know little about that behavior. The liminal is, second, dynamic or processual in that it involves crossing over (out of or in to) relatively stable or fixed structures or "grids." Or it may involve operating "betwixt and between" the margins of these recognized and accepted categories, rules, groups, and structures. Again because of my materials, I am concerned here mainly with liminality—with what mediates or is interstitial, not with what is totally beyond the pale. Third, liminality may involve persons, states, or even situations or statuses; these may be literally transitory, as in the case of persons who are adolescent, pregnant, on a hunt, senile, and so forth. It typically involves such stages of life and "rites of passage" (Van Gennep 1960) as birth, mating, disease, death, or natural and cultural transformations and disorders; in many cultures, for example, a woman going through her first menses is secluded in an isolated hut. Liminality may, on the other hand, involve relatively *permanent* but interstitial *states,* whether these are strongly based in biology, as in the case of a hermaphrodite, or consist of certain "fringe" or semioutcast or semioutlawed statuses, such as those (depending on the society) of the minstrel, burglar, prostitute, poet, or seer. Liminal figures, particularly liminal mythic figures, are often involved in murder, cannibalism, incest, adultery, or other acts in which "the elements of culture and society are released from their customary configurations and recombined in bizarre and terrifying imagery" (Turner 1967a: 577).

From another viewpoint, the theory of liminality is complexly related to language and linguistic categories. It seems to correspond to the moods of the potential, possible, desirable, unreal, and so forth that are coded in grammar by the subjunctive and optative. At a rationalistic level certain aspects of liminality become a purely logical or intellectual mediation between cultural and transcultural and universal categories (this is one burden of Lévi-Strauss).

The liminal figures and images of myth often deny or contradict or challenge the basic categories of society and the ethical norms of a culture. A summary idea of the scope of the liminal may be had from the following set of contrasts or antitheses, which I find suggestive, although, as I fully realize, they raise many new questions. Thus, liminality often entails the following:

1. Transition or "crossover" between grids, structures, etc.
2. A bridging or vaulting over, or simply operating between, such cultural (and universal?) oppositions as nature/culture, good/evil, and beauty/ugliness
3. Asceticism *or* strong sexuality
4. Extreme verbal purity *or* excessive profanity and obscenity
5. Silence *or* verbal efflorescence and brilliance
6. Foolishness and silliness *or* great wisdom, seercraft, prescience
7. Social homogeneity *or* simply absence of relative status
8. Nakedness *or* special costumes

The above traits and processes were suggested by the writings of Victor Turner (e.g., 1969: 106) but also reflect selection and adaptation on my part. For example, the dimensions of the liminal are obviously of different orders: number 1, above, is the most comprehensive, 2 is a subcategory of 1, and the others range from general conditions to the specifically physical (8) (granted that the physical has important aesthetic and psychological ramifications). I also part with Turner when he remarks that the liminal covers one extreme, for I would say that it covers both; for example, Turner links silence with the liminal and the verbal with structure, but I would link both extremes with the liminal (as two paths to ecstatic states). One reason for our partial differences is my focus on the early Greek Aphrodite, whereas his orientation is toward aboriginal Africa and medieval and modern India and Europe. My hope is that, by intensively studying a larger sample of cultures, we will be able to improve the theory of liminality.

One of the great works or jobs of myth, in any case, is to bridge or simply to assert contradictory categories, to split and rearrange and reclassify them, or, in other words, to make it possible for culture to be dynamic. The emotional mediation provided by liminal phenomena is one of the essential mechanisms by which man "constructs powerful, pervasive, and perduring moods and motivations . . . by clothing [his] conceptions with such . . . credibility as to make [them] uniquely realistic." But this interstitial or marginal action also unquestionably releases enormous social and psychological energies that may threaten or, in their consequences, actually destroy structures or, on the other hand, motivate the building of structures, art, and science; the historic role of Aphrodite in artistic, notably poetic, inspiration is of course consonant with this.

The theory of liminality has sometimes been carried too far (the fate of all constructive ideas), but it gets at some of the essentials of our subject. If the theory of liminality is ignored, the Aphrodite of the ancient Greeks cannot be understood theoretically. Her religious meaning springs not just from the fact that she symbolizes fertility and procreation, the joys and curses of love, but from her extreme liminality within a system of culturally specific religious categories. To adapt Turner: she bridges physical reality and metaphysical belief.

THE LIMINALITY OF APHRODITE

Aphrodite's liminality seems to be eightfold. It appears in association with (*a*) sexual intercourse without pollution, (*b*) sexual relations between a goddess and a mortal, (*c*) the naked goddess, (*d*) the active female, (*e*) the patroness of courtesans, (*f*) passionate sexual relations within marriage, (*g*) nature and culture, and (*h*) the "blessings" versus the "curse" of Aphrodite.

Sexual Intercourse without Pollution

Aphrodite's generous and carnal affection and her lack of ambivalence about sex made her, as we have seen, unique among the queens of heaven. What I have called her "sunlit sexuality" also implies a deeper freedom. In many cultures extramarital sex is regarded as polluting, particularly when engaged in by a woman, because of the common attitude that she brings the other man's seed back into the family. In Greek culture, sexuality in violation of the code of honor was as polluting as filth or death; and, as I think I have shown elsewhere, much of the epics involves a system of exchange between sex and death (1977). To take another example, the adulterous Helen, Clytemnestra, and the servants of Penelope are all compared with dogs, and dogs, in turn, are a master symbol of pollution on the battlefield. For some Greeks, such as Hesiod, *any* sex was dangerous and polluting: "Whosoever trusts a woman trusts deceivers" (*Works and Days* 375). While pollution through sex applies mainly to mortals, it also underlies the attitudes of the queens of heaven and seems to be epitomized by Artemis. In contrast, Aphrodite may be shamed through mockery but does not seem to feel polluted or to be afraid of pollution (I am indebted to L. Lamphere for originally suggesting this point). One of the bases for this is that the special Homeric vocabulary for shame and mockery is used of Aphrodite (as when Zeus wants to get back at her in the Fifth Homeric Hymn) but the specific terms for pollution and filth, such as *luma,* are not; one possible exception is when Hephaestus calls her "bitch-eyed," but in the context this seems more a term of simple abuse.

The fact that Aphrodite is not associated with pollution poses an interesting exception to the general rule that shame is caused by or implies pollution. The larger context is, first of all, the contrast which she poses with the antisexual Athena, whose essentially martial nature does not pollute her, despite the liminal and polluting force of war itself. Ares, on the other hand, is both highly sexual and highly martial and seems to incarnate pollution (particularly in Homer). These structural relations may be schematized as follows:

	Sex	War	Polluted
Aphrodite	+	−	−
Athena	−	+	−
Ares	+	+	+

Beneath this explanation in terms of structural contrasts lie deeper psychological roots: sexual intercourse and war, two concrete expressions of creation and destruction, are both potentially polluting, so that, when they are mixed or bridged, they become unequivocally so. Such deeper forces underlie the long-recognized and widespread patterns for hunters. Hunters and hunting are liminal, mediating between bringing life to man and death to animals (Lévi-Strauss 1955). In many, probably most, cultures hunters avoid sexual intercourse before the hunt and again, after the hunt, are careful to wash off the blood and otherwise depollute themselves before engaging in it. The liminal terrors of mingling blood and sex also motivate the horror in many cultures of murder combined with rape or even of intercourse during menstruation. The apparent lack of fear of pollution from rape during war, on the other hand, reflects a reclassification of enemy women as semi- or nonhuman.

Sexual Relations between a Goddess and a Mortal

Aphrodite is also liminal in that she mediates between the categories of mortal and immortal that are otherwise kept apart; indeed, the most usual Homeric noun for man is "mortal." Among the immortal goddesses we have, on the other hand, Hera and the fully virginal goddesses and the rule that a mortal man who has sexual relations with a goddess is punished by death or castration or, yet more horribly, as Ixion was; for he, having fornicated with a cloud he thought was Hera, is forced to spin, bound to a wheel, through space for all eternity. Aphrodite, on the other hand, is the potential lover of any god or hero and, like her cognate, Dawn, is sometimes seized by a desperate longing. More generically, she is the potential lover in the sense that the blinding subjective *state* of *aphroditē* can enter any human or immortal except Athena, Artemis, and Hestia (this, as we saw in chapter 5, was critical in Sappho's vision). By seducing mortals and providing a transcendent image of such seduction she mediates between the human and the divine in a way that gives man exceptional intimations of the immortality he can never attain.

The Naked Goddess

The liminality of Aphrodite is illuminated forcefully by the stories of her nudity. The background is the categorical taboo against seeing a goddess in the nude, accidental transgressors being punished by death' or blinding. Actaeon, as we have noted, was turned into a stag and torn apart by his own hounds for inadvertently seeing Artemis bathing (or, in another version, for boasting that his huntsmanship excelled hers). In early vase paintings and statues the goddesses are clothed (although one or both of Artemis' breasts may be uncovered).

In sharp contrast, Aphrodite may have been depicted nude (intermittently) from remote times. In early myth she, like the Vedic Ushas, may bare her bosom or even her entire body, as when persuading Paris to grant her the golden apple (in another version she simply promised him Helen). An Aphrodite or Aphrodite-like figure "appears in early times as a naked goddess" (Seltman 1956: 85) in a number of Mycenaean, Cycladic, and Minoan representations. Then, during the sixth and most of the fifth century there were no sculptures of *any* female in the nude; even the Aphrodites are fully clothed, or covered with a gown of sorts, and are often queenly and enthroned. Later in the fifth century the nude female reappears, though rarely. This group includes the *Venus Genetrix,* the first of the great statues of Aphrodite (probably by a student of Phidias); as one renowned art historian describes it, "the beauty that arouses physical passion was celebrated and given a religious status" (Clark 1956: 79). However, the sentiment that the beauty of Aphrodite should not be uncovered lasted into the fourth century until some (now lost) work by Scopas. Then Praxiteles, about 330 B.C., created a sensation throughout the Greek world (and some of its neighbors) by sculpting an Aphrodite who was at once nude and one of the masterpieces of all time. She was modeled after the courtesan Phryne. The citizens of Cos rejected her in favor of a more conservative, draped figure, but at Cnidus she was ensconced in a beautiful garden and became a source of great revenue—so great that the Cnidians refused to sell her to a king who offered in return to pay off their municipal debt. She has a "sensual tremor which, for five hundred years, led poets, emperors and boatloads of tourists to linger in the sanctuary of Knidos" (Clark: 1956: 84). Many other nude Aphrodites were done about this time, notably the *Crouching Aphrodite,* now in the Louvre; but whether the fourth-century sculptors saw the naked Aphrodites of earlier times as a precedent remains an open question; the idea "may have occurred quite naturally and spontaneously to the Greek artists of the fourth century" (Farnell 1897: 671–72).

The nudity of Aphrodite suggests a half-dozen generalizations. One is that it breaks a boundary between man and the gods: man looks across the boundary at a revelation of a divine female form that is uniquely direct. Second, her nudity well illustrates what has been called "the reduction of structure" in myth to more elementary and transgressing forms (Turner 1967a: 576). Third, through her nakedness she crosses over into the male realm or straddles the two sexes, since, otherwise, it was male mortals and gods, particularly Apollo, who were so represented. Fourth, her nudity is connected both with her frequent appearance as dressing or undressing

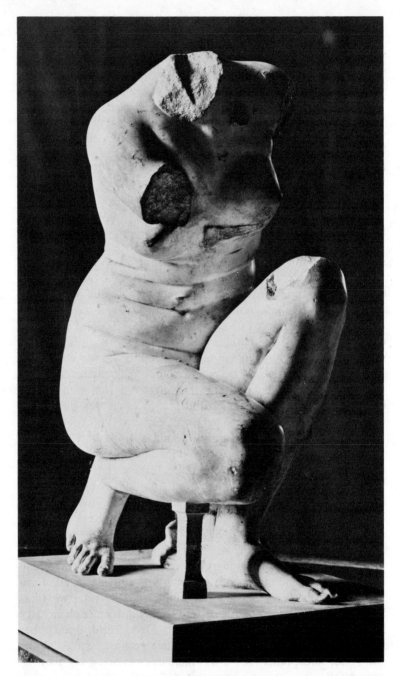

The Crouching Aphrodite (or Aphrodite Bathing). Roman copy of an original by Doidalses. Photograph reproduced by permission of the Musée du Louvre.

The Cnidian Aphrodite. Photo by Alinari, Florence. Reproduced by permission of the Monumenti Musei e Gallerie Pontificie, the Vatican.

and with all that is said about her clothing and cosmetics—all of which symbolizes interstitiality between the body and the external world (Lévi-Strauss 1963: 225). Finally, her nakedness, like her torso and her sexuality, results, by one myth, from an act of castration and so exemplifies how myth works through symbols in which the body is the microcosm of the universe (Turner 1967b: 107). Such corporeal symbolization particularly typifies the *most* liminal stages of ritual and myth when they bring together with intensity the sacred and "the all-too-human" (ibid., p. 580).

The Active Female

Many details of Aphrodite's sexuality add another dimension of liminality, that of the active female. In the Homeric system in general, men are often rapacious. Heroes divide up captive women and violate them. As Anacreon later put it, "Thracian filly . . . know well that I could easily put the bridle on you, and take the reins and race you around the goal of the course" (in Snell 1960: 58). At the level of myth, a seduction by gods, not only Zeus and Poseidon, but also Apollo and even Hermes, often consists of a hot pursuit followed by rape.

The arts of love are seen as mainly a feminine specialty, and an exception like Paris is cruelly mocked for his expertise: "What, you on the battlefield? Get back to the boudoir!" Or as Diomedes actually puts it, "Then your lyre won't be of use nor the gifts of Aphrodite / Nor your hair nor your form when you mingle with the dust" (*Il.* 3. 54–55). In another such exception, Odysseus, an (unmanly) competence in the arts of love is artfully masked or deemphasized. Aphrodite is properly sovereign in what was held to be essentially or at least primarily a feminine skill.

Two opposed attitudes are at play here (they were necessarily dealt with to some extent in chapter 3, under dimension 15, motion and proximity). On the one hand, Aphrodite is often waiting, receptively, as in many graphic representations or in the adultery scene in Book Eight of the *Odyssey*. On the other hand, she is often far from subordinate in wooing and seduction, love and love-making —as Helen implies on the walls of Troy—and one implication of her mastery of "wiles" is that she can be active and take the initiative. I would repeat, also, that she is never raped or, in Homer, assaulted by a male—she is so powerful sexually that this would be a contradiction in terms—but she herself does sometimes "seize up" handsome young men. Thus Aphrodite is both loved and loving, both active and passive. Smile-loving (or penis-loving—see the second part of Appendix 6), she presents an image of relative sexual equality and an active female role that dynamically contradicts the sexual double standard of the early texts. In a male-dominated culture like that reflected in Homer and Hesiod, even a relatively active woman defies and threatens and crosses over fundamental categories.

The Patroness of Courtesans

From a point of view that may strike some as irreverent and others as realistic, Aphrodite is also personified by members of the world's oldest profession. This raises a crucial question of wording and connotation. To some extent, she may have been the patroness of any prostitute, including whatever the early Greek analogues were of "the painted whore at half a crown" of our Victorian forebears or the "hookers" of contemporary America. But since such figures never appear in any of the texts on which my book is based, we are left with pure conjecture.

It is quite certain, on the other hand, that the early Greeks did see her in the temple courtesans at the religious centers of Aphrodite at Cyprus, Cythera, Corinth, Eryx, and elsewhere, who, we must remember, incarnated the goddess. And it is just as certain that they saw her in the self-confident and often beautiful and intelligent courtesans who captured the imagination and affection of the archaic and classical Greek world.

These courtesans must be seen in a historical and comparative perspective. The Sumerian Inanna and the Old Semitic Astarte seem to be echoed in some ways by the Greek Aphrodite and her hierodules. One may assume that courtesans and the institution of courtesanship were already known to the eighth-century Greeks of Homer's time, partly because of Greek commercial contacts with Lydia, Phoenicia, Egypt, and other centers, and the institution must have been further stimulated by the combination of trade, colonization, and political factionalism that lasted through the seventh century. Courtesans certainly do figure at a number of points in Sappho's poetry and, later, that of Pindar. By classical times they constituted an important social class in Athens and other cities, having special legal rights, an often inherited status (from mother to daughter), and close connections with the ruling classes. Many have compared them to the geishas of Japan, with their emphasis on music, dancing, entertaining conversation, and related arts.

Perhaps the closest modern representation in the West can be seen in the character of Garance in Marcel Carné's cinematic master-piece *The Children of Paradise*. All these courtesans—early Greek, Japanese, and French—are, like many burglars, poets, and even anthropologists, essentially liminal people.

Passionate Sex in Marriage

At another level, of wider and more popular significance, Aphrodite acted out or represented life at the core of the chaste and fully legitimate Greek family (as briefly treated in chapter 4 under dimension 8, "kinship"). Recall that even the Zeus of the *Iliad* pinpoints her primary function or business as the *himeroeis* works of marriage (5. 429; *himeroeis* is variously translated as "charming, delightful, desirous"). These delightful and pleasant works of marriage are not a euphemism for the arts of love outside marriage (like the adolescent "You want to get married?") but a reference to the fact that they were felt to be an integral part of marriage—particularly of the aristocratic and highly civilized married life depicted in the *Odyssey* and the Sapphic wedding hymns. The most famous episode illustrating this is Aphrodite's personal gift of a veil on the occasion of Andromache's marriage to Hector (*Il.* 22. 70), as im-mortalized in Sappho's poem (see Appendix 7, below). The earlier Greek representations of Aphrodite are often of a "draped figure having a certain stiff dignity" (Rose 1959: 27). The inclusion of this "refined cult of the goddess, as the patroness of married life" (Farnell 1897: 656–57) carried down into classical times when public rituals to her were observed throughout Greece; they were solemn and emphasized conjugal love, as various authorities have noted. She was also prayed to as a cherisher of children. Similarly, a key phrase in the Homeric Hymn to Demeter (line 102) evokes the natural link between artful love-making and child-rearing in wedlock: "cut off from child-bearing and the gifts of garland-loving Aphrodite."

What is at issue are the arts of love both within the legitimate fam-ily and outside it. While relations were entered into with concubines and courtesans (relations usually sexual but often much more than that), the legitimate ties of marriage were also, in both Homer and Sappho, of an avowedly and legitimately sexual nature in which what I have called "passionate conjugal sexuality" was highly valued (e.g., in the Homeric passages that refer to Aphrodite's "works of marriage" and the many Sapphic passages on love in marriage). To the large degree that Aphrodite symbolized and mediated between the sensuous courtesan, who is always liminal, and the passionate wife, who is liminal in many cultures, she posed an unusually intense liminality that as an explicit cultural ideal was fated to be eradicated from Greece chiefly during the Byzantine period.

Nature and Culture

What has been said so far raises the whole question of the role in a great religion of explicitness in the arts of pleasure—the charming, desirous, pleasing arts. They obviously rest on natural drives; Homer and Sappho make that clear, and it is illustrated by the way Aphrodite's power cuts across the categories of animal, mortal, and god. When I speak of "nature" in connection with Aphrodite's liminality, I am referring to fertility and procreation and to sexual drive, desire, and satisfaction.

"The works of Aphrodite" in early Greece are attested, or at least referred to, in the loci given above (e.g., Zeus's reference to "the works of marriage") and elsewhere; the phrase "the works of Aphrodite" occurs no less than three times in the first nine lines of the Fifth Homeric Hymn. But these works and arts of love and marriage—and I am going to stay with these literary terms—also have to be hypothesized to a large degree. They surely included the varied positions and movements of love-making. Such matters vary greatly from one culture to another; compare, for example, Ovid's *Ars Amatoria* and the *Kama Sutra* or, if your prefer, the contemporary folk patterns in rural Greece, France, and Sweden today. But despite such diversity and the fact that these matters are partly rediscovered by each individual, love-making is learned to some extent and is referred to in ordinary conversation; there is no reason to suppose that the Homeric and Mycenaean Greeks were unique exceptions.

Second, the arts of love certainly included the language of courtship and love-making (*oaristus*), with its hundreds or thousands of words and phrasings, special usages and intonations, distinctive and appropriate ways of expressing things. Of course, cultures vary, and, if we accept Basil Bernstein (1964), the British working classes have minimized the language of courtship. On the other hand, there are cultures in which this language is elaborated, and ancient Greece was probably one of them. This would be part of its typical concern with verbal power and socially appropriate and elegant speech. Here as in other ways it resembles Polynesia.

Third—and the texts here give us a great deal—the arts of love must have included styles of singing and dancing, the arts of coiffure, the use of oil and cosmetics, and lore about aphrodisiac drinks and foods, such as the pomegranate (i.e., the things dealt with in the young women's groups discussed in chapter 5). In the *Iliad* (14. 193–223), Hera, after consulting with Aphrodite, goes through a fairly standard sequence of washing, anointing with oil, combing, braiding, dressing, and so on. She also gets the love charm, "a pierced, embroidered thong."[1] Circe is a love witch, adept at making potions; Helen, another variant, is expert in drugs, including one that makes a person insensitive to any witnessed brutality (*Od.* 4. 219–34). It is Aphrodite who "made Jason wise in charm and incantation that he might loosen Medeia's shame for her parents" (Pindar's *Fourth Pythian*), and it is she who casts "a winsome shyness" over the love bed of her brother Apollo and a mortal woman (*Ninth Pythian*). In post-Homeric times perfumes and incense became central (Detienne 1972). The pleasing arts probably also included skill in composing and reciting certain kinds of poetry, especially the genres related to song, empathy, sensitivity, and weddings. Finally, they refer to a more diffuse realm of empathy, sensitivity, responsiveness, and skill in the give-and-take, the wiles and charms, of amorous relations. The "arts of love," then, constitute a rather complex learned system.

How were they transmitted? The extreme case may have been transmission through the hereditary courtesans of Cyprus and elsewhere and the standard mother-to-daughter transmission of the classical courtesans. Many of the related women's arts, as pointed out in chapter 5, were probably passed on to groups of premarital girls. A few ancient texts suggest some transmission by women from one generation to the next, and the probability of this is increased by the great number of cultures in which this occurs.

"The arts of love" were a set of practices, skills, sentiments, attitudes, and moral and aesthetic values that were learned and transmitted and that at once guided behavior and made it comprehensible and meaningful. These arts were ways *of* acting as well as *for* acting and were thus part of the *culture* of the early Greeks. Various parts of this system probably had antecedents in the Indo-European dawn goddess and the patterns of the early Semites; as already noted, Gilgamesh's friend is converted to civilization by a week of lying with the courtesan from Uruk. This developed idea of love-making as a civilized art contrasts with the physical violence and rapacity that is conspicuous in other parts of the Greek evidence.

This brings me back to an earlier point (semantic dimension 14) about the realm of nature, patronized by the wild and untamed Artemis, and the realm of culture, specifically Greek culture, which is personified by the civilized Athena. The drives of sexuality are natural; on the other hand, sophisticated love-making is highly cultural. Aphrodite mediates between the two, "puts them together." Or, better, she does not make them *identical* but interrelates them and makes them overlap to a high degree. To put it yet another way, we can agree that she is a "goddess of rapture" but ought to recognize that this rapture harmoniously blends natural and cultural ingredients. As Clark puts it, "Perhaps no religion ever again incorporated physical passion so . . . naturally that all who saw her felt that the instincts they shared with the beasts they also shared with the gods" (1956: 83). The fact that Aphrodite conjoins nature and culture through the arts of love enhances yet more her liminal and interstitial character.

To some degree my conclusion here simply translates and expands on Homer's insistence that sexual-amatory relations between man and woman are *themistos,* are part of the traditional and appropriate order of human affairs that is presided over by the goddess Themis, one of the most archaic figures in the Greek pantheon, a sister and spouse of Zeus. Themis, as a quality of human relations and, specifically, of man-woman relations, is argued most notably by Odysseus, the Homeric hero in the best position to speak on this subject. In the great scene in Book Nineteen of the *Iliad* he arranges the reconciliation between Achilles and Agamemnon; the latter must swear that he has not slept with Briseis, the former's concubine, although that would have been *themis* for a man and woman. Odysseus nicely suggests the conflict between the *themistos* quality of sexual relations between man and woman and the quality of Agamemnon's seizure of Briseis, which was not *themistos.*

The "Blessings" versus the "Curse" of Aphrodite

There is a final, enriching liminality. The arts of love have a double value for culture and organized, civilized life. On the one hand, they are strongly integrative in uniting man and woman in harmonious sexuality and, sometimes, a happy wedded life. On the other hand, these same arts can generate rivalries, jealousies, and passions that, moreover, acutely threaten the relations between individuals, kinship groups, and yet larger entities. The misogynous Hesiod is, of course, particularly insistent about these dangers, but they are explicit or alluded to in Sappho and are a grim moral of the sack of Troy and the carnage in Ithaca. The "blessings" of Aphrodite are thus seen to be matched by her "curse" in a way that exemplifies the eternal theme of love and death that, as we have seen, was already evident in the earliest Indo-European and Sumerian systems. And once again she is in an interstitial and ambivalently potent position.

Further Aspects of Aphrodite's Liminality

Aphrodite's liminality is expressed in yet other ways, which are of a different order. As we shall see in chapter 7, the queens of heaven and Demeter can be contrasted with each other in a paradigm of archetypes based on the features (1) active-aggressive, (2) identification with the mother, and (3) attitudes toward sexuality. Unlike the other goddesses, Aphrodite has to be marked as ambivalent (plus *and* minus) on all counts: both active and passive, both affirming her mother Dione but in Hesiod denying any mother, and (3) positive toward sex but threatening through its consequences.

Another way to comprehend the liminality of Aphrodite is to note the various ways it is symbolically concretized or condensed. Islands, aquatic birds, and the Morning Star, Venus, have already been discussed (chap. 4). Let us look at three more such symbols. First, in one of the origin myths she emerges from foam, which is itself, like dew, between air and water (Lévi-Strauss 1963: 225). Second, she is symbolized through the wolf or dog—as a she-wolf in some Orphic hymns, for example (Summers 1933: 67). In the epics Helen is referred to, by herself and others, as a bitch, bitch-eyed, and so forth (e.g., *Od.* 4. 137–41). Dogs link her to Ares; this feature may ultimately go back to Inanna. Finally, there are the sanctuaries on mountain peaks, shrouded in mist, the liminal country of shepherds and nymphs (Redfield 1975: 189–91) and the abodes of the gods in the early Greek and Phoenician world view. These symbols of islands, the star Venus, water birds, foam, dogs, and peaks (and yet others) masterfully concretize the liminality of Aphrodite.

CONCLUDING REMARKS

I have now sketched eight ways that Aphrodite is liminal (in a fairly loose and, I hope, suggestive sense that often overlaps with "ambiguity" or "ambivalence"). For ready reference to what follows, I repeat the list:

1. Sexual intercourse without pollution
2. Sexual relations between a goddess and a mortal
3. Nakedness of a goddess before mortals
4. Sexually active female
5. Patronage of courtesans, etc.
6. Sexual passion in legitimate marriage
7. Nature and culture combined in "the arts of love"
8. "The blessings" and "the curse" of Aphrodite

Two structurally interesting facts can be observed. One is that in all eight cases Aphrodite is liminal or intermediary in the fairly strict sense that she overrides (or, in one case, stands between) two categories that are opposed in the cultural system. These are:

1. (Extramarital) sex *vs.* purity (nonpollution)
2. Mortal *vs.* immortal (via sex, nudity)
3. Male *vs.* female (via nudity, sexual activeness)
4. Active *vs.* passive (sexually)
5. Legitimate marriage *vs.* prostitution
6. Nature *vs.* culture
7. Blessing *vs.* curse (dire consequences)

I would emphasize that in no case does her liminal, mediating, or transgressing role involve a set of transformations or other set of systematic, logical rules for getting from one category to the other. On the contrary, her role consists of an emotional assertion, or simply a pragmatic acting-out, that brings together what should be kept apart. She does not exemplify the "intellectualist" theory that "myths pertain to the understanding, and the demands to which it responds and the way it tries to meet them are primarily of an intellectual kind" (Lévi-Strauss, 1962, in Turner 1967a). Her mediation does, on the other hand, illustrate that "many mythic and ritual symbols belong to the class of nonlogical symbols" (Turner 1967a: 579) and, to a marked degree, that liminality creates "pure potency"; in other words, her potency is an output of structure as well as the specific content of her liminality.

A second interesting fact is that the eight kinds of liminality and the seven oppositions interact in many complex ways. Limiting ourselves to the order given above, we see that sex without pollution is a more general instance of a goddess having sexual relations with a mortal (which is otherwise polluting); that sexual intercourse with a mortal is a more intense version of naked exposure to one; that naked exposure is one aspect of being sexually active; that sexual activeness is more characteristic of courtesans or men. These many interrelations deserve a separate analysis.

The fact that the different kinds of liminality interact cybernetically increases the power of each and, in a strictly mathematical sense, enormously increases the quantum of Aphrodite's liminality and her pure potency. While this chapter has been a largely synchronic one, based on Homer, we must remember the complexity of Aphrodite's prehistoric and historic origins. She grew through time into a figure that both comprised and transcended categories and concepts that in the constituent cultures contradicted each other. Thus the synchronic liminality of Aphrodite is one more expression or consequence of her history. This history of liminality and of power through liminality was perpetuated in Aphrodite and in the closely related figure of Eros (Love) and is captured, for example, by the seeress Diotima of Mantinea, who, as quoted at the height of Plato's *Symposium,* says, "he is the mediator who spans the chasm which divides them [the gods and men], and therefore in him is all bound together" (Diotima is speaking specifically of Eros' function of interpreting prayers, sacrifices, commands, and replies). The many and complex ways that Aphrodite is liminal, which I hope this argument has somewhat clarified, should make it more understandable why the early Greeks, beneath their playfulness and their tales about the gods' irreverence toward Aphrodite, should have stood in awe of her mysterious power.

The liminality of Aphrodite rests ultimately on the foundation stone that sexual love is itself peculiarly liminal. But the liminality of our goddess must also be seen in context, the context of other divinities. *All* the gods are liminal in some ways, although Athena and Hera, for example, are minimally so. Nor does Aphrodite enjoy a monopoly, for she is nearly matched in liminality by Dionysus and Artemis; the latter seems to be more mobile, not because she is so charged sexually (albeit negatively) but because she is wilder. Hermes may actually be the most liminal in terms of specific components (e.g., twilight time, magic-controlling, sly eroticism, crossroads—see Appendix 8). But of all the Olympians Aphrodite is the most liminal because, as the divinity of sex and of the empathy and identification of love, she presides over the most liminal behaviors and emotions. In common parlance, "sex and love are the great levelers." In anthropological terms, sexual love is the ultimate *communitas,* the dyadic union that so often dissolves the grids and paradigms of life.

The Fifth Queen: The Meaning of Demeter

THE "EMOTIONAL GAP"

My detailed analysis of the queens of heaven, chiefly as they appear in Homer, has raised troublesome questions about what might be called their emotional economy or adequacy, particularly their motherhood and motherliness. It is true that all are in some sense concerned with the institution of motherhood, but in every case the role is offset by negative values and is thus ambivalent. Hera, for example, is the patroness of mothers and is mother of the goddess of childbirth, but these are less important than her functions as wife. And she is not depicted as loving her children, at least not typically; as I have noted, one may take as paradigmatic her hurling the child Hephaestus out of Olympus because he was so weak and ugly (granted that this incident also may symbolize the frequent loss of children through disease or the destruction of imperfect children through intentional exposure). Athena may be descended from a mother goddess, is sometimes called "Mother Athena" (particularly in Athens), and is often prayed to by women, as in Book Six of the *Iliad* (297–311), but she is neither a mother nor inspired by maternal love. Artemis certainly evolved from a prehistoric mother goddess, and she is a nature goddess and the official patroness of children and of labor pains; however, she is also the cause of those pains, is a frequent slayer of mothers, and does not play with children or nurse them or act motherly. There is here a symbolic link, already noted above, between the blood of menses, childbirth, and slaying, whether the victim is a stag or human.

Of the four queens of heaven, Aphrodite is certainly the most motherly, and it is she who displays love for children (some of the points that follow have been made in earlier chapters, but they bear repeating). She arranges for the upbringing of Aeneas and later saves him from the berserk Diomedes. She falls in love, as a *mother,* with the infant Adonis and then languishes over his loss to Persephone; her later love for the young man is analogous to Demeter's love for her daughter, Persephone. One of the major variants of Aphrodite, namely Thetis, also with a primeval, aquatic origin, is probably the most powerful symbol of maternal love in all of Homer (Bespaloff 1970: 51–59). In these and other instances Aphrodite and some of her variants stand for a motherly willingness to suffer for one's child and a motherly identification with one's offspring. In many local cults she was worshiped, not only as the patroness of the arts of love, but as a cherisher of children (Farnell 1897: 655).

The motherliness of Aphrodite, definite though it is, has to be qualified. For example, it is the convenient nymphs who tend to the upbringing of Aeneas (although that doesn't necessarily make her less motherly!). And some readers find "comical" the way she drops him after having snatched him from the fray, as described in Book Five of the *Iliad* (those readers may underestimate how terrifying an onrushing Diomedes must have seemed). She does not actually have any children by her husband, the lame Hephaestus, and in other ways the illegitimacy of her motherhood may weaken her image as a mother, as does her symbolic "denial of the mother" in the Hesiodic version. Her love of children is partly another expression of her playful and affectionate nature. And she is first and foremost the patroness, not of motherliness and motherhood, but of the arts of love and of longing and persuasion. The *relatively* secondary status of her motherliness/maternity and the symbolic conflicts between this and sexuality/sensuousness combine to keep her from filling the emotional gap that I referred to at the outset of this chapter.

Another way of approaching the problem is to say that the queens of heaven make up a paradigm of archetypes: (1) the matriarchal Hera, the "all-mother," (2) the erotic Aphrodite, who lacks sexual anxieties and, in Hesiod, origin from a mother, (3) the intellectual and masculinely professional Athena, who also lacks a mother but is antisexual, and finally (4), the wild "all-daughter," Artemis. Archetypes of this sort have been studied and defined (e.g., Jung 1973: 21–34), and we can profit by the specific insights of this model while denying some other aspects of the theory, such as the idea that archetypes are innate or genetically derived.

Similar archetypes are actually current in the contemporary vernacular, where the four queens would reduce to an "all-Mom," a "sex sweetheart," a sexless career woman, and a nun or "dyke." These labels are worth mentioning, partly because some of my most concerned readers will be recoding in this way what I am writing. Also, they may remind the more staid reader of the equally gross and simplifying classifications by the academics, to whom Aphrodite is "a pretty creature," a "good-for-nothing," and so forth. But let us turn to the more complex and tempered idiom and framework of ideas that I am trying to work out. No matter what idiom we choose, we have to conclude that the four queens of heaven are inadequate in some profoundly significant affective sense. In other words, *they leave an emotional gap.*

This lacuna, this lack of motherhood and motherliness, is filled by the great and awesome figure of Demeter, to whom the special epithet *semnē* is almost exclusively applied. (Our English glosses on *semnē* are usually the same as those on *aidoiē* [see chap. 1], but the connotations of the two words differ markedly.) Demeter resembles the other queens closely enough to be placed in the same matrix. She too is associated with a place, Eleusis, and, like Hera, is both a sister and a spouse (the fourth) of Zeus—and so is not a virgin. Like the others, she is beautiful and golden, with a "golden sword" and golden or blond hair, and she always appears fully clothed (contrasting maximally here with Aphrodite). But some of these features are irrelevant to her definition, and, from another point of view, she is more specialized than the other goddesses and also has more cosmic implications than Hera, Artemis, or Athena. I think the authorities have been justified in treating her as distinct from the other members of the Olympian family because she does not play a comparable role in the epics, Hesiod, or Sappho. She does not appear in the numerous councils, altercations, feasts, and other exchanges between the immortals on Olympus.

The relative neglect of Demeter-Persephone in Homer, Sappho, and Hesiod is problematical because a generalized loving, nurturing, strong mother figure is so widespread in the myths of the world as to verge on being an empirically universal archetype. It certainly is conspicuous in the archetypal theories of Jung, Campbell, and others, though the Greek figure may be unusual in its emphasis on grief and vengeance for the lost daughter. In sum, the neglect of Demeter-Persephone in our sources is significant on typological grounds.

Drastically different from Demeter-Persephone, both typologically and in a specifically Greek sense, is Aphrodite. To begin with types, there is surely no shortage of sex goddesses in, for example, Old Norse and Hindu myths or in those of many African and New

World groups (e.g., Mayan), to say nothing of myths from many other parts of the world. But I know of no close parallel to the full combination of sexuality, sensitivity, sensuousness, subjectivity, and fertility/procreation that emerges from a careful study of the early Greek texts. This absence of close parallels partly or sometimes involves the suppression of an Aphrodite archetype in both the actual myths and the theories of the mythologists. But it also involves the fact that our Aphrodite combination reflects unusual evidence and the poetic vision of several of the world's greatest poets and so is not strictly comparable to most other systems. In the second place, I do not think the Aphrodite combination is culturally universal in the way that the mother combination is. This leaves us with, or brings us back to, the apparent paradox of the extraordinary power of Aphrodite in our texts, particularly the Sapphic ones, and the deemphasis of Demeter in these same texts. Since this situation runs counter to what one might expect, an explanation is called for.

THE HISTORY AND STRUCTURE OF DEMETER

The relative neglect of Demeter in Homer is particularly significant because of her major role in early Greek religion. Let us briefly review this history.

Archeological, mythological, and other lines of evidence support a pedigree that resembles Aphrodite's in the remoteness of its origins. Part of the pedigree certainly goes back to mother-goddess figures of the Old European and Minoan-Mycenaean civilizations. These appear to have been synthesized with the Indo-European mother goddess or earth goddess who was linked with a sea-and-river god, the eventual Greek Poseidon.

The cult of Demeter probably came from northern Greece during the middle of the second millennium (Mylonas 1961: 14), and tombs and a settlement of about that date have been found at Eleusis. By late Mycenaean times her cult was already well established; a large megaron, an acropolis, a beehive tomb, and other architectural features of that period have been discovered (Nilsson 1950: 468). By Homer's time the Lesser Mysteries at Eleusis, like the earlier ones at Mycenae, involved double-ax symbols carried exclusively by women. Some people have argued that the Mycenaean Linear B *da-ma-te* stood for Demeter, but it is almost certain that it meant simply "an amount of land under grain." Mycenaean times seem to be depicted in the Homeric Hymn to Demeter, which, though sometimes dated at about 600 B.C., may be much earlier, as Wilamowitz argued (1931, 2: 47).

The cult of Demeter had probably become pan-Hellenic by the first Olympiad (776 or 760 B.C.—about the time the *Iliad* was composed). The increase in Demeter worship in the following century seems to have come in response to what I have called the "emotional gap" left by the queens of heaven in Homer and Hesiod. Even if we knew nothing of Greek religious or intellectual history, we would tend to predict the rise or intensification of something like a Demeter cult.

The strengthening of the Demeter cult was almost simultaneous with the rise of Orphism (an admittedly controversial term). Orphism was also of northern origin (Macedonia or Thrace), and the legendary and eponymous poet would have lived in the century before Homer. The beginning of the Orphic cult, however, is usually dated in the seventh century. In one tale of Orphic origin (Rose 1959: 51) Zeus covets Persephone and then has her in the form of a snake. A marvelous son, Dionysus, is born but is eventually dismembered by the Titans. Zeus eats the son's heart (which had been rescued by Athena) and fertilizes Semele (whose name may descend from that for a Slavic earth mother, Zemelo, Slavic *zemel-,* "earth"). Semele carries the embryo until her death by Zeus's thunderbolt, after which the transplanted Dionysus finishes his growth in the thigh of his father. The dismemberment of the first Dionysus and of Orpheus resembles the dismemberment of Adonis, lover of both Persephone and Aphrodite. Orphism and the cult of Demeter (and Pythagoreanism) are strongly mystical and much concerned with death, rebirth, and the underworld; the myth of Orpheus descending into Hades to retrieve Eurydice has been perceived as a transformation of the myth of Persephone's abduction.

By early classical times the vast center of Demeter at Eleusis, twelve miles northwest of Athens, annually witnessed the Lesser Mysteries in the spring and the Greater Mysteries in the fall, the latter marked by a five-day procession to Eleusis. The Eleusis center remained enormously popular through Roman times until it was destroyed, first by Theodosius' decree against secret rites, then by the ruinous onslaught of Alaric (395 A.D.), and finally by the Christians of the fifth century. But Demeter's staying power is demonstrated by her survival in Greek orthodoxy as the male Saint

Demetrius or as the noncanonical Saint Demetra in her home town of Eleusis (where she was worshiped as a grain goddess into modern times).[1] The contemporary Greek image of the Virgin Mary and the mother as "sacred" probably derives in part from the archaic Demeter.

The place of Demeter (and Persephone) in the paradigms of the gods is partly predictable in terms of what has been said so far, but it also brings some surprises. Let us summarize the facts that so contextualize her.

She became a wife of Zeus (or was raped by him) and gave birth to Persephone. Hecate helps her later. This is paralleled by the Arcadian myth of Demeter (in Rose and elsewhere): while searching for her abducted daughter she herself becomes the object of a pursuit by Poseidon; after several changes of shape the rape takes place as a stallion on a mare and results in a marvelous horse called Arion or, in another variant, in a daughter called Mistress *(despoina)*. This myth relates the equestrian Poseidon with Demeter in her equestrian aspect. By yet a third myth Poseidon couples with Medusa, a Mother Terrible of sorts, and she and the resulting daughter are eventually slain by Perseus; the name Persephone may result from Perse plus *phonē,* "murder, slaughter." Artemis is sometimes confused or identified with Hecate. As a fourth set in the paradigm we must add Persephone herself; here three brothers, Zeus, Hades, and Poseidon, combine in sexual assault. Finally, there is the myth of Zeus raping Leto in the form of a swan, which resulted in Artemis. In the chart, the first column contains the assaulting males, the second the assaulted women, the third the daughters, and the fourth a helping figure:

1. Zeus	Leto	Artemis	
2. Zeus	Demeter	Persephone	Hecate
3. Poseidon	Black Demeter	Mistress	Artemis
4. Poseidon	Medusa-Gorgon	Persephone	
5. Hades	Persephone		Hecate

The Black Demeter, or Demeter of the Furies, appears in Arcadia and in this formidable aspect seems related to Medusa. Hecate and Artemis are of course connected with the moon, the night, the underworld (caves, etc.), the occult, and the wild things of nature. Artemis is, in turn, associated with Demeter in many ways, such as the quintessentially female animals: the gravid sows in the case of Demeter (which were thrown into pits in the rituals of Eleusis), and the mother bears in some of the Artemis rites. The several variants schematized in the chart leave us with an underlying godhead of a vengeful mother or raped woman, a raped and/or slain daughter, and an antisexual, wild ally—a trinity of goddesses joined in their hostility and bitterness toward sexual aggression by males.

Since this discussion highlights one of the most basic and antagonistic confrontations in Greek mythology—that between Demeter and Poseidon—it seems appropriate at this time to adduce a few of the more relevant facts about the sea god. His name, well attested in the Mycenaean Linear B, probably goes back to a pre-Greek and even Proto-Indo-European compound for "master (husband) of the earth" *(potys dā)*. Recall that one of the more plausible etymologies of Demeter is "mother earth, earth mother" *(dā-mētēr)*. One of Poseidon's main symbols is the horse, as would be natural for a principal deity of the horse-breeding Proto-Indo-Europeans of the South Russian steppe. Horses are of course metaphorically close to water (the crests of waves, horses of the sea—I assume that our forebears were not blind to these obvious and indeed universal connections!). Horses are in fact second only to the sea as symbols of Poseidon. To the (frankly, bizarre) puzzlement of some scholars at the Proto-Indo-Europeans having a sea god, and to the apparently irrepressible doctrine that the early Indo-Europeans were landlocked I can only reply that the Oceanus of early Greek myth is simply the largest of the rivers (only later, in classical times, did it come to refer to "ocean" in the sense with which we are familiar). The Proto-Indo-European homeland was in fact intersected by vast rivers—the Danube, the Dnieper, the Kuban, the Volga, and others. It was over these that their "sea god" presided.

Structurally, Poseidon's riverine aspect appears to be a transformational counterpart of Demeter's ties to the land, and his blue hair parallels her blue robes; he also is tall and stately. Otherwise, he is wild, vengeful, and sexually passionate and rapacious; his swiftness of foot is a metaphor of his sexuality (and of course congruous with horses and the sea). Poseidon typically rapes nymphs, nereids, and harpies, and he even has a steady affair with Medusa, who was pregnant by him with Pegasus when slain by Perseus. Poseidon thus symbolizes the female analogue to castration: the physical traumas of defloration and sexual violence to which women are subjected. As such, he is the symbolic antithesis to Demeter. Unlike her, however, he was not developed theologically in later times.

Demeter was worshiped at Eleusis through cults or Mysteries, the dread secrecy of which still seems incredible. I am writing now not of the public rites, about which much is known (e.g., Van Gennep 1960: 89–90), but of the secret and mainly nocturnal ones. We do have some inklings of what went on, from a variety of sources: that the procession from Athens to Eleusis was punctuated by obscene and other liminal behavior; that women were the prominent and more numerous, if not the exclusive, officiants; that the rape of Persephone may have been enacted in some way, and that a high point was the holding up of a single ear of grain for some time in total silence. Van Gennep (following Foucart and Harrison) wrote that "the initiation included: (a) a voyage through a hall divided into dark compartments which each represented a region of hell, the climbing of a staircase, the arrival in brightly illuminated regions, and entrance into the megaron, where the sacra were displayed; and (b) a representation of the rising of Kore, containing elements unknown to the profane and not understood in the legend that was popularly known" (1960: 91; see also Mylonas' excellent study, 1961). But beyond these largely speculative details and additional speculation, and despite the popularity of the rites among myriad worshipers for over two millennia, the specific contents remain unknown.

Many anecdotes suggest the intensity of the underlying attitudes and feelings. The famous general, Alcibiades, was condemned to death in absentia and had all his property confiscated because he allegedly imitated some of the rites while drunk. Aeschylus was nearly killed by an outraged mob who mistakenly thought he had divulged some of the secrets in one of his tragedies. The degree of secrecy in the rites of Demeter probably explains why she is so deemphasized in Homer; since he took her seriously, he was aware of the consequences of making her or her mysteries too public through his playful depiction of the gods. He must have feared the fate that, much later, nearly befell Aeschylus.[2]

THE MEANING OF DEMETER

With this historical background, let us turn to what Demeter symbolized. At one level she certainly stood for plant growth—specifically, the principal grains, wheat and barley, and generally "the glorious fruits, the good gifts" (Homeric Hymn to Demeter, line 192). Hesiod is typical in again and again coupling her name with harvests and crops: "the sacred grain of Demeter" (*Works and Days* 806). That Demeter-Persephone are a Greek cultural metaphor for the agricultural cycle is obvious and is so stated in Greek terms in many texts. Interpreting her as a symbol of fertility does not necessarily conflict with a structural analysis.

Demeter also represents longing for a deceased relative, the fear of death, the problem of life and death. Persephone, the silent and enduring queen of the underworld, stands for a passivity that contrasts with the activism of Artemis; her rape is an allegory of man's helplessness before death. As already noted, Demeter-Persephone were central to "Orphic religion" and its concern with fertility and immortality. The symbolism of death and the annual cycle ally Demeter-Persephone with Dionysus, just as the latter resembles Aphrodite in the way he "enters into" those possessed by him. In some of these early Greek religions there was a mystic link between the earth's fertility and human sexuality or fecundity.

In terms of emotions and personal relations, which in a way is my focus, the most fundamental meaning of Demeter is what I have been calling "maternity" or maternal love. Two basic features have been identified by Deutsch and others concerned with female psychology. The first, which Deutsch calls "motherhood," involves the system of status and role, rights and obligations, that perdure and evolve over time; this is a slot for woman in the overall sociocultural system. Hera to some extent illustrates or projects motherhood, but the Homeric texts say little on this score about Demeter.

The second basic aspect is a "definite quality of character," a holistic set of emotions, a complex fabric of feelings and attitudes between the child and the mother that often demands considerable suffering, patience, and endurance from the latter. Yet the normal woman also identifies strongly with her child and takes vicarious pleasure in its growth, its qualities, its achievements. A crucial quality of these words and acts is perhaps conveyed by the term chosen by Deutsch: "tenderness" (clearly a translation of sorts of German *Zärtlichkeit* and of the idea of *nezhnost'* in Russian).

The tenderness of the motherly woman is instinctual to some extent and is widely paralleled by the tender behavior of animal mothers (e.g., dogs, monkeys) toward their offspring. But tenderness is also patterned, channeled, and encouraged through the patterns and symbols of a culture, and there are enormous ranges in the amount and quality of such tenderness—from the middle-class French and European Jewish women, who spend many of their adult years at it, to the extraordinary case of the Marquesas islanders, where, at least according to Linton (1945), motherliness was almost totally eliminated in favor of a hypertrophy of sexuality.

Motherliness ramifies into many related aspects of female experience. One of these is the desire for children, which may be a strong and simple thing in the case, for example, of a first child by a loved man. But the desire can be just as strong under other circumstances; when there is ambivalence, guilt may be compensated by fantasies of tenderness. Motherliness is diffused throughout the anticipation of the child during pregnancy and the excitement and sense of expectation when feeling the first movements inside the woman's "matrix sea." Tenderness and physical concern also come from the experience of birth, which, despite its pain, is for many a transcendentally meaningful experience that bonds a tenderness toward the child (L. Friedrich 1939). The long months of nursing and child care and watching and helping the child begin to walk and speak also call forth and reinforce this motherliness. I could elaborate further, but enough has been said to emphasize that it is the Greek Demeter, the loving, nurturing, grieving mother, who alone can be said to epitomize the tenderness and loyalty between mother and daughter, which reaches a sort of acme during the daughter's later childhood and early adolescence—precisely when Persephone was raped. She stands for motherliness just as Aphrodite stands for sensuousness, and in each case the meaning is partly Greek and partly universal.

Some of the sources of this motherly tenderness are well understood. In most cultures, including the Greek one, there is relative continuity in the growth of a female through childhood and adolescence. The girl normally stays in or near a home area, comparatively close to her mother or other older females while helping with the housework and the care of the younger children or simply conversing. During these years the daughter tends strongly to identify with her mother and, through this, with her eventual child; "she (re)experiences herself as a cared-for child" (Chodorow 1974: 47). Also, because she is more within the home during childhood in cultures like that of Greece, she is more involved in the "primordial triangle" of parents and child and more committed to recreating it. The relative continuity of growth among females and the greater commonality and embeddedness also encourage a distinctive set of attitudes involving cooperation between women, emotional solidarity, and verbalization of emotional questions and concerns. The ontogeny of women in these cultures inculcates the tenderness of motherliness, discussed above, which in various ways is symbolically linked with the "exquisiteness" of Sappho and the "gentle arts" of Aphrodite.[3]

Contrasting with the relatively strong continuity of the bond between mother and daughter and the relative gentleness between women is the sequence of experiences that threaten or even break down the boundaries between the woman's ego or self and the external world—the "I and the not-I." The crucial female experiences of menstruation, defloration, coitus, pregnancy and miscarriage, and lactation and nursing all directly or indirectly affect these boundaries. While the experiences are biologically based, since they are all associated with the reproductive cycle, all of them are classified and evaluated and experienced in terms of the cultural system. While some or all may be coded in negative terms, they also underlie a feminine openness to the external world and patterns of emotion that compensate and defend.

To the boundary-breaking experiences I would add another that is not biologically based: in many societies, including the Greek, marriage was by arrangement (recall Achilles' remarks on how his father would supply him with a bride in Phthia); the adolescent girl was taken out of her natal home and given away by her father. Speaking mainly for the peasants, Hesiod recommends a marrying age of thirty for the man and about sixteen or seventeen for the girl (*Works and Days* 695–98), and similar or greater differences were found at times in the aristocracy. After marriage the girl had to adjust to her husband, her husband's family, and other kinsmen in an environment that was strange and, often, far from home.

Let us return to the queens of heaven. Some of my results from the cultural analysis in chapter 4 can be reproduced as follows:

	Aggressive-Active	Relation to Mother	Attitude to Sex
Hera	+	+	−
Artemis	+,−	+ +	−
Athena	+	−(+)	−
Aphrodite	+,−	+,−	+(−)

What generalizations are implied? Both Aphrodite and Athena lack a mother (in some sense), but one incarnates sexuality while the other is a- or antisexual. Artemis is antisexual but is maximally identified with her mother (and in earlier myth was very much a mother figure herself). It is striking that nowhere, even when we add Demeter-Persephone, is a strong mother tie combined with strongly positive sexuality.

The most interesting conclusion brings us back to Aphrodite's liminality, which I so emphasized above. In the above scheme she turns out to be plus *and* minus on all counts, the minuses reflecting, respectively, her stances of waiting, receptivity, and passivity, the Hesiodic version of her birth, and, third, the latent, always potential "curse of Aphrodite." These and my other arguments for liminality are congruous with conclusions independently arrived at by Faber, who set up a four-cell typology based on the features of "erotic" versus "nurturing and mature" (compare "sensuous" versus "maternal" in chapter 9, below). Into this she was able to fit forty-seven female figures in Greek myth, but *not* Aphrodite, whom she characterizes as an "odd variation": "once Aphrodite, goddess of erotic love, enters the picture, the rules are not so easy to discern" (Faber 1975: 30, 41).

Let us now add the fifth queen and fit her into the above scheme:

Demeter-Persephone	(+) −	+	−

Demeter's overt response to the rape of her daughter is active and destructive, and in the Homeric Hymn she comes through as force-fully assertive. Nonetheless, she also symbolizes the suffering of mothers. Persephone stands not only for the suffering daughter but for passivity in the face of sexual aggression, for anxiety and hostility toward the aggressive spouse, and for disillusionment with an idealized father (to whom she keeps calling because she doesn't know he is in collusion). These passive or negative attitudes are combined with total identification with her mother. Four of the five queens, then, stand for anxiety and hostility toward sexuality.

A generalization that has been neglected by the mythologists is that these Greek goddesses do not suffer, tolerate, or endure patiently. This is congruous with the fact that they do not menstruate, get deflorated, or give birth (with two exceptions, and we can assume that these were painless?), or nurse their young (with one exception). They lack the biological problems that are said to make this ability to suffer biologically and socially adaptive. The two exceptions are only apparent. Demeter and Persephone are subjected to rape and similar torture by males, to forced betrothal, to betrayal by an idealized father, and to yet other things present in the experience or fantasy life of many or all normal women (particularly during adolescence) in most if not all cultures. But Persephone bitterly opposes her abduction, and Demeter has her revenge.

This raises a deeper issue. With the exception of Persephone, all the goddesses illustrate a facet of the real world that has been singularly neglected by female psychologists such as Horney and Deutsch and by anthropologists of the female such as Mead and Friedl, and that is female aggression and sadism (in the colloquial or literary sense that has been current for some decades rather than any specifically psychoanalytic one). Such aggression or sadism ranges from Artemis' torture of her innocent victims, to Hera's mistreatment of her children, to Aphrodite's "subjective cruelty," to the way Demeter ravages the land. The sadism of the goddesses may present a mythic antithesis to the social reality of ancient Greece but may well correspond to and reflect the realities of Greek child-rearing and the mother-son relationship; Slater (1968) has devoted an entire book to a Freudian analysis of the role in Greek myth of various destructive, devouring, entwining, castrating, blinding, and otherwise threatening females (incidentally, he hardly mentions Aphrodite).

That Demeter is a master symbol for motherliness does not entail a total negation of sensuous feeling for the opposite sex. In the myth of her affair with Iasion, according to Homer, she "yielded to her *thumos* (spirit, passion, feeling) and mingled with him in love-making and sleep" (*Od.* 5. 126); Hesiod uses the same phrasing (*Theogony* 970). In both authors the event takes place in a "thrice-plowed field." The scholiast even says that she came upon Iasion while he slept. The jealous Zeus slew this lover with one of his thunderbolts, but Demeter eventually bore Pluto. As Rose, following Frazer, correctly suggests, the myth "points to some rite of a real or simulated marriage in the cornfield" (i.e., British for "field of grain"; Rose 1959: 94). It is only in much later sources that Demeter is pursued and, in some, is forcefully violated by Iasion.

I have tried to show how Demeter, along with Persephone, fills an emotional gap in early Greek religion. But I have also pointed out many features that the five queens have in common. Perhaps the most important is the one shared by Demeter and Aphrodite.

Demeter, the *pietà* in this religion, has in common with the golden Aphrodite a complete lack of ambivalence—perhaps nowhere more vividly than when she runs "like a maenad" to meet her returning daughter. Her unbounded motherliness parallels the desires and longings that Aphrodite inspires between a woman and another adult and which she herself can feel toward a mortal like Anchises.

A fuller sense of their interrelation comes from the myth of Adonis, which is referred to by Sappho and appears in many later authors. Enlarging on Kerényi (1963: 179) I would say that the fervor of love between Demeter and Persephone is paralleled by that between the pairs of lovers Aphrodite and Adonis, Adonis and Persephone, and Orpheus and Eurydice. In each case, the loved one is irreplaceable—there can be no other Persephone for Demeter, Adonis for Aphrodite, Eurydice for Orpheus. Such irreplaceability implies identification. In their passion and lack of ambivalence, Demeter and Aphrodite contrast with the other queens of heaven. And yet at this same deep level they contrast with each other and raise universal problems (to which I will return). But first let us deepen our understanding of the meaning of Demeter by a careful reading of the main text.

8

The Homeric Hymn to Demeter

Our main text for Demeter is the long and extraordinarily beautiful and profound Second Homeric Hymn, one of the finest in the set and exhibiting so much internal integrity that most scholars agree that there was a single author. It was probably composed fairly early (about 650 B.C.) and, as already noted, is closer in its language to the Hymn to Aphrodite than to any other (and also very close to the *Odyssey*). I am going to give the full text in translation, with considerable commentary, for three reasons that I find decisive: (1) to illustrate the uses of a text in accord with my methodological position, set forth in chapter 3; (2) because so much of what we know about the early Demeter stems from this one source, as contrasted with the dispersal of information on Aphrodite (but note that the Aphrodite texts were summarized in some detail above); (3) because this source stands out from the other hymns and because some responsible scholars feel that within the Greek system it is extraordinary for its cosmic implications (Kirk 1975: 180, 203).

The translation that follows is adapted from those by Boer and Evelyn-White, with a great deal of additional work by myself, together with interspersed comments and suggestions, some of them from Allen, Halliday, and Sykes (the received authorities) but the majority from the students in a class on Homeric Greek, where (during the spring quarter of 1976) we went through the hymn line by line (using the Allen-edited Greek text). My understanding of the myth has been helped in many ways by the writings of Kerényi (I have in mind his specific insights).

"I begin to sing of Demeter, the awesome goddess, and of her beautiful hair." (The critical word here is "awesome," *semnē,* which does not occur in Homer proper; it is the epithet, almost exclusively, of Demeter; it is derived from the basic root, *sebas,* of uncertain etymology but with definite meanings of religious awe and shame.) "Of her and of her slender-ankled daughter, who was seized, with violence, by Hades. And it was Zeus the cloud-thunderer, who

163

gave her away." (Here the key word, already discussed in chapter 2, in connection with Dawn, is that for "seize with violence," *harpazō,* the standard verb for rape, kidnapping, and the like. Otherwise, the mythic collusion of Zeus with his brother Hades symbolizes the animosities, mostly latent, between a line of women, here a mother and her daughter, as against the men who dominate in the family and who, when they marry, take their bride away from the family circle in which she has been nurtured. We can assume that among the early Greek aristocrats the girl was often removed a considerable distance from her birthplace. The collusion also probably involves a mother and her daughters, as opposed, economically, to the father and the son-in-law, since the latter paid the bride-price to the former.)

"Far apart from Demeter of the golden sword" (probably a metaphor for the ear of ripe wheat) "and her good harvests" (or fruits or grain, all of which can be referred to by *karpos*) "[this daughter of hers] was playing with the deep-bosomed daughters of Oceanus, gathering flowers, roses, and beautiful violets in a soft meadow (or lowland), and also irises and the hyacinth and the narcissus, which (the goddess) Earth made to grow at the will of Zeus and to please the Host of Many to be a snare for the bloomlike girl—a marvelously radiant flower." (Allen and others claim that in early Greece young girls often [stereotypically?] were carried off while out picking flowers. It is of significance that she was wrenched away from her *friends,* since female friends are such an important part of the matrix of a woman's growth. The field of flowers was certainly already a fixed erotic context, as in the scene in Book Fourteen of the *Iliad,* where Hera seduces Zeus. Note the role of Earth here: although Demeter may derive from an earlier earth goddess, by the time of the hymn the bifurcation between her and Earth has become just as sharp—and marked by as much antagonism—as the bifurcation of the pre-Greek Dawn into Eos and Aphrodite.)

"It [the narcissus] was a thing of awe to all who saw it, to the immortal gods and to mortal men. From its root grew up a hundred blooms, and it smelled with a most sweet fragrance." (This narcissus is an obvious male phallic symbol, just as the earlier "soft meadow" is a specifically Greek female one. Otherwise, the narcissus "was the peculiar flower of the Great Goddesses" [Allen et al. 1936: 130]). "And all the wide heaven above and all the earth laughed, and the salt swell of the sea. And she was astonished and stretched out both her hands to take the lovely toy. But the earth with its broad roads in the Nysian Plain yawned wide, and from it leapt out the King, the Host of Many, with his immortal horses, the son of Kronos, He who has Many Names." (The many names of Hades probably arose from the desire to avoid naming him directly in some contexts, that is, as a type of taboo pattern.) "He seized her up, unwilling, on his golden chariot and bore her away, wailing. She screamed out shrilly with her voice, calling on her father Zeus, who is the most high and excellent." (There is extreme bitterness here in the contrast between Zeus as "the highest and best" and his collusion with Hades in the rape. Taking Persephone to Hades is a metaphor of the psychological distance that separates a raped girl from her family.)

"No one of the immortals or of mortal men heard her voice, nor the olive trees, bearing rich fruit." (The mention of olive trees in this context probably refers to the agricultural fact that they were normally *distant* from the lush marsh meadows, but it may also be connected with the fact that this is a basic fruit and that Demeter is "of the glorious crops." Finally, it may have some reference to Athena, the creator of the olive and rival of Poseidon in Athens. But, to continue: no one heard her) "except for tender-hearted Hecate, daughter of Perseus, in her bright headband, who heard her from her cave." (Hecate, Demeter-Persephone, and Artemis form a set in myth and iconic representations. In some myths Demeter is actually the mother of Artemis, in others she is the cousin of Hecate. All three [four] of them symbolize negative attitudes toward sexuality, and all three may derive from earlier mother-goddess figures. Hecate and Persephone are chthonic; Hecate and Artemis are strongly lunar [as is Demeter, to the extent that the moon is felt to influence vegetation].)

"And the Lord, the Sun, the glorious son of Hyperion [also heard] the girl crying to her father, the son of Kronos. He, on the other hand, was sitting apart from the gods, aloof in his temple, where many suppliants pray, receiving beautiful offerings from mortal men. And so it was that he, her father's brother, Son of Kronos, Ruler of Many, bore her away unwilling on his immortal chariot, by the promptings of Zeus."

"As long as the goddess could see the earth and the starry sky and the strong-churning, fishy sea, and the rays of the sun, and hoped to see her mother, who was so concerned [for her] and the families of the eternal gods—just so long did hope charm her great heart for all its grieving. And the peaks of the mountains and the depths of the sea rang with her immortal voice, and her queenly mother heard it. And a sharp pain seized her heart, and she tore with her hands the headdress on her immortal hair." (Here, as in the preceding line about Hecate with her bright headband, the key word is *krēdemna*; while mainly referring to a headdress, it was also used, metaphorically, for the battlements of a city and, more generally, for female chastity [including the hymen]. In this case the way Demeter rends her headdress reenacts her daughter's loss of her virginity; in the *Iliad* Andromache rends her headdress at the loss of Hector, the protector of her honor. Aphrodite, by contrast, is almost never described as wearing a *krēdemna*. The symbolism of the headdress has been dealt with excellently by Nagler 1967, 1974).

"And she threw off the dark blue cloak from her shoulders and sped like a wild bird over the dry land and the sea, searching." (As in the case of the olive trees, the comparison to a bird may link Demeter with Athena.) "But no one, either of the gods or of mortal men, wanted to tell her the truth; not even one of the birds, who are true messengers, came to her." (Athena sometimes brings news in the form of a bird.) "Then for nine days the queenly Deo wandered [went hither and thither] over the earth" (Deo is generally taken to be an affectionate nickname for Demeter, but there may be a crucial etymological relation with the name of Zeus) "holding the flaming torches in her hands." (These torches seem to suggest that she was also wandering by night, and they link her with Hecate. Many authorities agree that this scene constitutes a mythic charter of sorts for the bearing of torches by women during the ritual Mysteries of Eleusis and the Thesmophoria: "The object of both rites is mimetic, and their object undoubtedly was to promote the fructifying warmth of the earth" [Allen et al. 1936: 137]).

"Not once did she taste of ambrosia or the sweet draught of nectar, for she was grieving, nor once plunge her body into the baths." (Here I follow Boer's unorthodox translation rather than the accepted "sprinkle her body with water.") "But when the tenth luminous dawn appeared, Hecate, holding a torchlight in her hands, encountered her [Demeter] and told her the news." (Here Hecate's torch seems to stand for both chthonian and lunar aspects.) " 'Demeter, bringer of seasons, giver of fine gifts, who of the heavenly gods or of mortal men has rapt away Persephone and grieved your good heart? I heard a voice but didn't see with my eyes who it was. I will quickly tell you the whole truth.' So spoke Hecate, and the daughter of beautiful-haired Rhea said nothing in reply." (Rhea was the wife of Kronos and so mother of Demeter and also Zeus, Hera, Hades, Poseidon, and Hestia [the virgin goddess, patroness of the hearth]. The Greeks often identified Rhea with Cybele, the great fertility goddess of Phrygia, whom we met earlier, in connection with the Homeric Hymn to Aphrodite.)

"And swiftly she darted away with her, holding the flaming torches in her hands. They came to Helios, the watchman of gods and men." (There is an important parallel between the role of Helios as watchman and spy here and in Book Eight of the *Odyssey,* where he sees and reports Ares' wooing of Aphrodite. Because he is all-seeing, he is invoked in oaths.) "They stood before his horses, and the sacred goddess asked, 'Helios, you, at least, should respect me, if I have ever pleased your heart and soul with what I say. The girl whom I bore, sweet scion [of my body], glorious in her form—I heard her loud [thrilling] voice through the barren air, as if she were being overpowered, but I did not see her with my eyes. But you, who with your beams look down from the bright upper air over all the earth and the sea, tell me truly of my [dear] child, if perhaps you have seen someone, far from me, seizing her by force against her will and going away, whether of gods or of mortal men.' " (By the Greek theory of vision, man acts on his environment with beams from his eyes; in these terms, the sun, with its visible rays, would naturally be the great seer.)

"So she spoke, and the son of Hyperion answered her. 'Daughter of fair-haired Rhea, Queen Demeter, you shall know. I greatly revere and pity you, grieving as you are about your slender-ankled child. No one else of the gods is guilty but only cloud-gathering Zeus, who gave her to Hades, his own brother, to be called his blooming [buxom] wife. Seizing her, Hades took her, loudly screaming, down into the misty darkness. But, goddess, cease from your great lamenting. It is not right for you to hold on in vain to this insatiate anger. Aidoneus, the Ruler of Many, is not an unseemly son-in-law for you among the immortal gods, [since he is] your own brother and born of the same stock. As for his honors, he obtained his share back when the threefold division took place. He lives among those of whom he was allotted to be king.' " (This speech by Helios ironically underscores the theme of bitterness and injustice: the mother should *take heart* at her daughter's rape because the rapist is her brother and has great wealth and power. An important ambiguity lies here in the word *timē,* which means "honor" in Homeric Greek but also to some extent, and by the time of this hymn and, certainly, later, meant "material goods"; some scholars think that even Homeric "honor" [*timē*] consisted in material goods [Adkins 1972]).

"Thus speaking, he called his horses. They, at the sound of his voice, quickly bore the swift chariot [away] like long-winged birds. And a grief yet more terrible and savage came to her heart." (Here what is glossed as "savage" is literally "doggish," with strong connotations of sexual pollution.) "And then [she was] very angered with the dark-clouded Son of Kronos, and, staying far away from the gathering of the gods and from great Olympus, she went to the cities of men and their rich grasslands, disguising her outward form for a long time [by wasting it away]." (The Greek *eidos* here means "that which is seen, the outward form, the appearance," and not necessarily "beauty," as some would have it.)

"And none of the men who saw her recognized her, nor any of the deep-girdled women, until she arrived at the house of prudent Celeus, who at that time was ruler in the fragrant town of Eleusis. Grieving in her heart she sat down by the road, by the Virgin's Well, from which the women of the place were accustomed to draw water. In the shade overhead there grew a shrub of olives." (The exact well has been argued about by archeologists. More pertinent here is that the poet of the hymn chose to call it the Virgin's Well. The Greek word *parthenos* [see also chapter 4] can certainly refer to physical virginity in some contexts, as is illustrated later, when "virgin" and "unmarried" occur together, with the implication of either "unmarried and a virgin too," or "unmarried and therefore a virgin." Also, in Nausicaa's speech in Book Six of the *Odyssey, parthenos* seems to have this meaning. In other contexts the term refers to an unmarried woman and at some times could even be used for an unmarried concubine with children. Here the connotations of both "virgin" and "well" underscore the predicament of Demeter and Persephone.)

"She was like a crone of ancient times who is cut off from the gifts of the garland-loving Aphrodite, like the nurses of the children of kings, the guardians of traditional law and the housekeepers in those echoing halls. The daughters of Celeus, son of Eleusis, saw her as they came for the easily drawn water in order to carry it in bronze pails back to the home of their father. The four of them [were like] goddesses, having [still] their girlish flower: Callidice and Cleisidice and lovely Demo and Callithoë, who was the firstborn of them all. They didn't know [recognize] her—it is hard for mortals to discern gods—and standing nearby they spoke winged words: 'Where are you from, old woman, you who are of the folk born long ago? Why have you gone away from the city and [why] don't you approach the houses? For there in shady halls are women of the same age as you, and younger ones, who would be friendly to you in both word and deed.' Thus they spoke. She, that queen among goddesses, answered them, 'Dear children, whoever you are of women, of womankind.' " (This is awkward in English, no matter how translated, since it combines the standard word for "woman" with an equally standard adjective for "female, feminine.")

" 'Hail! I will tell you my story,' " [Demeter continued], " 'for it is not improper to tell the truth to you who ask. Doso is my name.' " (This pseudonym probably connotes "giver" and is related to the epithet of Earth as "giver of goods" [*dōtēr eaōn*].) " 'My mistress mother gave it to me. Just now I came from Crete over the wide back of the sea, not willingly, for pirates brought me away unwillingly, by force, under compulsion.' " (This bit may hark back to the early worship of Demeter on Crete, and there may be some irony, based on the fact that Crete was famous for its liars.)

" 'After that they put in with their swift craft at Thoricus, where [their] throngs of women, and the men, went ashore and prepared a meal by the stern cables of the ship.' " (Thoricus was one of the twelve independent towns of Attica.) " 'But I had no desire for the honey-hearted wine and, secretly rushing across the dark [shore] land, I fled those arrogant masters, so that they should not take me across the sea unpurchased and have the pleasure [use, enjoyment] of my price [ransom].' " (The verb, *aponinēmi,* can be translated variously. Here "ransom" again plays on the ambiguity of the word *timē* which, as noted above, can mean either "honor" or "price" and the like, so that another translation would be "to have the pleasure of my honor," that is, by getting a price though they themselves had not paid. Yet other ambiguities suggest themselves. Demeter's tale of the pirates, finally, reiterates symbolically the basic theme of the rape and the dishonoring of women by men.)

" 'And so I have come here, wandering. I do not know what sort of land it is or what sort of people are native to it [live here].

But may all those who live on Olympus grant you lawfully wedded husbands and to bear children, such as parents want.' " (This well-wishing is of course bitterly ironic, since Demeter herself has just lost a child "such as parents want.") " 'Take pity on me, maidens, and show me [this] clearly, that I may learn to whose house I may go, of man or of woman, so that I may work for them, with a will, at such tasks as are proper to a woman of my age. And, holding a newborn child in my arms, gladly [beautifully] would I nurse it and oversee house and spread [make] the master's bed in a recess of the well-built chamber, and teach the women their work.' The goddess spoke, and straightway answered Callidice, the virgin, the unmarried, the goodliest in form of the daughters of Celeus." (As noted above, the juxtaposed terms "virgin, unmarried" may have contrasting referents, but it is also possible that they simply reiterate reference to the same status.) " 'Mother, we mortals endure the gifts of the gods by necessity, even though we suffer. For they are indeed much stronger. I will teach you these things clearly and will tell the names of the men who have great power and honor here, who are chief among the people and guard the headdress of the city with their true [straight] laws [judgments]: wise-minded Triptolemus and Diocles and Polyxeinus and peerless Eumolpus and Dolichus and our own proud father, all of whom have wives who keep house [prepare and share their bed].' " (The symbolism of headdress [as battlement, etc.] has already been discussed; the use of that culture-specific metaphor at this point certainly associates Eleusis itself with Demeter and with the violation of female chastity. Here and elsewhere the emphasis on human *dikē,* "justice, law," and *themis,* "customary, traditional law," also underscores the injury done to Demeter and Persephone by the high gods. Otherwise, the list of the proper names of the leaders in such a small town suggests an aristocracy or oligarchy rather than a kingdom. But, to continue with Callidice.)

" 'Of them not one, after the first sight of you, would turn you away from the house, dishonoring you, but [rather] they will receive you. For indeed you have the appearance of a goddess. If you wish, remain here until we come to our father's house and tell all this fully to our mother, deep-girdled Metaneira, so that she may bid you to come to our home and not search the homes of others. Her son, late-born, is growing up in our well-built house, much prayed for and welcome. If you could bring him up until he reached the full measure of youth, any one of womankind [of women, of females] who saw you would envy you. Such gifts would our mother give for his nursing.' So she spoke, and Demeter nodded her head in agreement. Filling the shining vessels, they carried them off gladly [rejoicing]. Quickly they came to their father's house and immediately told their mother what they had seen and heard. And she then immediately told them to go and summon [Demeter] for an enormous salary. Like deer or like heifers in the season of spring, who leap about in the meadow when they're glutted with food, so they, holding up the folds of their lovely garments, darted down the hollow path. And their hair streamed out around their shoulders like crocus flowers." (There is an association here between the hair of the girls, the flowers that were being plucked when Persephone was seized, and the narcissus, which first tricked her and, later, is compared to a crocus.)

"They found the good goddess near the road where they had left her earlier. And they led her to the house of their father. She walked along behind, distressed in her heart, and veiled from the head down. A dark blue cloak waved about the slender feet of the goddess." (Here the emphasis on her veil, like the earlier one on her headdress, underscores her own chastity. This interaction between Demeter and the girls of Eleusis is reminiscent of the famous section in Book Six of the *Odyssey* where Odysseus encounters Nausicaa and her companions while they are washing clothes and playing ball on the shore.)

"Soon they came to the house of Celeus, cherished by Zeus, and went through the portico to where their queenly mother was sitting by a pillar of the well-built roof, holding her son in her lap, the new scion. They ran over to her. But the goddess crossed the threshold with her feet, and her head grazed the ceiling and filled the doorway with divine radiance. Then respect and religious awe and the green-yellow fear seized Metaneira." (This apparition of Demeter, grazing the ceiling and gleaming, parallels the view of Aphrodite in the Homeric hymn when she stands before Anchises just after he wakes up.)

"Metaneira got up from her seat and asked the goddess to sit down. But Demeter, the bringer of seasons, of the glorious harvests, did not want to sit down in the shining seat but waited in silence, casting down her beautiful eyes, until perceptive Iambe placed a jointed chair for her and threw a silver fleece over it. Sitting down there, she held her veil before her with her hands. She sat for a long time on this seat, speechless and grieving, and greeted no one by word or with an embrace, but, without laughing and without partaking of food or drink, she sat wasting away with longing for her deep-girdled daughter until, once again, the perceptive Iambe, with [her] jesting and quipping, made the holy lady smile and laugh and be cheerful."

(Since satirical and abusive poetry was written in iambics, at least from the time of Archilochus on, some persons may have connected this with the name of Iambe, the jesting daughter, or even with the story that this daughter invented iambics—a sort of mythic charter for this branch of poetry! The more relevant possibility is that iambic verse figured importantly in the Eleusinian Mysteries. Otherwise, Iambe's jesting and quipping may involve a symbolic role reversal by a maid and so constitute a mythic precedent or charter for the obscene badinage and other liminal behavior among women, or individuals of both sexes, that characterized the Thesmophoria and the Eleusinian Mysteries; such verbal behavior, common in fertility rites in general, is thought to stimulate the productive powers of the earth.)

"And it was Iambe, too, who pleased her later in a moment of anger. Metaneira filled a cup of sweet-hearted wine and gave it to her. She nodded her head upwards in refusal. It did not seem lawful [proper] to drink the red wine. She ordered them to give her barley water to drink, mixed with soft mint. And she [Metaneira] made the mixture and gave it over as she had been bidden. And the all-powerful Deo received it because of the rite." (This is a mythic charter for the communions with mixed drinks, usually without wine, that were important in the Mysteries of Demeter and sometimes those of Dionysus. Drinking of this mixture was part of the initiation ritual, according to Clement of Alexandria, who, in the course of excoriating the Greek pagans, gave us some information on the Eleusinian Mysteries.)

"And among them the well-girdled Metaneira took the lead in speaking. 'I do not suppose that you are born of common parents but of noble ones, for truly dignity and grace are conspicuous in your eyes—as of kings who administer traditional justice. Yet we mortals must bear, by necessity, the gifts of the gods, for the yoke is set on our necks. Now you have come here, and as much as I have is at your disposal. Raise my child here, whom the gods have provided, lastborn and unhoped for and much prayed for by me. If you raise him up to the measure of his youth, anyone of womankind who sees you will be jealous, so great is the reward I would give for his upbringing.' "

"And rich-haired Demeter answered her once again, 'And all hail to you, lady, and may the gods give you good things. I will take your child eagerly, as you command. I will nurse him, and I am sure he will never suffer from the carelessness of a nurse or from bewitching or "the undercutter." ' " (The undercutter or woodcutter is probably "the worm," the cause of toothlessness and the toothache.) " 'I know an antidote stronger than "the woodcutter," and I know an excellent safeguard against the witchcraft that gives many pains.' Thus speaking, she took [received] the child into her lap with her immortal hands. And the mother's heart was glad." (Demeter's offering to nurse one of her host's children of course reinforces her image as a motherly mother and adds yet another bitter comment on her search for her own child.)

"And so she reared up Demophoön in the palace, the splendid son of Celeus, whom well-girdled Metaneira bore. And he grew up like a god [*daimōn*], not eating food or feeding from his mother's breast, for by day rich-crowned Demeter anointed him with oil as if he were born from a god, breathing sweetly down on him as she held him in her lap. By night she would hide him like a brand in the heart of the fire, in secret from his parents." ("Hide" here is in the sense of "as a log is hid in the ashes," and there may be some ethnographic connection with the [early Greek?] practice of passing an infant over the fire to prevent infection and disease. By this time in the hymn we have a complex of superimposed metaphorical relations between the torches of the Eleusinian ceremonies, the torches with which Demeter seeks Persephone, the torches of Hecate, and Demeter's holding the infant "like a torch." Fire is of course the main purifying element, so that we have here a metaphor of the promise of immortality, with Demophoön as a metonyn of humanity. At yet another level he is a metaphor of a grain to be roasted.)

"And great wonder grew among them to see how he grew so precociously. Indeed, he resembled the gods. And she would have made him ageless and immortal if deep-girdled Metaneira in her foolishness, looking out by night, had not spied her. She cried out and struck both her thighs, fearing for her child and outraged in her heart. Wailing, she spoke winged words. 'My child, Demophoön, the stranger woman is hiding you in all that fire, and she makes grief and bitter sorrow for me.' " (The word for "grief" here has strong connotations of "funeral," and the "sorrow" is mainly for relatives.)

"Thus she spoke, mourning. And the queen of goddesses heard her. And the fair-wreathed Demeter, with her immortal hands snatched the child from the fire, the unhoped-for, whom Metaneira had born in the palace, and cast it from her to the ground. She was terribly angry in her heart. And at the same time she said, 'Witless mortals, and [too] brainless to foresee the lot that is coming upon you, whether of good or of evil, now by your foolishness you have done something irreparable. For—and may the oath of the gods, and the implacable waters of the Styx be witness—I would have made your son immortal and ageless for all time and would have given him undying honor. Now there is no way he can escape death and the Fates. Yet shall undying honor always be his, because he lay on my knees and slept in my arms. When he comes into his prime with the passing of years, the sons of Eleusis will wage war and terribly and continually strive with one another. I am Demeter, the holder of honor, who has produced the greatest blessing and cause of rejoicing among mortals. But come, let all the people build me a great temple and an altar below it beneath the city and its sheer wall and above Callichorus upon the rising hillock.' " (The well mouth, excavated in 1892, is surrounded by concentric circles —no doubt marks for the Eleusinian women who danced around the water in honor of the goddess.)

"Thus speaking, the goddess changed her size and form, thrusting away old age. And beauty drifted around her, and a lovely fragrance spread out from her sweet-smelling robes. And a light shone far from the immortal skin of the goddess, and her blonde hair fell down over her shoulders, so that the strong house was filled with the ray[s] as with lightning. She walked through the rooms. Metaneira's knees buckled, and she became silent for a long time, nor did she think to take up her late-born child from the floor. But his sisters heard his pitiful voice and sprang down from their well-spread beds. One took up the child in her arms and put [held] it in her lap. Another revived the fire. A third sped with her tender feet to help her mother to stand and to take her from the fragrant room. And gathering around, they washed the gasping [struggling] child and they embraced [fondled] him lovingly. But his heart could not be soothed, for inferior nurses and handmaids were holding him now."

"All night, quaking with fear, they sought to appease the glorious goddess." (This passage probably refers by implication to the all-

night festivals in the cult of Demeter that were confined to women.)
"But when dawn appeared, they told all truthfully to Celeus, whose
power is wide. And he, summoning the boundless populace into
assembly, ordered a rich temple to be built to Demeter and also an
altar on the rising hillock. They listened to his voice and obeyed right
away, and did as he had ordered. And the temple grew according
to the will of the goddess."

"When they had finished and had retired from their labor, they
went off, each one to his home. But blonde Demeter sat down there,
far from the blessed gods, and wasting away with yearning, recalled
her deep-girdled daughter. And she fashioned a terrible and savage
year for mankind over the all-nourishing earth. The ground would
not make the seed sprout, for rich-crowned Demeter kept it hid.
And much white barley fell in vain on the ground. And now indeed
she would have destroyed the whole race of mankind with a painful
famine and deprived those who have houses on Olympus of the
glorious honor of gifts and sacrifices if Zeus had not noticed this
and thought about it in his heart. And first he stirred up golden-
winged Iris with her lovely form to call rich-haired Demeter. So he
spoke. And she obeyed dark-clouded Zeus, the son of Kronos, and
quickly sped the entire distance with her feet. She reached the city
of fragrant Eleusis and found blue-robed Demeter in the temple and,
speaking to her, uttered winged words. 'Demeter, father Zeus, whose
knowledge is everlasting, calls you to go among the families of the
eternal gods. But come, lest my word from Zeus be unfulfilled.'
She spoke, begging her. But the heart of Demeter was not persuaded.
So then the father sent out the blessed and eternal gods, all of them.
Arriving in turn, they kept calling to her and gave her many most
beautiful gifts and honors, such as she might wish to choose among
the immortal gods. But no one was able to persuade her mind or
purpose, so angry was she in her heart. She firmly rejected their
words, [saying] that she would never set foot on fragrant Olympus
nor ever cause fruit to be sent up from the earth until she saw her
fair-faced daughter with her own eyes."

"Now when deep-thundering, wide-seeing Zeus heard all this,
he sent the Slayer of Argus, he of the golden wand, into Erebus so
that, having won over Hades with dulcet words, he might lead holy
Persephone from the dark mist up into the light, among the gods, so
that her mother, on seeing her with her eyes, would put aside her
anger." (The critical epithet here, *hagnē,* "holy, pure," is also commonly applied to Demeter and Artemis; they and Persephone are

the three goddesses who are particularly concerned about chastity and sexual pollution.)

"Hermes obeyed and, leaving the seat of Olympus, sprang down and sped under the hidden places of the earth. He encountered the king inside his house, sitting on his couch with his revered [venerated] wife, who was very unwilling because of her mother. But she [Demeter] was far off, brooding on her terrible design because of the deeds of the blessed gods. Standing near, the powerful Slayer of Argus said, 'Blue-haired Hades, ruling among the deceased ["Blue-haired" probably suggests some association with Poseidon, whose stock epithet it is], Zeus the father has ordered me to lead holy Persephone from Erebus and among them [the gods], so that her mother, when she sees her with her eyes, will desist from her anger and terrible wrath against the gods. For now she plans an enormous act: to destroy the weak tribes of earthborn men, hiding the seed beneath the soil and wiping out the honors of the gods. She holds a fearful anger, and she does not mingle with the gods but, far removed, sits within her fragrant temple, dwelling in the rocky city of Eleusis.' " (The reference to "weak tribes of man" is consonant with the position of Orphism, with which the Demeter-Persephone myth is so closely allied.)

"So he spoke, and Aidoneus, the king of the dead, smiled with his eyebrows ['grimly'] and obeyed the behest of Zeus the king." (That is, he smiled superciliously, without relaxing the grim lines of his mouth.) "Immediately he called the wise Persephone."

" 'Go back to the side of your blue-robed mother, Persephone, keeping a kind spirit in your breast and heart. Do not despair excessively. I am not an unworthy spouse for you among the gods, the own brother of your father, Zeus. While [you are] here, you will govern over all, as much as lives and moves, and will have the greatest honors [rights] among the immortals; and there will be punishment for all time for those who defraud you, who do not appease your heart with sacrifices, performing them reverently and making appropriate gifts.' "

"So he spoke, and wise Persephone was happy and quickly jumped up with joy. But he personally slipped [gave] her a pomegranate in secret, to eat, taking care [apportioning it] lest she remain at all times by the side of the revered blue-robed Demeter."

(This part of the myth seems to be based on the wider belief that the living may visit the world of the dead and return as long as they don't eat there, which is part of a wider belief that eating together unites people. The pomegranate was believed to have sprung from the blood of Dionysus and to stand for love and death, rebirth and fertility, and so on. In this passage the pomegranate may well symbolize the marriage of Persephone and Hades; but, at the more bitter stratum which runs through the whole myth, the blood-colored fruit and juice remind the reader of Persephone's rape and defloration.)

"And Aidoneus, the Ruler of Many, harnessed [hitched up] his deathless horses in front of their golden chariot. Persephone mounted the chariot beside the strong Slayer of Argus, who took the reins and the whip in his hands and sped out through the palace. The horses flew willingly. Quickly they covered the long road. Neither the sea nor the water of the rivers nor the grassy bends of the valleys nor the tops of the mountains contained the rush of the immortal horses. In their going above these things, they cut through the deep air. And Hermes, who was driving, stopped them where the fair-crowned Demeter was waiting before the fragrant temple. Seeing them, she darted forward like a maenad down a mountain shadowy with forest." (This famous scene is paralleled in Book Twenty-two of the *Iliad* when Andromache reacts to the news of Hector's death; it suggests the relationship, which I argue in chapter 9, between a woman's love for a man and her love for her daughter.)

"Persephone, on her part, when she saw the beautiful eyes of her mother, left the chariot and leaped down to run forward. She fell on her [Demeter's] neck, embracing her [falling all over her]. But Demeter's heart, even while she was holding her beloved child in her arms, suddenly sensed a trick; she trembled terribly and ceased from her fond caressing and asked her, 'Child, I hope that you didn't partake of any food while down there below. Speak out, conceal nothing, so that we both may know. For if you have not, then, back from dread Hades, you would dwell by me and your father, the dark-clouded Son of Kronos, honored among all the gods; but if you have partaken of it, you will go back again to the secret places of the earth and dwell there a third part of the seasons of the year and two parts among men and the other gods. When the earth blooms with sweet-smelling spring flowers of all kinds, then up from the misty darkness you will come again, a wonder to gods and to all mortal men.'" (The division of the year into two or three seasons was ancient. According to the most likely [Stoic] view, Persephone is to be identified with grain and her absence with the sojourn of the grain underground [in storage repositories]. In these terms, the rape would have to be construed as taking place in the spring.) " 'Tell me how you were rapt away under the misty darkness and by what trick the strong Host of Many deceived you.' Then Persephone, the most beautiful, responded to her, answering, 'To you, mother, I will tell the whole truth. When luck-bringing Hermes came, the swift messenger from my father, the Son of Kronos, and from the other Olympians, to make me come out of Erebus, so that, seeing me with your eyes, you would cease from your anger and terrible wrath against the gods, I immediately jumped up with joy. But he secretly put a seed of pomegranate [in my mouth], a sweet food, and made me eat it by force, against my will.' " (Note that Persephone claims that force was used, in contrast to the description above. This symbolization of enforced oral sex compounds the bitterness that has been building throughout the poem.) " 'And I will also tell how, having seized me by the shrewd plan of my father, the Son of Kronos, he went off beneath the ends of the earth. I will tell all, as you ask. All of us were playing in a lovely meadow, Leucippe and Phaeno and Electra and Ianthe, Melita also, and Iache, with Rhodea and Callirhoë and Melobosis and Tyche and Ocyrhoë, fair as a flower, Chryseïs, Ianeira, Acaste and Admete and Rhodope, and Pluto and charming Calypso; Styx was there, too, and Urania and lovely Galaxaura, with Pallas who arouses battles and Artemis delighting in arrows. And we were playing and gathering sweet flowers with our hands, soft crocuses mixed with irises and hyacinths and rose-buds and lilies, a wonder to see, and the narcissus which the wide earth caused to grow like a crocus.' " (Far from being "not clear," as Allen and others say, the point of the comparison is the force, or vernal energy, of the first blooming of the crocus.)

" 'But I plucked one in my happiness. The earth yawned beneath me. From out of it there sprang the king, the strong Host of Many, and he went beneath the earth, carrying me all unwilling. I cried out with a shrill cry. Of these things, though I grieve, I am telling you the whole truth.' " (Allen et al. [1936: 176] in an almost incredible bit of ideology, claim that "the emphasis laid on Persephone's shriek here, 38 and 57, suggests that it was not idle, but to save the appearance of consent to the abduction.")

"Thus the whole day, in harmony of feeling, they greatly cheered each other's hearts and breasts, embracing each other. The spirit stopped its grieving. They gave and received joy from each other.

And bright-coifed Hecate came near them. And many times she embraced the daughter of holy Demeter. And from that time Hecate was minister and comrade to Persephone."

"And deep-thundering, far-seeing Zeus sent a messenger to them, rich-haired Rhea, to lead blue-robed Demeter among the families of the gods, and he promised to give them honors, such as she might choose among the immortal gods. And he agreed that her daughter [should remain] a third part of the year beneath the misty darkness and two parts beside her mother and the other gods. Thus he spoke. And the goddess obeyed the message of Zeus. Quickly she darted down from the heights of Olympus and came to Rharion, once a fertile udder of the earth but now not at all fertile; all the plants lay fallow, for the white barley was hidden by the design of fair-crowned Demeter. But after that it began to wax with long ears of grain, as spring came on; and on the ground the rich furrows were heavy with the ears, which were tied in sheaves. There the goddess came down first out of the barren air. They looked at each other happily and rejoiced in their hearts. And fair-coifed Rhea spoke first to Demeter. 'Come, child, deep-thundering wide-seeing Zeus is calling you to go among the families of the gods, and he promises to give honors such as you would wish among the immortal gods. And he has agreed that your daughter should spend a third part of every year beneath the misty darkness and two parts with you and the other immortals. So he said that it would come to pass and nodded his head in assent. But come, my child, obey, and don't be angry too continuously with black-clouded Zeus. Make fruits fertile again among men.' Thus she spoke. Fair-crowned Demeter did not disobey but sent the fruit up again on the rich lands. All the wide earth was heavy with leaves and with flowers. And going to the kings who administer traditional law and to Triptolemus and to Diocles the horse-driver and to Eumolpus and to strong Celeus, the leader of the people, she showed the conduct of the sacred rites and taught the rites to all of them—to Triptolemus and to Polyxeinus and to Diocles also, awesome rites, which may not be transgressed or pried into or uttered, for great awe of the gods checks one's voice." (Note that the hymn ends as it began, with emphasis on the religious awe [*sebas*] that is so particular to Demeter. The early initiates into the rites of Demeter thought that actual communion with the deities of the underworld was essential to salvation.) " 'Happy [prosperous] is he among earth-dwelling men who sees them; but whoever is not initiated in these sacred rites and has no part in them never has a share of similar good things once he is dead and beneath the misty darkness.' "

"But when the divine goddess had taught all these things, she went to Olympus, to the company of the other gods. And there they dwell beside Zeus, who dwells in thunder, awesome and revered. Blessed is he among earth-dwelling men whom they graciously favor, because they immediately send Plutus, who gives wealth to mortals, as a guest to the man's great house." (The key word, *olbios,* implies both happiness and physical prosperity, often, as here, with an ambiguity similar to that which surrounds *timē,* "honor, material wealth." Plutus, the son of Demeter and Iasion, was generally depicted as a boy with a basket of grain. The identification of Plutus and Pluto [Hades] came later.)

"And come, holding the people of fragrant Eleusis and sea-girt Paros and stony Antron, o queen, you of the wonderful fruits, bringer of seasons, Queen Deo, you yourself and your daughter, the most beautiful Persephone. Graciously grant me heart-nourishing food in exchange for my song also."

9

Sex/Sensuousness and Maternity/Motherliness

INTRODUCTION: THE LOVER-MOTHER AS SUPPRESSED ARCHETYPE

In exploring the meanings of Aphrodite and comparing her with the other goddesses, I focused on her unique synthesis of sexuality, sensuousness, subjectivity, fertility-potency, and, in the vision of Sappho, her sensitivity and heightened subjectivity. I then found the meaning of Demeter in her maternal feelings and sense of unity or identification with her daughter. There now comes the question: Can we trace these two goddesses of love back to a common source? My question might be schematized as follows:

1. Aphrodite *vs.* Athena, Artemis, Hera

2. Aphrodite *vs.* Demeter-Persephone
   $X?$

Let us explore this question by comparing a woman's sensuous love for a man with her motherly love for a child. Let us also hypothesize an archetype that combines the erotic with the motherly and ask why it has been suppressed.

I turn first to myth and religion and to the great literary masterpieces that in many ways function as their analogues or surrogates in modern urban, highly educated cultures.[1] I have in mind, for example, *Don Quixote, Madame Bovary, Anna Karenina,* and *The Brothers Karamazov.* Above all, the major plays of Shakespeare, with their human archetypes, revelation of emotional problems, semi-sacred status, and rituals of study, performance, and attendance certainly have, in the English-speaking world, many of the functions that ritual and myth have in primitive societies; Shakespeare also has a special, archaic language that is linked connotatively with the King James Bible. In our own time certain great films have been providing major integrative myths, and they have wider audiences than the novels (compare the popularity of the Greek theater in classical times and Shakespeare's among the Elizabethan workers and artisans). All such normative representations in novels, films, and theater are, in any case, complexly related to the moral, social, and psychological concerns of the educated elite—in short, to a large part of their world view. It is therefore additionally significant that they also dichotomize so sharply between sensuousness and motherliness.

It is at this level of myth, religion, and high literature that we find a strong tendency to disassociate the complexes that I have been referring to as "sex/sensuousness" and "maternity/motherliness." It is true that there are some divinities, such as the Mayan moon goddess, who do synthesize the two complexes to some degree (Thompson 1939). The late Babylonian and Phoenician Ishtars might also be included if we keep in mind that the synthesis in this case was only part of their all-around, all-functional nature. I have already pointed out (chaps. 2, 4, and 7) that the Greek Aphrodite and Eos figures (and the Proto-Indo-European Dawn), though primarily erotic, were also maternal. Much more usual and widespread than such "exotic" syntheses, however, is a strong segregation of the two complexes from each other. The erotic, sensuous figures in Greek myth tend to be segregated from the "mature," maternal, or motherly ones. Gods and heroes are usually mothered by females who, as one authority sees it, "have hardly any other role in the myth" (Faber 1975: 35); the same sorts of authorities perceive the erotic figures as "immature." While the disjunction is transparent, even "analytical" in Greek myth, it is widespread elsewhere. A more extreme example, in fact, is the Virgin Mary versus the former courtesan Mary Magdalene (and even she has been sublimated into holy love for god-in-man). Let us look at other cases where close harmony or even the suggestion of it is absent from literature and similar representations.

In classic works of Western literature the Gretchen of Goethe's *Faust* is cited as a sort of bourgeois Aphrodite-Demeter. Joyce's Molly Bloom is sensuous enough, but her motherliness, such as it is, is for the middle-aged Leopold. Dante's Beatrice is maternal only in a theological sense; if she arouses eros in the bard, this hardly makes her a sensuous lover. Still, granted the high theological tone, she does combine the two roles, and this contributes to her power. Two of Tolstoy's heroines are sometimes advocated, but the striking thing about Natasha in *War and Peace* is her drastic shift from being an erotic adolescent to being a Slavic *Urmutter;* there is never a balanced synthesis between them. Anna Karenina certainly houses the two complexes within herself, but it is precisely the conflicts they engender that lead to her suicide. The later Tolstoy, incidentally, would have objected violently to the claim that his great heroine synthesized eroticism and maternity in some ethically or religiously acceptable sense. Anna's tragedy is part of the more humdrum and extensive truth that the culturally patterned and indeed enjoined antithesis between sensuous sexuality and motherliness often leads women (and men) to play the two roles in different families; witness the many women who combine deep motherliness toward their children with a series of clandestine extramarital affairs, or the male stereotype who never confuses love and marriage.

The one major exception to the antithesis seems to prove our generalization. The two complexes may well be combined and directed toward one object, that is, toward the same man, but with consequences that are usually tragic. In the Oedipus tale, for example, the sensuous/maternal woman has the same man as both son and lover, with disastrous results. The many permutations on this theme provide an unrelieved panorama of tragedy, pollution, shame, conflict, guilt, and death which reinforces for many the already deeply ingrained sense of antithesis.

A different picture presents itself when we consider actual women, whether or not they belong to the elite. Some of the possibilities have been summarized by a leading female psychologist as follows:

> Sexuality and motherliness are sometimes in close harmony, yet at times they appear completely separate.... In many cases the presence of one permits us to infer the presence of the other, and variations in one produce variations in the other. There are women who are both unerotic and unmotherly, and others who combine extraordinary erotic intensity with the warmest motherliness. The split between sexuality and motherliness can assume innumerable forms. For instance, each of these components can relate to different love objects. A given woman sexually desires one man or has the exciting wish to be desired sexually by him, but chooses another man as the father of her children and tenderly and faithfully loves him in this capacity. A sexually integrated woman can gratify both sexuality and motherhood through the mediation of one man. Either component may completely dominate the conscious life while the other remains hidden in the unconscious (Deutsch 1945: 24).

And there are an infinite number of additional shades and permutations.[2]

This close harmony between maternal and erotic love has a physical basis. It is well known that maternal experiences, such as nursing, may arouse a woman erotically. It is also well known that love-making can be linked to maternity (as when, for example, a woman's milk "lets down" during erotic play). The sensuous love of a woman for a man can have a maternal flavor when she worries about him as though he were a child or experiences him as a substitute for a child. Such motherliness typically involves a woman who is older than the man, but it may also involve a woman whose man is her own age or even older than she, since the attitudes in question are prior to the specific ages in a union. Or the man may play an erotic and quasi-maternal role vis-à-vis the woman. Close harmony between these two kinds of love clearly depends on the individual, but in Europe and the Americas a significant minority of women do achieve it (or perhaps I should say, "reflect" it). It is a matter of values and attitudes, moods and motivation; like "the arts of love," it is a complex set of alternatives or options in most cultures (and it is ruled out in some). Given the fact that the two constituent complexes are not infrequently in close harmony, it would seem that both have their source in a single deep emotional and symbolic stratum. This possibility has received almost no attention from anthropologists or even psychologists (but see Appendix 9).

A BIOLOGICAL VIEW

The biological aspect of these relations has been exhaustively researched, stated in dozens of publications by biologists and physicians, and distilled by Niles Newton, Alice Rossi, and others.

Their basic argument can be summarized, adapted, and partly criticized as follows. Adult females have three major "acts of interpersonal reproductive behavior"—(1) coitus, (2) gestation and parturition, and (3) lactation—which are closely related to each other. About a dozen specific behaviors are shared by "undisturbed, undrugged childbirth" and "sexual excitement": (1) deep breathing in early stages, followed by rapid and/or interrupted breathing; (2) similar vocalization (e.g., gasps); (3) strained, concentrated facial expression; (4) rhythmic contraction of the upper segment of the uterus; (5) loosening of the mucous plug from the cervix;

(6) periodic abdominal contractions; (7) loss of inhibitions and the "veneer of conventional behavior"; (8) exertion and strength often beyond the individual's normal capacities; (9) anaesthesia (of the vulva, of the entire body); (10) differential "insensitivity to surroundings" (amnesia, unconsciousness); (11) a flood of joyful emotion and a sense of well-being as the emotional response. Other details include marked clitoral engorgement during the latter stages of dilatation in the case of some women.

As a nonbiologist with some biological background, I have reservations about this list of "behaviors." For one thing, I am disturbed by the silence about what they do *not* have in common. It is true that for some women sex is painful and birth pleasurable, but I think that for most women the primary thing about sex is pleasure and the primary thing about birth—or at least one primary element in it—is pain (whether or not the cries of the woman engaged in these two activities sometimes sound similar).

The biologists are also silent or naive about the cultural factor. For example, the physical position of the woman in the two behaviors is said to be on the back, whereas in most cultures women deliver, or prefer to deliver, in a kneeling position. In many cultures female orgasm is almost unknown, and in any culture "sexual excitement" may lack one or more of the alleged behaviors. A more general cultural fact is that sexual orgasm and birth orgasm are not systematically and explicitly equated in any culture that I know of, and the idea of such an equation would be rejected by many women (except parts of the natural-birth subculture in our Western society). A third and yet more general criticism is that the biologists tend to ignore or obscure the major cultural fact, which I have repeatedly emphasized in the latter part of this book, that the complexes sensuousness/sexuality and motherliness/maternity are primarily attitudes, feelings, and beliefs that hold over long time spans; that is, they are not short-lived behaviors. Still, despite these reservations, the many behavioral analogies between the two orgasms—sexual and birth—are a striking embodiment of the connection between the two complexes. They correspond to what many women have often reported about the similarities between these two "moments of truth."

The three "female acts"—coitus, parturition, lactation—are similar both in their sensitivity to environmental stimuli and in the fact that they are based on neurohormonal reflexes.[3] Women who have not borne children, for example, have skin-color changes in the labia minora from pink to bright red, but in women who have borne children the labia typically vary from bright red to a deep wine color (Masters and Johnson 1966). This neurohormonal base, with which the female child is endowed at birth, survives in adult women despite the modeling power of culture, which, as noted above, can enormously weaken both sexuality and motherliness.

The specific actions of the hormones have been determined, but much remains unknown, particularly about the key hormone, oxytocin (which in its artificial form, pytocin, is given to delivering mothers to stimulate uterine contraction). A strong statement on oxytocin is made by the distinguished expert, Alice Rossi:

> it is a clear link between sexuality and maternalism: it stimulates uterine contractions that help the sperm on their way to the oviduct; at high levels it produces the stronger contractions of childbirth; and it causes nipple erection during either nursing or loveplay. . . . The interconnection between sexuality and maternalism makes good evolutionary sense. By providing some erotogenic pleasure to the mother of a newborn baby, there is greater assurance that the child will be nursed and the uterus restored to pre-pregnancy status. . . . Pregnancy and childbirth in turn improve the gratification women derive from coital orgasm, since orgasmic intensity is directly related to the degree of pelvic vasocongestion, and vasocongestion increases with each pregnancy (Rossi 1977: 17; cf. Campbell and Petersen 1953).

Since the close connection between sexuality and maternalism, that is, between Aphrodite and Demeter, is supported both scientifically and by the ordinary experience of life, we must again wonder why it has been subject to widespread taboo or repression. As Newton notes:

> The reason the sensuous nature of breast feeding is so seldom recognized in our society may be the same reason birth orgasm is so seldom seen. Current social patterns are very effective in inhibiting the psychophysical reciprocity of lactation. Mother and child are usually kept separated except for brief contacts during their hospital stay. Rigorous rules about duration and timing of each sucking period have been invented and are enforced by persons who usually have never successfully breast fed even one baby. Probably most people in our society would be willing to concede that we would cause coital frigidity if we prescribed the act only at scheduled times and laid down rules concerning the exact number of minutes intromission should last (1973: 84).

Two Explanations for the Antithesis in Myth

Thus we are still left with the question: Why is there such an antithesis between erotic and maternal love in myth, religion, and high literature? What are the motives, the causes?

Two explanations suggest themselves. In probably the majority of cultures sex and sensuousness are associated with wildness, evil, lack of control, both external and internal, and, more generally, with an animal or primitive order of being (let us not forget that, for example, the word "hysteria" is derived from the Greek word for "uterus"); Ortner has distilled some of this in her article, aptly entitled "Is Female to Male As Nature Is to Culture?" (1974: 68). A biological basis for this is that a woman's reproductive cycle is much more complex and has more components than the man's. Motherhood and maternity are also generally classed as more physical and emotional and closer to the earth and to nature and, correspondingly, removed from the intellectual, the capacity for making abstractions, for "strategic reasoning," and so forth. These dichotomies are vividly exemplified by Athena, whose mental and professional powers are coupled with a denial of the mother, of motherhood on her own part, and of sexuality and sensuousness of any kind whatsoever.

The folk classifications that I have been discussing, widespread though they are, are unrealistic psychologically because they imply a sharp division between mind and body, between the emotions and intellectual power, and between men and women, in that the latter are alleged to be more sensuous and fertile. On the other hand, since it is a fact of life that most people in most cultures class women as closer to nature than men, then Aphrodite and Demeter epitomize two crucial sides of that naturalness.

Another consequence of the classification is that sexuality-sensuousness and maternity-motherliness tend to be kept as far apart as possible in many cultures and literatures. To conjoin them would, to put it simply, entail or imply too great a concentration of power. Also, the wildness and lack of control that are associated with sexuality would contradict and conflict with the moral stature and maternity of the *materfamilias* ideal in at least some cultures.

A second explanation for the antithesis is that a conjunction would threaten the male's image of his authority by bringing into the open the sexual and emotional power of the female; the antithesis, then, is another instance of "keeping women in their place." This seems valid in part. For example, a close harmony between the two kinds of love is more often achieved in situations where women are encouraged to express their feelings, to develop emotional maturity, and to enjoy rights and obligations that are more or less commensurate with the men's. On the other hand, the overwhelming majority of myth-makers and authors of normative representations that dupe women into keeping their place are men. Myths and theories contrived by men tend to mold the growing woman, including future female myth-makers, psychologists, and anthropologists; the very idea of the technical term "female castration complex" reflects the ingrained custom of theorizing about women by analogy with men. In cases where women myth-makers break loose from such indoctrination (for example, Sappho and the authors of *The Three Women*), they tend to speak for and even idealize the close harmony between the two aspects of love in woman.

The explanation of the dichotomy in terms of male dominance also ignores certain complications. For one thing, in societies where women *are* relatively dominant (e.g., among the Isthmus Zapotec, the eighteenth-century Iroquois, the nineteenth-century Tuareg), the mother is disjoined from the lover, or at least one of the two roles is curtailed. On the other hand, the classic Maya, the Assyrian, and the Proto-Indo-European cultural schemes, though they appear to have known a synthesis of the two complexes in an All-Mother-Lover, have not been proposed by anyone as female-dominant cultures (they were male-dominant). Moreover, dominance of *any* kind varies enormously, even within the Western world, where it ranges from the extreme patriarchy of many Mediterranean folk cultures to the quasi-matriarchal patterns found in many American families. The variables in question do not seem to covary in any simple, predictable manner. The male-dominance hypothesis also tends to get into the pitfall of trying to explain deep symbolic structures in terms of superficial observations or statistics; in fact, the antithesis between sexual sensuousness and motherliness/maternity seems to be encouraged by *either* male dominance or female dominance (in the case of female dominance the split is between the lover [e.g., the transient husband] as against the brother [or mother's brother]). Finally, the male-dominance hypothesis often sounds like the familiar explanation of all social evils through patriarchy, male chauvinism, and kindred devils. Actually, a large number of women in many cultures dichotomize men just as sharply into what is a mirror image of the lover versus the mother: into the sensuous (and relatively irresponsible) male lover versus the positive and nurturing father-husband.

Once it is established, the antithesis becomes integral to the emotional life of the individual. Infant and child naturally tend to confuse heterosexual love and parent-child affection but, through open injunctions or more subtle cues, learn to keep the two apart. One vast and almost unexplored phase of this learning lies in language. Within our own lives we know of an enormous realm of idioms, intonations, special words and ways of using them, syntactic styles, and the rest that are used in courtship and love-making and also in the breakup of emotional and sexual ties between men and women. This language or style of adult love is largely distinct from the style of parent-child relations and is kept so by an enormous system of refined controls; a crucial part of growing up is to learn the codes for these styles and the differences between them. Once the system is established, it operates cybernetically, with the language style and the values of the culture influencing each other over time (although the cultural system is by far the more determining of the two). Many studies of parent-child language have shown how it differs from the language adults normally employ with each other, but the focus has all too often been on a few phrases or on objective referential meanings and all too seldom on nuances and the finer shades of meaning and form. The language styles of love remain almost totally unknown or even recognized in such fields as sociolinguistics and psycholinguistics (for an exception see Friedrich 1967).[4]

I have already said that the divide or disjunction between a male lover and a loving father is just as great as the divide between the female lover and the nurturing mother. One apparent and partial exception is Odysseus, who, one supposes, combines the affection, understanding, and experienced wisdom of a good father with the vigor, empathy, and skills of a "beautiful lover"; the picture, however, is most incomplete, for we do not see him, for example, making love or playing with small children (or even particularly aware of them). I find it fascinating, incidentally, that James Joyce's clearly unsuccessful attempt to rival Homer's full portrait of a well-rounded man missed on precisely the disjunction at issue here, the mores of his Irish Catholic past not being irrelevant. And it is also fascinating that the only major exception to the male disjunction was created by the world's greatest poet.

Perhaps one reason for the disjunction between sensuous and paternal love in myth and literature is that so many authors, prophets, and poets have had personal problems with one or the other of the complexes; their vision is incomplete, and we are left with

Don Quixote and Madame Bovary (or Moby Dick!). An exception is the modern Russian, Anna Akhmatova, who synthesized in her person and projected to her readers both of the complexes dealt with in this chapter as part of a more general image of the artistically creative woman.

THE INCEST FACTOR

The antithesis found in myth and literature between the two kinds of love is also motivated by forces more profound than male dominance, the defects of myth-makers, or even the conflicts between the symbols of a given culture. The basic locus of the problem is in a universal or transcendental paradox, or really set of such paradoxes, that have to be dealt with fairly hypothetically in this book.

A human being may want both of two relationships but cannot have them simultaneously with the same person. This happens when the ways of enacting the two roles, while within the range of a single person, are felt to be inherently mutually exclusive within the given system of cultural definitions; combining the roles, or even allowing them to overlap too much, would destroy the exclusivity of one or the other. For example, a man may love a woman as a mother, with all that that implies in its specific symbolism, and so cannot be imaginative or fully realistic about her sensuousness—to say nothing of accepting it. He may want another woman as a lover or at least a sexual partner and cannot face up to the full implications of her maternal love and what it might deprive him of; this is instanced by the not uncommon cooling of a man's affections after his partner becomes pregnant (or his recourse, sometimes desperate, to other women). In other cases he may desire a woman to produce and care for "his" children but not respect or satisfy her sexually. The two complexes and the disjunction between them are, in sum, an extension of the more intense situation mentioned above, where the roles actually converge in one person: where the same woman is both mother and lover.

While our immediate view is of the actual mother and the mother-child relation, the relations and implications carry far beyond this in all cultures. For one thing, the "maternity" involves not only literal birth but a wider emotional domain, where "the woman who bore me" shades into "the woman who raised me." Breast feeding can have many implications, as among the Russian peasants and the Wolof of Africa, where sex is tabooed between those who have suckled the same woman, between "milk brother and milk sister." "Maternity" can also ramify to include not only mother and children but the daughters of sisters and yet more far-flung matrilineal relations; for example, sex or marriage between the children of sisters is almost everywhere tabooed despite the even wider prevalence of preferred sex and/or marriage with cousins of various sorts. A final example is the almost universal "mother-in-law avoidance," which can range from the sense of constraint in our society to strict rules against conversation or even being in the same room; in at least one celebrated case, the Djirbal of Australia, there is a distinct "mother-in-law language" (Dixon 1974). Intimacy with a wife's mother can suggest, so to speak, an untoward mingling of sensuousness and maternity. All these facts point toward the larger idea that incest primarily reflects or expresses feelings and attitudes about the mother-child bond; as one anthropologist puts it, "incest expresses the violation of motherhood by sexuality" (Martin 1976), and another, speaking of the Nuer of Africa, notes "the disgust . . . at any association of sex with the mother" (Evans-Pritchard 1951: 37).

What I have been calling the disjunction between sensuousness and maternity is part of this larger symbolism of incest and other sexual taboos. Their great power partly accounts for the normally positive attitudes toward mother-daughter and man-woman bonds. Ultimately the main sphere of both complexes is not in rules *for* marriage between groups, or *against* first-cousin marriage, and the like, but *within* the primary triangle of the nuclear family, such as our own.

The power of the taboo against mixing sensuousness and motherliness is shown by the fact that the early poets say little about Demeter's sensuousness in contrast to her maternity and motherliness (aside from the affair with Iasion). Aphrodite's maternal love is significant but minor compared with her erotic subjectivity. Perhaps some future titan of the novel or epic will create a full synthesis of the meanings of Demeter and Aphrodite that will recapture the archaic synthetic imagery of the early Mayans and Indo-Europeans. Perhaps, also, we can hope for a future that will recognize, accept, and encourage the deep and natural connections between sensuous sexuality and motherliness-maternity. The split between them should be healed in the world view, or by the religion, by the system of ideas, whatever it is called, that connects our concrete lives with the awesome powers beyond our control.[5]

Appendixes

APPENDIX 1
HYMN TO DAWN (RIG VEDA 1. 113)

1. Here to this place the most beautiful light of lights has come,
   An expanding, brightly colored apparition has arisen.

   Night, as if driven, has yielded up a place, a womb for Dawn,
   That Savitar the sun may set the world in motion.

2. Shining brilliantly, the White One with her brilliant calf has come;
   The Black One has surrendered her abode.

   Of common kinship, deathless, these two halves of day
   Move in succession, each displacing the other's color.

3. The two sisters have the same endless path,
   Directed by the god, each moves over it in turn;

   Well-fixed, they do not meet nor do they ever stand:
   Night and Dawn, like of mind but different in appearance.

4. The luminous one has appeared, bringing in generous gifts;
   Brightly colored, she has opened the doors for us;

   She has lighted up our riches and roused the living world—
   Dawn has awakened all creatures.

5. One, sprawled out, that he might move,
   One to seek for food and wealth,

   Others, seeing little, that they might see far—
   Generous Dawn has awakened all creatures.

6. One to seek dominion, one fame,
   One greatness, one to go about his work,

   Diverse living beings to look about—
   Dawn has awakened all creatures.

7. The daughter of the sky has appeared,
   A radiant young woman in dazzling white,

Sovereign mistress of all earthly goods.
O prosperous Dawn, shine out here this day.

8. First of the dawns coming without end,
She goes off after the herd of dawns departing—

Radiant Dawn, arousing the living,
But not awakening anyone dead.

9. O Dawn, since you made men kindle the fire,
And shone forth through the glance of the sun,

And awakened men who will sacrifice
You have earned a handsome reward among the gods.

10. When will she be midway
Between those who have shone forth and those who will shine out
from now on?

Lowing after previous dawns she forms herself after them—
Looking forward in her mind, she goes willingly with the others.

11. They have gone, those mortals
Who earlier saw the radiant Dawn;

To us she has just now appeared;
And they are coming, who shall see her in the future.

12. Warding off enmity, guarding order, born within order,
Dispensing favors and creating numerous gifts,

Auspicious, bearing the invitation to the gods,
O Dawn, most beautiful of all, shine forth here today.

13. The goddess shone forth in the past without fail,
And here today the bountiful lady has shone forth,

And she shall shine out in all the days to come.
Undecaying, undying, she moves with her own laws.

14. She has flashed bright on the porticoes of the sky in streaks of rouge;
The goddess has drawn back the black robe.

Waking men up with her ruddy horses,
Dawn comes with her well-yoked chariot.

15. Bringing copious treasures, growing brighter and brighter,
She makes a brightly colored flag.

The last of those gone by, the first of those
Shining out forever, Dawn has shone bright.

16. Stir yourselves! A life-giving breath has come upon us—
The darkness has gone, light is coming;

She has left the way so the sun can travel it—
We have come to the place where men extend their lives.

17. Like a charioteer, the praising bard
Rouses the radiant dawns with the lash of the holy word—

So shine today, O generous lady, upon the one extolling;
Bestow on us long life with progeny.

18. Those dawns rich in cows and mighty heroes,
Which shine forth for the mortal who honors the gods—

May the man sacrificing with Soma and giving away horses receive
them
When the final chant of the sacrifice brings forth the generous gifts,
like those of the Wind.

19. Mother of the gods, face of Aditi,
Banner of the sacrificial rite, vast one, shine forth.

Shine forth, bestowing praise upon our prayer,
O you, who hold all good things, make us prolific among men.

20. That brightly colored, handsome reward which the dawns bring
To him who sacrifices with care—

Let Mitra, Varuṇa, Aditi, the River, Earth, and Sky
Bestow it on us.

(trans. James Fitzgerald)

Notes (by James Fitzgerald)

References below are to verse and quarter-verse (a, b, c, d); when two
letters are given, e.g., 8b/a, the first refers to the quarter-verses of the
translation, the second to the quarter-verses of the original text. The
discrepancies arise because I have occasionally transposed the order of
phrases within a verse, as, for example, in 8ab.

1a. Here to this place—*idám*: This adverb is the very first word of
the hymn, and it represents a significant idea that recurs in this
hymn several times. Throughout, the poet refers to Dawn's shining out "here" and "now, today" and uses the first person plural,
referring to the relation of himself and his own group to Dawn
and her generosity. The hymn is rooted in an immediate and
personalistic rather than a universalistic perspective. In the
context of this emphasis even the general terms "the living
world" (9c) and "all creatures" (4d, 5d, 6d) must be understood as confined in their reference to the world circumscribed
by the poet's "here."

1d/c. That Savitar (the sun) may set (the world) in motion—
savitúḥ savā́ya: Dative of purpose with subjective genitive.

3b. Directed by the god—*devā́siṣṭe*: That is, by Savitar.

4a. Generous gifts—*sūnṛ́tā*: See Louis Renou, *Etudes védiques et pāṇinéennes* (Paris: de Boccard, 1957), vol. 3, p. 17 (on Rig Veda 1. 48. 2). Renou accepts Hermann Oldenberg's conclusions from "Vedische Untersuchungen, 2. *sūnára, sūnṛ́tā,*" *Zeitschrift der deutschen morgenländischen Gesellschaft* 50 (1896): 433–43.

8b/a. Herd—*pā́thas*: This word is quite problematic and uncertain. Again I follow the lead of Renou, who accepts the results of Klaus Janert, who first proposed this interpretation in *Sinn und Bedeutung des Wortes dhāsi und seiner Belegstellen im R̥gveda und Awesta* (Wiesbaden: Harrassowitz, 1956), p. 10, note. (Unfortunately this book was not available to me.)

9a. Fire is significant as a symbol chiefly because of its central role in the Vedic sacrificial ritual, and much Vedic poetry is directed to the personified fire, Agni, in this role. At the same time, fire signifies warmth and light and thus has obvious affinities with the dawn, the day, and the sun, affinities we know were highly significant in some later Brahmanical thought.

11b/a. Earlier—*pū́rvatarām*: This word is an adjective modifying Dawn (*uṣásam*) and resonates with "previous (dawns)" (pū́rvāḥ) in 10c. I have translated it as an adverb for the sake of the flow of the line in English.

14a. Porticoes of the sky—*divá ā́tāsu*: That is, amidst the columns (*ā́tā*) which form, on the horizons, the frame supporting the sky over the earth (cf. R̥g Veda 1. 56. 5).
Streaks of rouge—*añjíbhis*: I do not find F. B. J. Kuiper's argument (*Vāk* 2 [1952]: 78 f.) against the sense "makeup, rouge," convincing. The context supports the notion of coloring applied to the face (by anointing) much more strongly than the notion of ornamentation.

APPENDIX 2

PROTO-INDO-EUROPEAN **ǵhár-i-s*

One interesting etymology for Proto-Indo-European **ǵhár-i-s* was proposed originally by Max Müller (1864: 368–69), who dealt mainly with some of the Greek and Indic evidence. It merits a brief discussion in contemporary terms.

The comparison is between forms in four Indo-European stocks. (1) The *Harits* in the Rig Veda are the winged horses of the sun, usually seven in number, ruddy in color, bright and dripping with fat, and the bringers of wealth and prosperity. They are mentioned in only five hymns (plus one additional occurrence as the horses of Agni and another as the horses of Soma). (2) The *Charites* in Homeric and other Greek myth are beautiful young maidens whose typical role is to wash Aphrodite and anoint her with oil; these "Graces" are generally agreed to belong to the early, or pre-Olympian, stratum of Greek myth. (3) The Proto-Slavic word *zórja* yields the word for dawn (the natural kind) in all the Slavic languages. (4) Lithuanian *žarijà* means "burning coal." Note that these correspondences are from the same stocks that provide the main evidence for the Twins and Dawn, plus Slavic (but "Balto-Slavic" is a superstock in the opinion of some scholars).

Let us begin with the phonology. The correspondences are quite regular. PIE *ǵh- may be reflected by Sanskrit *h* and is normally reflected by Greek *ch,* Slavic *z,* and Baltic *ž.* PIE *a regularly goes to Slavic *o.* All four stocks point toward an i-stem. *s* is the PIE nominative singular ending. One can posit a PIE *ǵhár-i-s. This noun was probably late and probably a deverbative from the verbal root *ǵhér-, "to bring, carry."

At the morphological level there is independent evidence for such a nominal form. *Harites* is taken as an independent nominal by some Sanskritists. The corresponding Sanskrit verb, *hr̥-* (third person singular *hárati*) is, in the Rig Veda, strongly associated with the sunrise, with the dancing-place of Ushas, with the web of Ushas dispelling the night, and similar images (Boedeker 1974: 57–60); it has one or the other of these meanings about half the time. Ultimately these Sanskrit forms derive from PIE *ǵhér-/ǵhár-. As for the Greek *Charites* or Graces, Frisk, who would have opposed Müller's suggestion, says that "the substantive, *charis,* stands by itself, independent of the verb" (he is speaking of Greek only). This *charis* is regularly derivable from the verb *chairō,* "to please, like," and similar meanings. I would propose that at some point, early in the prehistory of Greek, there was a convergence or conflation of the singular of *charis,* "grace," and the plural form, *charites,* with its meaning "bearers or attendants of the sun." One result of the conflation was the unusual but not anomalous pairing of an abstract singular and a concrete plural.

Let us turn, third and last, to the Slavic form. It is usually treated independently, as an independent nominal, by standard authorities, such as Max Vasmer, with only some reference to the verbal root, *zr-,* "see." On morphological and related semantic grounds, then, from Indic, Greek, and Slavic, *ǵháris was already an independent noun in PIE times, although clearly connected with its verbal source in the well-established PIE verbal root *ǵhér-, "take, bring."

The semantic developments from this posited noun also seem plausible. I suppose that it orginally meant "bringers, takers, bearers," and the like and then became ritually or formulaically specialized to mean "bearers of the sun" (still reflected in Sanskrit as "the horses of the sun"). In pre-Greek the derivation was limited to "attendants of the sun," then to attendants of Eos, and, finally, to the attendants of the Dawn-derived Aphrodite. In Slavic the shift went to "forerunners of the sun" and thence to "rays, dawn," and related meanings like "flash" and "light"; in Bulgarian, however, *zorá* shifted to (or stayed as?) "morning and evening star."

If we admit *ǵháris* as PIE, we have the original name for the attendants of the dawn goddess who are mentioned in most of the early texts. The problem is of methodological interest because it poses in acute form the conflict between a semantically based as against the traditional approach to Indo-European. On the one hand, the etymology proposed above is well motivated both semantically and mythologically and works reasonably well in terms of linguistic criteria. But my solution would be ruled out by the Indo-Europeanist who ranks a strict (and, I would say, unrealistic) phonology over semantics and mythology—and, indeed, over everything else. He would derive the nominal forms independently from the verbal roots in each of the three stocks (Sanskrit *hári-*, Greek *chairo-*, "to please," Slavic *zr-*, "to see," and so forth). (The etymology proposed above is not mentioned in any standard grammar or etymological dictionary.)

APPENDIX 3
HERODOTUS 1. 199, ON TEMPLE PROSTITUTION

199. The foulest Babylonian custom is that which compels every woman of the land once in her life to sit in the temple of Aphrodite and have intercourse with some stranger. Many women who are rich and proud and disdain to consort with the rest, drive to the temple in covered carriages drawn by teams, and there stand with a great retinue of attendants. But most sit down in the sacred plot of Aphrodite, with crowns of cord on their heads; there is a great multitude of women coming and going; passages marked by line run every way through the crowd, by which the stranger men pass and make their choice. When a woman has once taken her place there she goes not away to her home before some stranger has cast money into her lap and had intercourse with her outside the temple; but while he casts the money, he must say, "I demand thee in the name of Mylitta" (that is the Assyrian name for Aphrodite). It matters not what be the sum of the money; the woman will never refuse, for that were a sin, the money being by this act made sacred. So she follows the first man who casts it and rejects none. After their inter-

course she has made herself holy in the goddess's sight and goes away
to her home; and thereafter there is no bribe however great that will
get her. So then the women that are fair and tall are soon free to depart,
but the uncomely have long to wait because they cannot fulfill the law;
for some of them remain for three years, or four. There is a custom like
to this in some parts of Cyprus.

(trans. Godley 1960:251–52)

APPENDIX 4

PINDAR'S EULOGY FOR XENOPHON OF CORINTH (FRAG. 122 [87])

["Xenophon of Corinth, before competing for the Olympic crown in
464 B.C., vowed that, in the event of his success, he would devote a
hundred courtesans to the service of the temple of Aphrodite in that
city. On the occasion of the fulfilment of his vow, the following ode
was sung in the temple of the goddess, while the hundred women
danced to the words of the song. The same Olympic victory was celebrated in the thirteenth Olympian ode."—Sir John Sandys, in his introduction to this eulogy in the Loeb edition.]

Young girls, hospitable to many guests, servants of
Persuasion in wealthy Corinth, you who burn the golden
tears of fresh frankincense, many times soaring upward
in your thoughts to Aphrodite, heavenly mother of loves:

To you, girls, she has granted blamelessly on lovely beds
to harvest the fruits of delicate spring, for under love's
necessity all things are fair. . . .

Yet I wonder what the lords of the Isthmus [of Corinth]
will say of my devising such a prelude to sweet-sounding
song to be the pleasure for women who belong to all in common. . . .

But we have tested their gold with pure touchstone. . . .
O Lady of Cyprus! Here to your grove sanctuary Xenophon
has brought a herd of one hundred girls, like fillies from
the pasture, glad for the fulfillment of his vows.

(synthesized from Sandys and Seltman)

APPENDIX 5

ETYMOLOGY OF *áwsōs*

The Greek reflexes of *áwsōs* include not only the Homeric *ēōs* (with
its regular Attic-Ionic shift of long alpha to eta) but also Doric and
Aeolic forms; the loss of the *s* between vowels is the rule for Greek.

The corresponding Latin is *aurōra;* the shift to *r* reflects the Latin "rhotization" of *s* between vowels. Latin also has *Auster,* "East," and the Latin *ostra,* "eastern" (which enters into the first part of Ostragoth). PIE *áwsōs* is reflected in Sanskrit *úshās,* with the "reduced grade" of the initial element (*w* for *aw*), and with the long *ō* going to long *ā* by a rule that is exceptionless in this stock. In Baltic there are the Lithuanian forms *Ausra* and *Ausrine* and the Latvian *Auskelis,* all meaning "morning star" (also "dawn" in the case of *Ausra*). We have a cognate in the Iranian *usait,* "to brighten" (of morning), and others that reflect a PIE *us-sk̑-.* And there are Celtic cognates, such as Middle Irish *fāir.*

The Germanic reflexes strongly support the reconstruction. They include the Modern English "east," which comes from Old English "east," etymologically "from the direction of the sunrise"; the Old English is cognate with Old High German *ōstan,* also "east." A second, related set includes Old English *ēasterne,* "eastern," and Frankish *ostra,* "eastern." Scholars have posited the form *austrōn-* as the name for the Germanic dawn goddess, whose holiday was celebrated at the vernal equinox (hence our word Easter; see Watkins 1969: 1507). Yet another set of Germanic forms may include the Gothic *ūhtwa* and the Old English *ūhta,* though this is doubtful.

Thus we have excellent correspondences of form and meaning in five highly valued stocks: Greek, Italic, Indic, Baltic, and Germanic (with somewhat weaker evidence from Iranian and Celtic). In all five stocks at least some of the forms refer to *both* the natural phenomenon and a goddess. The formal variations *aws-, ws-,* and so forth all exemplify typical early "vowel gradation." The PIE noun *áwsōs* was probably derived from the verbal root *ăwes-/aws-* and the commuted *wos-/wes-,* a derivational tie that is still transparent in the Vedic terms *vás-,* "to shine," as against *vásara,* "morning," and *úshās,* "dawn."

In addition to the exemplary set just discussed there is a second, with an intrusive *r* element: *ws-r-,* as reflected in Greek *aurion,* "tomorrow," Sanskrit *usrá,* "morning," and the Latin, Lithuanian, and Germanic forms already referred to. Within this context we must consider the Proto-Slavic word for "morning," *útro,* which is reflected in all the Slavic languages, for example the Russian *útro;* closely related are the widespread forms for "tomorrow" such as Old Slavonic *za ustra* and Russian *závtra.* This Slavic word probably arose by the following steps: (1) a reduced-grade version *wsos,* with the *r* increment, went to (2) *ustro* in Proto-Slavic, with an intrusive *t* (which is irregular but has parallels), and then shifted to (3) *útro,* with loss of the *s.*

The Slavic meaning was narrowed down to the natural phenomenon, although dawn is still anthropomorphic to some extent in Slavic folklore. The same narrowing has occurred in the cognate forms in Greek, Latin, Indic, and so forth, since the descendant forms in modern French, for example, no longer refer to a goddess. The main reason for the difference in reference in the Slavic, then, is that the Christianized texts of the late first millennium B.C. are being compared with the much earlier pagan ones of Greece, Rome, and India.

The excellent semantic case for "dawn, Dawn" is supported by the phonological one for the form *awsos, which, indeed, is one of the several hundred "good cognates" that are accepted by specialists, being quite on a par with such favorites as the terms for "beech," "wolf," "sweet," "to be," and "kill." The only other female divinity who can be posited with some certainty for Proto-Indo-European is Mother Earth, and that case is much weaker.

The evidence on *awsos* raises the general issue that language is a set of relations between a system of sound and a system of meaning, both of which it includes. Of these I think that the semantic one is primary. By the same token, correspondences of meaning between myths always have potential value for reconstruction, particularly when borrowing can be ruled out and when the correspondences are complex and many-sided. Mythological systems should be reconstructed giving *somewhat more* weight to the semantic than to the phonological (or other grammatical) evidence. We should avoid the fallacious practice of the Indo-Europeanist linguist who relies primarily or exclusively on phonological criteria and rules (since the latter are themselves probabilistic historical generalizations of great variability). We should also avoid the fallacious practice of some mythologists who reconstruct with little attention to linguistics and philology.

APPENDIX 6

ETYMOLOGIES ASSOCIATED WITH APHRODITE

The Etymology of the Name Aphrodite

The etymology of the name Aphrodite has naturally provoked alternative explanations. Some of these less likely sources need not be reviewed here (e.g., *a Phrygite,* "from Phrygia," or "the April goddess," etc.). Many think it ultimately goes back to some version of Ashtoreth or Astarte after considerable transmogrification through gradual transmission; of course this hypothesis is motivated by the assumption that the goddess herself is of exclusively "Oriental" origin (Frisk 1960: vol. 1, p. 197). Given the goals of the present study, great importance attaches to the view of Hesiod: "The 'foam-born' [*aphrogenea*] goddess and the 'well-crowned' Cytherean men call [her] because she grew amid the foam" (*aphros; Theogony* 196–98). Certainly many early Greeks thought this, too, and, after the seventh century, cited Hesiod, their inspired and authoritative synthesizer of religious and mythological traditions. Along the same lines, I find cogent the earlier comparison of Greek *aphros,* "foam," with the Indic *abhrá-,* "cloud," as mentioned in Frisk. The phonetic correspondences are excellent, including those for the accent; the semantic transition is entirely natural (although rejected by Frisk in another exemplification of his egregious conservativism). An even finer semantic point, well argued by Boedeker (1974:9) is that *aphros* rarely meant "sea foam" in the actual texts but did imply extreme vitality (sic!) in a number of key contexts. Finally, to the *aphros/abhrá* set we can add the Armenian *p'rp'r,* "foam," and tentatively reconstruct PIE *abhrós* (using *a* for the second laryngeal). On the other hand, this same set must be cognate to the long-accepted one for "cloud" and the like (Greek *nephelē,* Latin *nebula,* and German *Nebel,* three forms which represent a full-grade realization of an earlier syllabic *n* as *ne,* whereas *aphros* represents vocalization of the same syllabic as *a;* both sets go back to some pre-PIE *nbh-).

The second part of Aphrodite's name—assuming it is a compound—either consists of *hoditēs,* "wanderer," as Kretschmer thought (thus "foam wanderer"), or is built on *di,* "bright, white, brilliant." The latter suggestion has much in its favor, including the frequent use of the word *dia* as an epithet for Aphrodite and the frequent thematic association of Aphrodite with clouds in both erotic and martial scenes in Homer; note also the traditional formula of "white cloud" in just such contexts. Since this *di* comes from Proto-Indo-European *dey,* we have a genuine PIE source for the name of the goddess. (I believe this latter etymology originated with G. Nagy.)

Philommeidēs, "SMILE-LOVING"

One of the most frequent epithets of Aphrodite calls for a detailed discussion. The standard translation of *philommeidēs* as "smile-loving" is beyond reproach, but the same cannot be said of the common mistranslation "laughter-loving." Let me emphasize that "smile-loving" was doubtless *one* of the meanings in all the passages. While some occurrences of the word seem to be purely ornamental, it is usually found "in contexts which explicitly (or implicitly) emphasize Aphrodite's aspect as a goddess of sexual love" (Boedeker 1974: 32)—for example in the Fifth Homeric Hymn, when Zeus explains why he wants to humiliate her, when Aphrodite falls in love with Anchises, when she then adorns herself, and when she follows him to bed. Moreover, the root, with its "smile" meaning, has cognates in five other Indo-European stocks (e.g., Germanic, in English "smile"). The fact that the four cases of Vedic Sanskrit *smi-* are used of Ushas suggests strongly that the "smiling Dawn" is a PIE syntagm.

A second translation of *philommeidēs* is "loving a (man's) penis (or genitalia)." This translation is almost universally rejected as "patently false" by classicists and Indo-Europeanists, even when they cite and emphasize the passages for which this erotic gloss seems appropriate. Let us take a second look at this possibility.

First, the purely formal grounds. One common type of compound in Greek and Proto-Indo-European is of the V(erb) O(bject) order, as in the Greek adjective *helkesipeplos,* used of one "who drags her robe." One of the most productive verbal roots used in this kind of compound formation is *philo-,* which means "to like, to love" in Attic and, to some extent, in Homeric Greek (Benveniste 1969, vol. 1: 335–55). Also from the derivational morphology comes the fact that -*ēs* is a highly productive suffix for forming substantives (nouns and adjectives), usually agentives, or for referring to occupations or characteristic activities. It reflects an underlying -*tēs* and is one of the set of "dental suffixes" (as contrasted, e.g., with the nasals), the -*t* being absorbed by the preceding *d.* Within this morphological framework, *philommeidēs* could be "penis-loving."

Second some lexical facts. The Homeric Greek *mēdea* means "testicles, male genitals," and it occurs four times (all in the *Odyssey*). This reference seems to have disappeared in classical times but has a good parallel in Celtic; Middle Irish *mess* (from Proto-Celtic **med-tu*) means "acorn" (Frisk 1970: 222). This is congruous with the fairly standard (essentially universal) association between the acorn and the head of the penis, reflected, to take another case, in the English medical term *glans penis* (*glans* being the Latin word for acorn). Thus on lexical grounds the second part of the epithet fits into the Greek (and universal) categorical structure.

The third consideration concerns the sounds and letters. The first *m* in *mm* may reflect the former *s* of *philos* that I referred to above, but there is an additional, synchronic, motivation. A single *m* would result in a word with two short syllables followed by two long syllables, and that does not fit into a dactylic hexameter line if it stands *before* the name Aphrodite, whereas the double *mm* yields the appropriate sequence $\cup / — — / — \cup \cup / — —$; the final spondee also makes it possible to end the line at this point, and, in fact, this "smile-loving Aphrodite" occurs as a line-finishing formula five times (all in the *Iliad;* Schmidt 1885: 229). Finally, both *ei* and *ē* (the diphthong and the long vowel) occur. The Hesiodic form, *philommeidēs,* which is closest to *mēdea,* may be specifically Boeotian (Allen, Sykes, and Halliday 1936: 353). Since both spellings are found in the ancient sources—*ē* for the isolated noun and *ei* in the compound—we are at liberty to assume some orthographic juggling on the part of the later scribes, corresponding to an ambiguity or play on words in the earlier, purely spoken tradition.

Finally, the proposed second meaning, "penis-loving," seems cogent on psychological grounds and in terms of Aphrodite's historical connections with the Ishtars and the PIE *awsos,* her own sexual activeness (as referred to, for example, in *Iliad* 3), and, finally, the way the gods speak of her "arts and wiles." In both Homer and Hesiod, Aphrodite is represented as a female figure with interest and delight in male sexuality. We must also recall that in one major myth she sprang from the castrated parts of Krónos. In other words, the *themes* in the texts seem congruous with the specific philological arguments here advanced.

This brings us back to the meaning of *philo-.* While it often does mean "like, love," as just noted, the more common Homeric meaning is "to own inalienably," with typical reference to a spouse, a body part, one's home, personal weapon, blood (but not affinal!) relative, and the like (Rosén 1967). Thus, by an inversion of the usual meaning of "inalienable," she did not *possess* these genitals but arose from them (I assume that one would always be in a *philo-* relation to the part of a parent's body from which one came). Historically, what is involved is a conflation of the PIE roots for *glans* and for "smile," as they were inherited in early Greek—with a resulting ambiguity.

My final point is the essentially anthropological one of considering "what the natives say." Hesiod obviously cannot provide us with a scholarly analysis, but he is perhaps our best authority on myths of origin among the eighth-century Greeks, a source of truth and wisdom about the mythic past. What Hesiod said was (*Theogony* 200): "She was called *philommēdea* because she sprang from the members," or, in our periphrasis, is one related by *philos* to the male genitals. *Philommeidēs* as "penis-loving" illustrates a more general fact about language, and poetic language in particular, namely, that the lexical symbols have more than one meaning, depending on context, and that they can simultaneously mean two or more things in one and the same context. This is the multivocalism of the symbol that underlies the rich ambiguities of all poetry. The *double-entendre* also illustrates the operation of verbal taboo, since the epithet in question could always be taken as "smile-loving."

Appendix 7

Sappho's Fragment 66, "The Wedding of Andromache"

Kypros.
A herald came, racing powerfully on swift legs,
came quickly to the people of Ida with tidings

of imperishable renown in the rest of Asia:
"Hektor and his comrades bring a dark-eyed girl
from holy Thebe and the streams of Plakia;
splendid Andromache coming with the navy

over the salt sea. They bear many gold bracelets
and purple gowns and odd trinkets of rare design
and countless silver goblets and pieces of ivory."

So the herald spoke; and Priam sprang to his feet
and the glowing news was carried to his friends
throughout the wide city. Instantly the sons of Ilios
harnessed the mules to the finely-wheeled chariots,
and a throng of wives and slender-ankled virgins
climbed inside. Priam's daughters rode alone,
while young men led their horses under the carts
and drove them out of the city . . .

Like gods . . . holy . . . they all set out for Ilium
to the confusion of sweet flutes and crashing
          cymbals,
and the virgins sang a loud heavenly song
whose wonderful echo touched the sky. Everywhere
was laughter in the streets and bowls and chalices.

Myrrh and cassia and incense rode on the wind.
Elder women shouted and all the men sang out
with thrilling power and raised a paean to Apollo—
O mighty bowman and skillful player of the lyre—
singing of Hektor and Andromache as of gods.

(trans. Barnstone 1965: 59)

APPENDIX 8

HERMES AND APHRODITE; ODYSSEUS AND HELEN

The details of Hermes' liminality have been clarified by Otto (1954: 104–24); they include his moving by night (the time of love, dreams, and theft); his cunning and deceit (conjoined with friendliness à la Aphrodite); his magical powers (wings, wand, and magical hat, like Aphrodite's love charms and girdle); his patronage of traders, thieves, shepherds, and heralds (all of them marginal, like sailors); his own mobility and the location of his phallic herms on roads, at crossroads, and in groves; his particular brand of stealthy and sly eroticism; and, perhaps above all, his status as a guide across boundaries, including that between earth and Hades (otherwise performed by the Twins, the brothers of Helen and Dawn). Hermes is also a popular god of fertility. Small wonder that he and Aphrodite were eventually synthesized as the Hermaphrodite figure of classical and Hellenistic times.

Hermes is akin to Aphrodite in yet other ways. Like her he stems from the more archaic, pre-Olympian, stratum of Greek myth and, like her, goes back to yet more remote origins: his numerous and complex analogies to the Pushan of the Indic Vedas guarantee his status as a Proto-Indo-European god of cattle, paths, the night, exchange, transitions, and so forth (Watkins 1970: 345–50). Both Hermes and Pushan are probably cognate with Odin of Old Norse. If we go downward in time, on the other hand, he is tied in to the epics, not only as an actor himself but as the mythic source for Odysseus, who is resourceful and witty, verbally skilled, mobile, typically on thresholds and in boundary areas, and is a wanderer and changeling. Genealogically, Hermes is the grandfather of Odysseus and was first married to Ameirake, who, after being rescued by a duck (*pēnelops*) was called Penelope; the fact that the two Penelopes are associated with an Aphrodite bird is symbolically critical.

The affinity between Hermes and Aphrodite is also brought out through the personal interaction between their faded variants, Odysseus and Helen. As the poet of the *Little Iliad* (seventh century) has it, "Odysseus disfigures himself and goes in to Ilium as a spy, and there being recognized by Helen, plots with her for the taking of the city" (Evelyn-White 1967: 511). In Homer, Odysseus enters Troy disguised as a beggar and is recognized only by Helen, who takes him home and bathes him and anoints him with oil (*Od.* 4. 244–64) (one wishes the bard had given us some of their conversation!). On the other hand, when Helen later imitates the voices of the wives of the heroes who are hidden inside the Trojan horse in order to make them betray themselves, it is Odysseus alone who is able to keep full control over himself and prevent the man who breaks down from crying out (4. 274–89). In each case, when one simulates, the other responds adequately and, indeed, most appropriately. (I am indebted to James Redfield for this point.) Once again, Homer is not explicit or even conscious of this relation between epic and the mythic subtext, but he seems to intuit and even suggest it through his portrayal of empathy. On the potential empathy between Helen and Achilles the poet of the *Cypria* (seventh century) says, "Achilles desires to see Helen, and Aphrodite and Thetis contrive a meeting between them" (Evelyn-White 1967: 495); see also Hilda Doolittle's *Helen in Egypt*.

APPENDIX 9

TWO STRUCTURALIST VIEWS OF THE RELATION BETWEEN APHRODITE AND DEMETER

One Structuralist View

Let us turn to a last interpretive glance at the Greek myths. In the view of structuralists such as Vernant and Detienne the meanings of

Aphrodite and Demeter-Persephone are generally and often emphatically counterposed. It is impossible and unnecessary to recapitulate the scholarship and harmonics of Detienne's study, in particular, but to my summary near the end of chapter 3 we can now add the following list of contrasts between (1) the seductive, perfumed, feasting courtesans of Aphrodite, sowing their ephemeral, eight-day Gardens of Adonis, *as opposed to* the abstemious, legitimate, family-oriented matrons of Eleusis and the Thesmophoriae, who have their men sow basic grains in season in rich soil.

Aphrodite The Gardens of Adonis		Demeter-Persephone The Thesmophoria
1. Heat, dryness ("dog days of Sirius"), growth out of season	*versus*	Cold, wet, moist; growth in season
2. Superficial growth, without roots, in baskets or pots on roofs, for eight days	*versus*	Cereal crops maturing over eight months in rich soil
3. Courtesans and concubines	*versus*	Matrons and virgins
4. License, "perversion," feasting, play	*versus*	Abstinence, rule of law, fasting, seriousness
5. Myrrh and other perfumes	*versus*	Lettuce (symbol of death)
6. Disequilibrium	*versus*	Equilibrium
7. Aphrodite and Adonis	*versus*	Demeter and Persephone

I have synthesized this list from Detienne (1972: 157, 200). Despite the many problems it leaves us with, it is extremely interesting and also parallels the overt public opposition in the rituals of classical and Hellenistic times.

Phryne's Stand: Aphrodite *vs.* Demeter-Persephone

The structuralist opposition argued by Detienne and Vernant actually was enacted dramatically during one of the more remarkable episodes in the symbolization of the emotions. I have already discussed the celebrated courtesans of ancient times (chapters 5 and 6). Perhaps the most famous was Phryne, "The Toad."[1] Though born in Boeotia, she lived in Athens, where, in the words of the *Encyclopaedia Britannica,*

she earned so much by her beauty and wit that she offered to rebuild the walls of Thebes, on the condition that the words "Destroyed by Alexander, restored by Phryne the courtesan" were incribed upon them. At a festival of Poseidon and also at the festival of Eleusis she walked into the sea with her hair loose, suggesting to the painter Apelles his great picture of Aphrodite Anadyomene ("rising from the sea"), for which Phryne sat as model. She was also (according to Athenaeus) the model for the statue of the Knidian Aphrodite [discussed above, under liminality] by Praxiteles, whose model she was; copies of the statue survive in the Vatican and elsewhere. When accused of blasphemy (a capital charge) she was defended by the orator Hyperides. When it seemed as if the verdict would be unfavourable, he tore her dress and and displayed her bosom, which so moved the jury that they acquitted her; another version makes Phryne tear her own dress and plead with each individual juror.

The above scene requires some contextualization. As a courtesan, Phryne was allowed to appear in court—but not to speak. Her offer to rebuild the walls of Thebes gets a lot of its meaning from the Greek symbolic equation: city walls are analogous to a woman's veil or headdress, which in turn is analogous to the hymen, which symbolizes female integrity (Nagler 1972: 298). In other words, in a pragmatic sense, the great Phryne was saying: "I, the greatest of courtesans, and so *the* symbol of erotic love, will rebuild the walls of the fairest city (which stand for the integrity of any woman) that were torn down by that sacker of cities (and women), and lover of men, Alexander the Great." This remarkable woman was a devotée of Aphrodite—in many ways another incarnation. Perhaps she was affirming, or indeed flaunting, the meaning of Aphrodite against those of Demeter. As a beautiful, wealthy, and relatively free woman, she might have been subjected to mockery by the matrons of Eleusis and by the Thesmophoriae.

A Different Structuralist View

A different structuralist view can lead us toward a fuller appreciation of the communality, whether obvious or latent, between the complexes of Aphrodite and Demeter.

A number of symbols are shared by the two goddesses: (1) the pomegranate and the poppy; (2) goldenness; (3) nonmartiality; and (4) great (or the greatest) beauty.

In other cases the symbolism of one is an analogue of the other; compare the birth of Aphrodite with the rape (symbolic death) of Persephone: (1) ascent at (2) birth (3) from the genitals (4) of her father, (5) seen as an immanent source (middle voice) (6) out of the sea or foam, is some analogue of Persephone's (1) descent, at her (2) rape (3) by the genitals of (4) her father's brother (and father), (5) seen as an aggressive act (active voice), (6) into the underworld. This kind of transformational relation, incidentally, is typical of structuralism and makes people suspicious of it, but it may have some heuristic value.

Many other such "transformational relations" could be elaborated with the appropriate accompaniment of formulas and diagrams, but I think for the present it will suffice to list a few more of the major contrasts between the two complexes.

Aphrodite	Demeter-Persephone
1. Solar, astral, insular	Chthonic
2. Water, navigation	Drought, desert
3. Never virgin	Virgin in spirit; chaste
4. Seduces men in the mountains	Gets raped by gods in meadows
5. Passionate lover	Anxious and hostile about sex
6. Arts of love (linking nature and culture)	Arts of agriculture (linking nature and culture)
7. Maternal love for son	Maternal love for daughter
8. Human and animal fertility	Agricultural fertility
9. Mobile/immobile	Mobile (Demeter); immobile (Persephone)
10. Near	Distant

These relations do not begin to exhaust the possibilities of this powerful (and permissive) way of analyzing these myths. For transformations can be established on the basis of the following relations: equivalence, inversion and other permutations and commutations, conjunction, negation, class inclusion, and, at a more substantive level, name relations (e.g., homonymy), shared origin, same or opposite direction, any polarity, quantity (more/less), expansion/contraction, and any basic quality such as intense/lax. Such multi-based transformations clearly relate Aphrodite and Demeter-Persephone. But the very permissiveness of such structuralism raises the question of its indeterminacy.

Myth and Ritual

Let us try to ground the mythic relation between Aphrodite and Demeter-Persephone by considering the ascertainable facts about ritual objects because, as Victor Turner has said, the *sacra* are "the heart of the liminal matter" (1967b: 102). The better-known objects in the Lesser Mysteries of Eleusis were an apple, a bone, a ball, a fan, a mirror, a tambourine, a top, and a woolly fleece (Harrison 1903: 144–60). The *sacra* in the Greater Mysteries were said to have included pyramidal and spherical sesame-seed cakes, balls of salt, a serpent, and "pomegranates, fig branches, fennel stalks, ivy leaves, round cakes, and poppies" and symbols of Themis, such as "marjoram, a lamp, a sword, and a woman's comb, which is a euphemistic expression used in the mysteries for a woman's secret parts." We know from another source that wheat, poppy, and fennel were integral ingredients in the rites of Demeter (Detienne 1972). The list of sacra is suggestive and, even more than that, extremely ambiguous.

"Clement's Hypothesis": Aphrodite Equals Demeter-Persephone

I think this is the point at which to bring up the exhortation against the Greeks by Clement of Alexandria (150–220 A.D.), who, because of his hatred of their paganism (and, I would say, of women) was motivated to break the taboo against revealing the content of the Greater Mysteries (or at least to conjecture publicly about their contents). Clement claimed that the Greater Mysteries celebrated both Aphrodite, the "lover of lustful members," and the Demeter of motherhood, with ritual enactment of her rape by Zeus and then the rape of her daughter by Zeus and Hades. Clement's accusation does mesh with many things: with the patently phallic *and* reproductive symbolism of the Eleusinian *sacra;* with the fact that the poppy, shared by the two goddesses, is shown in second millennia B.C. representations of "poppy goddesses" with its pods cracked as they are for the extraction of opium (thanks to N. Spencer for this point); with the probable use of incense; with the fact that the nocturnal procession to Eleusis stopped at an Aphrodite shrine and was generally marked by obscene and other liminal behavior; with the psychological fact that it is Aphrodite who has to mediate between Demeter and a man and Persephone and a man if they are to realize their mythic roles; and, finally, with the fact that Aphrodite and Persephone in later myth are identified with each other through their competitive love for Adonis, both as a beautiful baby boy and, subsequently, as a sperm-rich youth—in other words, by the symbolism of incest.

In sum, the female-dominated Greater Mysteries of Eleusis were marked by hallucination through narcotics, by androgynous and incestuous symbolism, and by nocturnal, liminal behavior. They confronted and flouted the artificiality of the antithesis between sexuality and maternalism that was upheld in all public cult in the male-dominated society. In modern terms, we would say that the focus of the Mysteries was on the mystic union of the complexes of sexuality and maternalism, of Aphrodite and Demeter-Persephone. Precisely because of this they were under such a categorical and successful taboo. This exhortation-redone-as-hypothesis strikes me as interesting, to say the least—if largely hypothetical.

Notes

CHAPTER 1

1. Further examples of avoidance include a major 1950 book, with six references of one sentence or less, and Nilsson's major works of 1950 and 1972, the first of which contains a few brief mentions of Aphrodite, while the latter devotes part of one sentence to her. Murray (1925) rarely mentioned her. I could cite many other examples. The main mythologist of Indo-European myth, G. Dumézil, has avoided mention of Aphrodite during most of his long and extremely productive scholarly life. Lévi-Strauss says little.

A pragmatic index of the neglect of Aphrodite is the fact that Chicago's great Regenstein Library has only one serious work on the subject—Fauth (1967)—and a second partly about it—Schroeder (1887).

2. *Aidōs,* from which comes the adjective *aidoiē,* labels one of the key value complexes in Homeric Greek. *Aidōs* is a kind of shyness, shame, or shrinking about one's actions vis-à-vis another who is cognizant of them. One feels *aidōs* about being seen naked, doing something cowardly or ungenerous, and the like. In this sense it is about intrusions into one's private life or criticisms for something shameful. It is particularly inspired by cowardice, perjury, irreverence, sexual transgressions, or mistreatment of the helpless—strangers, suppliants, the old, the blind, and children. It is felt before a guest, a close relative, a superior in age, and persons of superior status, such as kings, sages, elders, or even excellent workmen. Above all, it is felt toward the gods and their criticisms of something as shameful. *Aidōs* contrasts with *nemesis,* the sense of outrage or indignation felt toward another (Redfield 1975).

CHAPTER 2

1. Gimbutas and the others who use the term "script" in this context seem actually to be referring to a large number of signs, most of them iconic to some extent, that may be taken to stand for certain ideas; for example, the meander stands for streams or, more generically, for water. The fact that Gimbutas' inferred scheme resembles that of the Dogon and other peoples increases their naturalness. I have to state, though, that many archeologists reject many of her inferences.

2. The inference of this symbolism from archeological remains is often fascinating in its details. Gimbutas, for example, points out that the "steatopygia" of some of the figurines is simply a misnomer for what turns out to be an abstract representation of the (cosmic?) egg within; many clay images

of the Bird goddess and other goddesses were found to contain clay *eggs* within their "steatopygous" buttocks! (Gimbutas 1974a: 106–7).

3. In abstracting from Gimbutas' work (1974a), I am aware of methodological errors in her argument. Some of her initial interpretive hypotheses seem to come from Greek mythology, but the statement is organized as though it had been based on a long series of purely archeological inferences which, near the end, had been felicitously corroborated by the Greek legends. Still, I find that her 1974a text, including its illustrations, contains many sound insights.

Other flaws in Gimbutas' work are shared by many, apparently the great majority, of the scholars working in this area. One misses a modern theory of meaning (e.g., regarding polysemous interpretation) and insights from modern anthropology, particularly with regard to the crucial differences between matrilocality (that is, residence with the wife's mother after marriage), matrilineality (tracing descent through the mother), and matriarchy (control of the home or the community by women; it might be noted that the only culture with community-level matriarchy known to anthropologists is that of the eighteenth and nineteenth-century Iroquois). The two concepts of matriarchy and matriliny tend to be particularly confused in discussions today. Yet it is important to differentiate them because, for one thing, they are not correlated as one might expect: many cultures, for example, combine patriarchy with a predominantly matrilineal-descent rule. Peggy Sanday (1974), in a carefully controlled study, has shown that, "whereas there is a high correlation between [the] percentage of deities who are female and [the] female contribution to subsistence ($r = .742$), there is no correlation between the percentage of female deities and female status ($r = .039$)." So the conspicuous role of female deities in the Old European and Minoan civilizations makes it probable that women had a major role in subsistence, but it tells us little about matrilineality and almost nothing about matriarchy.

I think we also have to go beyond Sanday's work. More research is needed on the correlations between rules of descent and of residence and the role of females in the pantheon. Matrilineality (albeit not matriarchy) and goddesses go together in some parts of Africa and North America. And I would wish for more rigor in stating the *direction* of implications between variables: rather than x "correlates" with y, we need more generalizations of the shape "if x, then y (to a certain percentage); whereas, if y, then x (to a certain percentage)." In many cases unidirectional implications can be arrived at, and these are, of course, much more powerful.

4. "Brother" here may stand for the king, "house" for his palace (Kramer 1969: 104); on the other hand, since Sumerian kinship terminology is of the Hawaiian type, "brother" could have been used toward any cousin, including those preferred for marriage or as lovers.

5. Masturbation is never referred to in the Homeric texts, although, as one reader reminded me, "they must have had it." Presumably this feature was subject to the same Homeric taboo as other items to be discussed below.

6. It is of course necessary to distinguish more general or universal features of these goddesses from ones that are diacritic. Thus, while goddesses are generally associated with washing and anointing, Aphrodite is so more than any other, and, moreover, golden ornaments, deceit in love, and (except in Homer) astrality are specific to her.

The conjunction of bloody sadism and sex is not as anomalous as it might seem to some modern eyes—indeed, it must strike *some* modern eyes as totally natural! The main linking symbols are often fairly balanced in what they stand for. Blood, for example, typifies the wounds of war but also menstruation and childbirth and, ultimately, strongly symbolizes both life and death. Consider also the instinctive violence of the lioness, bear, and other females in defending their young.

7. Another figure who conjoins sex and sadism is Lilith. She first appears as a Sumerian she-demon, roughly contemporary with Inanna (and mentioned about 2400 B.C.). She is beautiful but barren, a vampire and a harlot. She is still present in the late Babylonian period and was probably well known to the Hebrews, although she is mentioned only once (Isaiah 34:14). She becomes much more important in the Talmudic and, even more, in the Kabbalistic period (Patai: 1964). By this time she is often nude, sexually aggressive, a child-killer, liminal, very red (lips, hair, robe), and the procreatress of a whole race of demons. In some ways, but only some, the medieval Hebrews distinguished sharply between two aspects of sensuousness (roughly Eve versus Lilith) that had been fused in Cybele, Astarte, and even some of the Greek Aphrodites. This distinction corresponds roughly to the one in many contemporary cultures between a wife and a whore (i.e., *either* a wife *or* a whore). (I am indebted to Nella Fermi Weiner and E. Mutri for directing my attention to Lilith.)

Some variant of the Babylonian goddess was seen by the authors of Revelation 17 as a woman with whom the kings of the earth had fornicated "and the inhabitants of the earth have been made drunk with the wine of her fornication. . . . A woman upon a scarlet-colored beast, full of the names of blasphemy, having seven heads and ten horns . . . arrayed in purple and scarlet color, and decked with gold and precious stones and pearls, and having a golden cup in her hand full of abominations and the filthiness of her fornication." The passage continues with further descriptions of the great mother of harlots.

8. Some think the Egyptian goddess Isis was a major independent source for the Semitic Ishtars, the Minoan goddesses, and the Aphrodite of the Greek-speaking world. For an inspired and suggestive literary statement see Hilda Doolittle's *Helen in Egypt,* where the equation Isis = Thetis = Aphrodite is insistently repeated (whereas Ishtar, Hathor, and Astarte are rarely mentioned).

My own study of secondary sources has convinced me that in both her specifics and overall gestalt Isis is much closer to the Greek Demeter—tender mother, queen of wheat fields, pillar of familial solidarity, and so forth. She too was often depicted with sheaves of wheat, and her symbol was the sow. In Greek texts, most of the time, she is actually identified with Demeter. There is some overlap between Isis and Astarte, since the latter is also a patroness of maternal love; and of course there is a structural parallel between Isis and Osiris, Astarte and Tammuz, Orpheus and Eurydice, and Demeter and Persephone, and here, indeed, there is a close analogy to the post-Homeric Aphrodite and Adonis, for in each pair a protective mother and/or lover is bonded to a figure who spends part or all of the year in the underworld. But in terms of overall gestalt it is Hathor who, more than any other Egyptian divinity, resembles Aphrodite. Speaking more generally, the influence of the somehow introverted and chauvinistic Egyptian system on the Greeks should not be exaggerated, despite what we know about the considerable contact between the two cultures through much of the second millennium. I tend to agree with another poacher in this highly specialized scholarly field: "Egyptian influence on Greek mythological thought seems for these reasons to be negligible" (Kirk 1975: 209).

9. One more familiar reflex is the Polish-American name Wanda, which originally referred to a female water spirit who killed herself by drowning. Much Slavic and Germanic lore was revitalized in the great ballets.

10. A good sample of the Müller style runs: "The dawn, which to us is merely a beautiful sight, was to the early gazer and thinker the problem of all problems. . . . What we simply call the sunrise brought before their eyes every day the riddle of all riddles, the riddle of existence . . . ; their youth, their manhood, their old age, all were to the Vedic bards the gift of that heavenly mother who appeared bright, young, unchanged, immortal every morning. . . . The whole theogony and philosophy of the ancient world centered in Dawn, the mother of the bright gods" (1861: 498–99). While we may smile knowingly today, a reading, not only of the Vedas but many other mythologies, particularly that of the American Indians, leads one to think that there is considerable empirical support for Müller's position.

A related and rather contemporary point might be made about Müller. In his early twenties, and in Paris, he (like F. Bopp), went through a sort of Copernican revolution while studying Sanskrit. From then on the basic question always was: what would it be (have been) like as a Vedic poet-priest? This contrasts drastically with the sociological positivism of Dumézil and the taxonomic and rationalistic concerns of Lévi-Strauss. Müller's basic position resembles the "phenomenological" one, and both of these represent a development from Romanticism.

11. Homer, in the most relevant passage, says, "The life-giving earth holds them both below alive, having honor from Zeus underground. One day in turn they live, and one day in turn they are dead." Most translators and other authorities interpret this to mean that the Twins have alternate days above and below earth, although it has been speculated that the meaning is that one Twin (Hesperus) goes underground with the sun, while the other (the Morning Star) rises with the sun and follows it around the earth. What Pindar says in the *Tenth Nemean* is that Zeus, speaking to the surviving brother, Polydeuces, says: "half the time you may breathe under the earth, half the time in the golden houses of the sky." Since the purpose of Zeus's grant is to enable the Twins to be together, the speculation that they were to move separately would seem to be vitiated.

12. In addition to the Latin and Celtic forms cited above, we have Proto-Slavic *sĭln- and of course, Greek *hēlios*. All of these go back to Proto-Indo-European *sū/sāwe-*, "sun." This is a nominal root and belongs to the so-called heteroclitic class, characterized by alternation of a stem-formative r/n; other members of this class are generally thought to belong to the oldest stratum in the PIE vocabulary, and I think the same is true of this particular member. Its r/n alternation is best illustrated in Iranian, Celtic, and Germanic—for example, in Old English *sōl* and *sunne*. That this archaic PIE word was originally used for a divinity is also made more probable by the early Vedic and

Greek usage already cited, by the meanings of the Baltic term in question here, and by the Italic (i.e., Umbrian) name for Zeus-Sol, that is, Iuve Zal. The reader should note that the special intersection of the two sets in Baltic resulted from the early and "northern," that is, Baltic and Germanic, gender switch whereby the moon became masculine and the sun feminine (both grammatically and, in some cases, lexically).

13. Yet another Vedic dawn figure is Saramâ, who is associated with dogs, good fortune, love, cows, and light; she is quick-footed (*su padi*) and crosses water unhurt. She seems to dovetail with the *awsos* that we infer from Greek and Vedic evidence and, even more specifically, with the Homeric Helen(a) —whose name itself may be cognate.

14. I cannot leave the comparative Indo-European evidence without mention of certain suggestive data from Old Irish. Three war goddesses, beautiful young women with "marked sexual characteristics," frequently symbolized by birds, "figure with impressive frequency throughout the earliest stratum of Irish mythological tradition" (Ross 1967: 219). They are often associated with the color red—with red clothes, red cattle, and so forth. In the major epic, the *Táin,* "The Morrigan" (one of these women), after her explicit offer of love-making has been rejected by the hero, Cuchulain, comes against him, successively, in the form of a "white, hornless, red-eared heifer," then an eel, and then a "grey-red, bitch-wolf" with wide-open jaws. Cuchulain successively breaks the leg, smashes the skull, and puts out the eye of these assailants (Dunn 1914: 169–70), but he is eventually tricked into giving them back, and so healing the Morrigan. The Morrigan somewhat resembles Aphrodite and may have an Indo-European source, but her combination of aggression, magic, and carnal sex suggests even more the Ishtars of the Phoenicians, who, of course, were traders in Ireland in the pre-Christian centuries (particularly for tin); still, diffusion seems relatively unlikely.

The Armenian evidence is also tantalizing. Rural customs and rituals emphasize dawn, both its connections with brightness, female divinities, and so forth, and its opposition to evening. The Armenian word for dawn, *ayg-,* is, according to Dumézil (1938), a regular reflex of PIE **aiw-*. Earlier, Benveniste, in his important work on IE root structure, had shown that Latin *aeuum,* "age, eternity," and *iuuenis,* "youth," were variants of this same root **aiw-* (with full and zero grades of the root: H₂ei-w- and H₂y-eu). **aiw-* is strongly attested in many IE stocks and, according to Benveniste, had the earlier, more basic meaning of "vital force." If **aiw-* could be related to **awsos,* which neither Dumézil nor Benveniste suggests, the case for the formal status and the cultural importance of the PIE dawn goddess would be given greater depth and scope.

CHAPTER 3

1. Hesiod obviously differs from Homer in many ways, particularly in his misogyny and peasant outlook, but he also resembles Homer at many points—for example, in his description of Aphrodite as golden, shedding grace, causing cruel cares, etc. The myth of origin in the Fifth Homeric

Hymn is picked up at the point where the western wind is wafting Aphrodite toward Cythera.

The Hesiodic myth raises another fascinating question of Near Eastern connections. Part of a striking Hittite myth has been summarized as follows (I quote in part Gurney 1961: 190–91):

> And the king of heaven reigned for nine years, and in the ninth year
> Kumarbi made war on the king. The latter abandoned the struggle and
> flew like a bird into the sky, but Kumarbi seized his feet and pulled him
> down. Kumarbi bit off the king's member (called euphemistically
> his "knee") and laughed for joy. But the king turned to him and said:
> 'Do not rejoice over what thou hast swallowed! I have made thee pregnant
> with three mighty gods.'

The main editor of the text, Hans Güterbock (1948, 1961), has pointed out many parallels with Hesiod, including other elements not quoted above, such as the three generations of kings and the eventual disgorging of the swallowed elements and their rebirth in Earth. Güterbock (largely supported by Goetze 1949) thinks that the myth was originally Hurrian, from which it was adapted by Hittite scribes. According to this widely accepted hypothesis, the myth may have been Babylonian (although no Babylonian version actually exists). If it was ultimately Hurrian, on the other hand, it would have passed from there into Babylonian and from there to Hittite; this second hypothesis depends heavily on the fact that some of the Hittite names in the text are of Babylonian origin (but so are *so many* Hittite names!). The same authors contend that, in the west, the myth passed to the Phoenicians (Güterbock 1948: 133) and from them to the Greeks, during the first part of the first millennium B.C.

Güterbock's hypothesis—and it is not yet a theory—has been challenged, among others, by Kirk: "The plain conclusion is that neither [Hurrian and Greek] borrowed from the other, but each is a distinct form or portion of a complex set of mythical themes" (1975: 219). The hypothesis has to be judged by standard diffusion theory, taking account of such critical variables as areal contiguity and the number and internal organization of the elements in a myth (see Boas 1891, in Boas 1940). On the one hand, the Greeks and the Hittites were *not* contiguous, and the amount of *direct* transmission from one to the other was decidedly limited. On the other hand, the Hittite and Greek versions share many analogous (homologous?) items organized in about the same way, so that inheritance from a common PIE source seems to be a reasonable hypothesis.

More specific arguments have been provided by Pisani (1930: 65–73), cited in and supplemented by Boedeker (1974: 15–16). The original PIE *dyews* was a sky god strongly associated with stone (there is a great deal of other evidence on this, incidentally); even in PIE myth the dawn goddess, *awsos,* was born from *dyews.* As *dyews* shifted in function to being a god of rain and light and, eventually, toward the highly personified Zeus of the Greeks, he was replaced in myth by a surrogate sky god called Uranus. Concomitantly, Aphrodite as the new "hypostasis" of Dawn acquired the name Urania (or at least the latter became more important); this latter cult title, like her association with a chariot, reflects her Indo-European celestial origins.

Thus the Hesiodic version of her birth, which has seemed exotic to so many and which has been treated as "Oriental" (Hurrian, Babylonian), often by persons who accept Güterbock uncritically, may with greater probability reflect the archaic Indo-European system. This Indo-Europeanist hypothesis, so brilliantly propounded by Pisani, does not preclude some limited mutual influence or even reinforcement as a consequence of contact between Greeks and the Phoenicians and other eastern peoples during the second or first millennium B.C.

2. Whether or not we agree with the Analyst consensus, as exemplified by Wilamowitz, that Book Five is the oldest book of the *Iliad,* we must respect many of the subtle arguments regarding the traditional antiquity of many of its constituent elements, including those that involve Aphrodite (e.g., her birth from Dione and Zeus).

3. All the quotes in the discussion of the Fifth Hymn are from Allen et al. 1936: 349–51; the technical points about the language of the hymn, including some not mentioned above, were discovered by Deborah Kaspin in our Homer class.

CHAPTER 4

1. Many scholars have attempted to derive Aphrodite from *one* place only; Herter (1960), for example, and others before him, argued for Cyprus. Some of these theories of one limited origin are methodologically interesting, but they all suffer from a sort of fallacy of misplaced concreteness that is reminiscent of the attempts to pinpoint the PIE homeland in the Prussian plain, or the Ukraine, or some similarly small area. Otherwise, some of the theories about pre-Hellenic associations are well-founded: Athena was a local goddess of Athens who evolved into a war goddess; Artemis had many local cult centers in the eastern Mediterranean and in Asia Minor; Hera was the pre-Greek goddess of Argos and originally the spouse of Heracles (her union with Zeus being a bit of theological reshuffling to fit the sociopolitical realities).

2. It is interesting in this connection that Gladstone (1858), in his work on Homer's colors, does not treat "gold" or "golden" as *in any sense* chromatic. This is part of the author's fruitful but limiting physical bias.

3. The fact that her marriage is incestuous does not imply conflict, since divine siblings can make love and even marry (e.g., Ares and Aphrodite are also half-siblings). One crucial factor is Homer's apparent aversion to Hera (as contrasted with his affection for Hermes, Athena, and Aphrodite). This aversion is usually masked because he had to be in nominal conformity with the attitudes of his audience.

4. Stanford (1968) in his third and fourth chapters gives a sensitive analysis of Athena's friendship with Odysseus. Her role as a friend of heroes may descend from her earlier one as a palace goddess in Mycenaean myth (Nilsson 1950: 500).

5. Lucretius begins: "Mother of Aeneas and his race, delight of men and gods, life-giving Venus, it is your doing that under the wheeling constellations of the sky all nature teems with life, both the sea that buoys up our ships and the earth that yields our food. Through you all living creatures are conceived and come forth to look upon the sunlight. . . . Since you alone are the guiding

power of the universe and without you nothing emerges into the shining sunlit world to grow in joy and loveliness, yours is the partnership I seek in striving to compose these lines ON THE NATURE OF THE UNIVERSE" (*trans.* R. E. Latham).

6. The subjective "curse of Aphrodite" is of greater significance in the present study than the objective dangers of the Black Aphrodites who flourished locally in Sparta and Cyprus and elsewhere and became more important after the sixth century. They haunted cemeteries, slew men, and figured as local patronesses. The Black Aphrodites also rose to a national level as war goddesses. Perhaps the most famous example of their power occurred when the prostitutes of Corinth offered a group prayer that was held to be partly responsible for the great naval victory at Salamis (Farnell 1897: 668). Just what Aphrodite did to confound the Persian sailors is not said. Simonides wrote about this (Seltman 1956: 81):

> For the Greeks and for their hard-fighting armies
> These girls stood forth to pray to the Lady Cypris,
> And Aphrodite willed that none should betray
> To Persian archers this citadel of Hellas.

Be it noted that Corinth, founded in myth by a Phoenician, was also visited by Phoenician traders and was hence probably most open to the martial connotations of the Semitic Ishtar figure (i.e., Anat).

7. Another feature, which I have not studied, is the frequency and type of invocation. Yet another source of insight would be to *independently* compare Aphrodite, the most marked queen, with each of the other three queens of heaven.

CHAPTER 5

1. For reference purposes I have adopted the numbers that appear in the Loeb edition edited by J. M. Edmonds (*Lyra Graeca,* vol. 1, 1963), for three reasons: (1) it is readily available in libraries (although temporarily out of print); (2) it contains both the Greek texts and English translations; (3) it is widely used for such reference by other scholars. Readers wishing to familiarize themselves further with Sappho are urged to consult the translations by Barnstone, Davenport, and Roche.

2. For this stanza I have not transliterated the *h* of *ph, th,* and *ch,* because in Sappho's time the sounds stood, not for something like English *f, th* (as in "thin" or "that"), nor for *ch* (as in "child"), but, on the contrary, for sounds rather close to the contemporary English "voiced aspirates" in initial position, that is, *p, t,* and *k.* Similarly, Greek *ss* is transcribed as *sh,* since that is how it was pronounced in *lissomai.*

CHAPTER 6

1. Long shrouded in mystery, the nature of this love thong has recently been greatly clarified by the research of Father Frederick E. Brenk, S.J., who, after studying numerous graphic and plastic representations, has shown that it was a cord or thong that hung either around the loins and then to a

pendant or knot below the navel, or over the shoulders and then down to some point between the breasts.

CHAPTER 7

1. A statue dating from pagan times was worshiped as Saint Demetra until carried off in 1802, in the face of rioting peasants, by Clark and Cripps; it now languishes in the British Museum (Fermor 1958: 180).

2. I owe this suggestion to Mrs. R. Ross Holloway. Wilamowitz, on the other hand (1931: 319), thinks the deemphasis of Demeter simply reflects the male-aristocratić purposes and audiences of the author(s) of the *Iliad*.

The three brothers, Zeus, Poseidon, and Hades, in their relation to Demeter-Persephone, seem to be paralleled in Germanic myth by Odin and his two brothers and their consorting with Frig (the love goddess, daughter of the Earth Mother). When her beautiful son Baldr ("prince") dies and descends into the underworld, she weeps. These and other complex parallels between Greek and Germanic myth need to be exhaustively explored. I am indebted to Deborah Friedrich for these points.

3. This chapter is focused on cultures like that of the Greeks. Obviously, there are cultures where the men have as much continuity as the women and as much tenderness (much of the excellent discussion by Chodorow and others is concerned with modern urban society). Similarly, the fact that men have to deal with all sorts of human interactions outside the home may create sensitivities and awareness that more than equal those of the woman.

CHAPTER 9

1. This chapter refers mainly to written forms. There has always been more synthesis in the plastic and graphic arts—examples being the *Venus Genetrix* and the *Crouching Aphrodite;* the latter goes back to the "great age of plastic energy," that is, fourth-century Greece (Clark 1956: 89).

2. I am aware that Deutsch's concepts of motherliness and tenderness are partly culturally specific matters and that her discussion has a variously Slavic, Germanic, and Jewish ring (my own kinship in blood and marriage includes these components). I find it preferable to work with such ideas as best I can rather than follow the widespread practice of ignoring them.

3. The classic experiment that demonstrated the reality of neurohormonal reflexes involved a ram and a ewe whose circulatory systems were artificially joined. Masturbation of the ram triggered, in thirty seconds, the milk-ejection reflex in the ewe (Debackere et al. 1961).

4. In terms of contemporary scholarship, the questions about the language of love (whether maternal or heterosexual) belong to the field called "the ethnography of speaking" that was considerably reorganized, and named, by Dell Hymes. This field is part of, or overlaps with, the field of sociolinguistics, and the research of Basil Bernstein has dealt with mother-child and woman-lover relations. But in general there is almost nothing on the language of love, largely because of the researchers' own concern with cognition and social structure. Another reason is the absence of texts or of a precedent for gathering such texts. For example, my own Tarascan was unusually fluent

in 1967–69 and was learned in many contexts, but I have no texts, recorded or taped, of tender communication between mother and child.

5. Calhoun's somewhat Victorian evaluation of Aphrodite should not be left out:

> Aphrodite for example, was clothed in infinite variety; she was one among the supreme rulers of the universe, arbiters of human destiny, defenders of moral values; she was also a figure in ancient, grotesque myths and naive tales, and at the same time one of the principal actors in the drama at Troy; she was sexual passion and also spiritual love, the deity of procreation and the personification of the impulses into which love and passion are translated; she was the vision of a bright effulgence moving in the heavens, a gracious presence instinct with loveliness; she was the music that breathes . . . (Calhoun 1937: 23).

APPENDIX 9

1. Phryne is said to have been called "The Toad" because of her pockmarks, her sallow complexion, or the cultural (Balkan area) metaphor between the shape of the amphibian and the human uterus. The partially global distribution of this metaphor is suggested by a documented anecdote involving an anthropologist and his "most Indian" informant: Q: "Is a toad a fish?" A: "No, a toad isn't a fish." Q: "What *is* a toad?" A: "A toad is a woman."

The life of Phryne ends on an optimistic note. As Clark puts it (1956:83): "It was a triumph for beauty; and to the Greek mind this beauty was not simply created by Praxiteles, but was already present in the person of his model, Phryne. She shared with him the credit for the beautiful figure with which he enriched the Greek world; a nude statue of her in gilt bronze, openly a portrait, was erected in the sacred precincts of Delphi by a grateful community."

Bibliography

Adkins, Arthur W. H. 1972. "Homeric Gods and the Values of Homeric Society." *Journal of Hellenic Studies* 92:1–19.

Albright, William F. 1953. *Archeology and the Religion of Israel*. Baltimore: Johns Hopkins University Press.

Allen, T. W. 1969. *Homeri Opera*. Oxford: Clarendon Press.

————; Halliday, W. R.; and Sikes, E. E. 1936. *The Homeric Hymns*. Oxford: Clarendon Press.

Amory, Ann. 1969. "The Reunion of Odysseus and Penelope." In *Essays on the Odyssey*, ed. Charles H. Taylor, Jr., pp. 100–122. Bloomington: Indiana University Press.

Arthur, Marylin. 1978. "Erinna and the World of Women." Lecture delivered at the University of Chicago.

Auerbach, Ernst. 1953. "Odysseus' Scar." In *Mimesis: The Representation of Reality in Western Literature*, trans. Willard R. Trask, pp. 3–23. Princeton: Princeton University Press.

Balzac, Honoré de. 1842. *Mémoires de deux jeunes mariées*. Paris: Béthune & Plon.

Bamberger, Joan. 1974. "The Myth of Matriarchy: Why Men Rule in Primitive Society." In Rosaldo and Lamphere, pp. 263–80.

Barreno, Maria. 1976. *The Three Marias: New Portuguese Letters*. New York: Bantam Books.

Barnstone, Willis. 1965. *Sappho: Lyrics in the Original Greek, with Translations by Willis Barnstone*. New York: New York University Press.

————. 1975. *Greek Lyric Poetry, Including the Complete Poetry of Sappho*. New York: Schocken.

Barthes, Roland. 1972. *Mythologies*, selected and translated by Annette Lavers. London: Cape.

Beauvoir, Simone de. 1957. *The Second Sex*. New York: Knopf.

Benveniste, Emile. 1935. *Origines de la formation des noms en indo-européen*. Paris: Maisonneuve.

————. 1969. *Le Vocabulaire des institutions indo-européennes*. 2 vols. Paris: Minuit.

221

222 *Bibliography*

Bernstein, Basil. 1964. "Elaborated and Restricted Codes: Their Social Origins and Some Consequences." In *The Ethnography of Speaking* ed. John J. Gumperz and Dell Hymes, pp. 55–69. *American Anthropologist,* special pub. no. 66.

Bespaloff, Rachel. 1970. *On the Iliad.* Bollingen Series IX. Princeton: Princeton University Press.

Bloomfield, Maurice. 1908. *The Religion of the Vedas, the Ancient Religion of India (from Rig Veda to the Upanishads).* New York: G. P. Putnam's Sons.

Boas, Franz. 1940. *Race, Language and Culture.* New York: Free Press.

Boedeker, D. 1974. *Aphrodite's Entry into Greek Epic. Mnemosyne,* supplement 32.

Boer, Charles, trans. 1970. *The Homeric Hymns.* Chicago: Swallow Press.

Brenk, Frederick E., S.J. Lecture, "Aphrodite's Thong," delivered at the University of Chicago.

Brown, Norman O. 1966. *Love's Body.* New York: Random House.

———. 1969. *Hermes the Thief.* New York: Random House (Vintage).

Budge, E. A. Wallis. 1904. *The Gods of the Egyptians.* Vol. 1. New York: Dover Press. (Reprinted LaSalle, Ill.: Open Court, 1969.)

Bury, J. B. 1937. *A History of Greece.* New York: Modern Library.

Butterworth, G. W., ed. and trans. 1919. *Clement of Alexandria: Exhortation to the Greeks.* London: Heinemann.

Calhoun, George. 1937. "Homer's Gods: Prolegomena." *TAPA* 68:11–25.

Campbell, B., and Peterson, W. E. 1953. "Milk Let-down and Orgasm in the Human Female." *Human Biology* 25:165–68.

Campbell, Joseph. 1959. *The Masks of the Gods.* New York: Viking.

Chadwick, John. 1970. *The Decipherment of Linear B.* Cambridge, Eng.: At the University Press.

———. 1976. *The Mycenaean World.* New York: Cambridge University Press.

Childe, V. Gordon. 1958. *The Dawn of European Civilization.* New York: Knopf.

Chodorow, Nancy. 1974. "Family Structure and Feminine Personality." In Rosaldo and Lamphere, pp. 43–66.

Clark, Kenneth. 1956. *The Nude: A Study in Ideal Form.* Bollingen Series XXXV.2. New York: Pantheon Books.

Cohen, Percy. 1969. "Theories of Myth." *Man* 4:337–53.

Cox, George W. 1887. *The Mythology of the Aryan Nations.* London: Kegan Paul & Trench.

Davenport, Guy. 1965. *Sappho: Poems and Fragments.* Ann Arbor: University of Michigan Press.

Debackere, M.; Peters, G.; and Tuyttens, N. 1961. "Reflex Release of an Oxytocic Hormone by Stimulation of Genital Organs in Male and Female Sheep Studied by a Cross-Circulation Technique." *Journal of Endocrinology* 22:321–34.

Detienne, Marcel. 1972. *Les Jardins d'Adonis*. Paris: Gallimard.

Deutsch, Helene. 1944, 1945. *Psychology of Women*. New York: Grune & Stratton.

Dixon, Roland M. W. 1974. "A Method of Semantic Description." In *Semantics*, ed. D. Steinberg and L. Jakobovits, pp. 436–72. Cambridge: At the University Press.

Doolittle, Hilda ("HD"). 1961. *Helen in Egypt*. New York: New Directions.

Dorson, Richard. 1955. "The Eclipse of Solar Mythology." In Sebeok, pp. 15–39.

Douglas, Mary. 1966. *Purity and Danger: An Analysis of Concepts of Pollution and Taboo*. Baltimore: Penguin.

Dumézil, Georges. 1938. "Jeunesse, éternité, aube: Linguistique comparée et mythologique comparée indo-européennes." *Annales d'histoire économique et sociale* 52:289–301.

———. 1952. *Les Dieux indo-européens*. Paris: Presses Universitaires.

———. 1973. *Mythe et épopée: Histoires romaines*. Paris: Gallimard.

Dunn, Joseph. 1914. *The Ancient Irish Epic Tale "Táin Bó Cúalauge."* London: David Nutt.

Durkheim, Emile. 1915. *The Elementary Forms of Religious Life*, trans. Joseph W. Swain. New York: Macmillan.

Edmonds, J. M. 1963. *Lyra Graeca*, Vol. 1. Loeb Classical Library. Cambridge, Mass.: Harvard University Press.

Eliade, Mircea. *Myths, Rites, Symbols*, ed. W. C. Beane and W. Doty. New York: Harper/Colophon.

Evans-Pritchard, E. E. 1951. *Kinship and Marriage among the Nuer*. Oxford: Clarendon Press.

Evelyn-White, Hugh G. 1967. *Hesoid, The Homeric Hymns, and Homerica*. Loeb Classical Library. Cambridge, Mass.: Harvard University Press.

Faber, Ada. 1975. "Segmentation of the Mother: Women in Greek Myth." *Psychoanalytic Review* 62:29–47.

Farber-Flügge, Gertrude. 1973. "Der Mythos 'Inanna und Enki' unter besonderer Berücksichtigung der Liste der me." Rome: Biblical Institute Press.

Farnell, Lewis R. 1897. *The Cults of the Greek States*. Vol. 2. Oxford: Clarendon Press.

Fauth, Wolfgang. 1967. *Aphrodite Parakyptusa*. Mainz: Akademie der Wissenschaften.

Fermor, Patrick L. 1958. *Travels in the Southern Peloponnese*. London: John Murray.

Finley, M. I. 1972. *The World of Odysseus*. New York: Viking/Compass.

Foucart, Paul François. 1895, 1900. "Recherches sur l'origine et la nature des mystères d'Eleusis." *Mémoires de l'Académie des inscriptions et des belles lettres,* nos. 35, 37. Paris: Klincksieck.

Fraenkel, Enrst. 1962. *Lithauisches etymologisches Wörterbuch*. Heidelberg: Carl Winter.

Frazer, James. 1935. *Adonis, Attis, Osiris: Studies in the History of Oriental Religion* (part 4.2 of *The Golden Bough*). New York: Macmillan.

————. 1951. *The Golden Bough*. Abridged ed. New York: Macmillan.

Freud, Sigmund. 1954. *A General Introduction to Psychoanalysis*. New York: Doubleday Permabooks.

Friedrich, Deborah. n.d. "Odin, God of War, Magic, Poetry." Ms. of Ph.D. diss., University of Chicago.

Friedrich, Lenore. 1939. "I Had a Baby." *Atlantic Monthly* 163:461–69.

Friedrich, Paul. 1967. "Structural Implications of Russian Pronominal Usage." In *Sociolinguistics,* ed. William Bright, pp. 214–59. The Hague: Mouton.

————. 1970. *Proto-Indo-European Trees*. Chicago: University of Chicago Press.

————. 1973. "Defilement and Honor in the *Iliad*." *Journal of Indo-European Studies* 1:119–27.

————. 1976. *Neighboring Leaves Ride This Wind*. (Poems.) Chicago: Published by the author.

————. 1977. "Sanity and the Myth of Honor." *Ethos* 5:281–305.

————. 1978. *The Bastard Moons*. (Poems.) Chicago. (In press.)

————, and Friedrich, Deborah. 1978. "Poetry and Myth." Ms.

————, and Redfield, James. 1978. "Speech as a Personality Symbol: The Case of Achilles." *Language* 54:263–88.

Frisk, Hjalmar. 1960, 1970. *Griechisches etymologisches Wörterbuch*. 2 vols. Heidelberg: Carl Winter.

Geertz, Clifford. 1966. "Religion as a Cultural System." In *Anthropological Approaches to the Study of Religion,* ed. Michael Banton, pp. 1–47. London: Tavistock.

Geldner, Karl F. 1951. *Der Rig-Veda*. Cambridge, Mass.: Harvard University Press.

Gerber, Douglas E. 1976. "Studies in Greek Lyric Poetry: 1967–75." *Classical World,* vol. 70.

Gimbutas, Marija. 1962. "The Ancient Religion of the Balts." *Lituanus* 4:97–109.

————. 1963. *The Balts*. New York: Praeger.

————. 1974a. *The Gods and Goddesses of Old Europe. 7000–3500 B.C.* Berkeley and Los Angeles: University of California Press.

————. 1974b. "An Archeologist's View of PIE in 1975." *Journal of Indo-European Studies* 2:289–309.

Gladstone, William E. 1858. *Studies on Homer and the Homeric Age.* Vol. 3. Oxford: Oxford University Press.

Godley, A. D. 1960. *Herodotus.* Loeb Classical Library. Cambridge, Mass.: Harvard University Press.

Goetze, Albrecht. 1949. Review of Güterbock (1948). *Journal of the American Oriental Society* 69:178–83.

Gordon, Cyrus H. 1949. *Ugaritic Literature: A Comprehensive Translation of the Poetic and Prose Texts.* Rome: Pontificum Institutum Biblicum.

———. 1955. *Ugaritic Manual.* Rome.

———. 1961. "Canaanite Mythology." In *Mythologies of the Ancient World,* ed. Samuel N. Kramer, pp. 181–219. Chicago: Quadrangle.

———. 1966. *Ugarit and Minoan Crete: The Bearing of Their Texts on the Origins of Western Culture.* New York: Norton.

———. 1975. "Ugarit and Its Significance." In *Biblical Studies in Contemporary Thought,* ed. Miriam Ward, pp. 161–69. Somerville, Md.: Greeno, Hadden.

Graves, Robert. 1966. *The White Goddess.* New York: Farrar, Straus & Giroux (Octagon).

Greenberg, Joseph. 1966. *Language Universals.* The Hague: Mouton.

Griffith, Ralph T. H. 1897. *The Hymns of the Rig Veda.* Benares: E. J. Lazarus.

Griswold, Henry De Witt. 1971. *The Religion of the Rigveda.* Delhi: Motilal.

Grube, G. M. A. 1951. "The Gods of Homer." *Phoenix* 5:62–78. Reprinted in Nelson (1969).

Gurney, O. R. 1961. *The Hittites.* Baltimore: Pelican Books.

Güterbock, Hans. 1948. "The Hittite Version of the Hurrian Kumarbi Myths: Oriental Forerunners of Hesiod." *American Journal of Archaeology* 52:128–34.

———. 1961. "Hittite Mythology." In *Mythologies of the Ancient World,* ed. S. N. Kramer, pp. 139–81. Chicago: Quadrangle.

Guthrie, W. K. C. 1962. *The Greeks and Their Gods.* London: Methuen.

Haas, Mary. 1942. "The Solar Deity of the Tunica." *Papers of the Michigan Academy of Sciences, Arts, and Letters* 28:531–35.

Hallo, William W., and Van Dijk, J. J. A. 1968. *The Exaltation of Inanna.* New Haven and London: Yale University Press.

Harrison, Jane. 1903. *Prolegomena to the Study of Greek Religion.* London: Cambridge University Press.

———. 1912. *Themis: A Study of the Social Origins of Greek Religion.* Cambridge, Eng.: At the University Press.

———. 1921. *Epilegomena to the Study of Greek Religion.* Cambridge, Eng.: At the University Press.

Harsh, Philip Whaley. 1950. "Penelope and Odysseus in *Odyssey* XIX." *American Journal of Philology* 71:1–21.

Hatto, Arthur. 1965. *Eos: An Inquiry into the Theme of Lovers' Meetings and Partings at Dawn*. The Hague: Mouton.

Heidel, Alexander. 1973. *The Gilgamesh Epic and Old Testament Parallels*. Chicago: University of Chicago Press.

Herter, Hans. 1960. "Die Ursprung des Aphroditenkultes." In *Eléments orientaux dans la religion grecque ancienne*, pp. 61–76. Paris.

Hofling, C. 1975. "The Mayan Goddess." Ms.

Horney, Karen. 1917. *Feminine Psychology*. New York: Norton.

Hutchinson, R. W. 1962. *Prehistoric Crete*. Baltimore: Pelican.

Jaeger, Werner. 1945. *Paideia: The Ideals of Greek Culture*, trans. Gilbert Highet. Vol. 1. New York: Oxford University Press.

Jakobson, Roman. 1939. "Signe zéro." In *Readings in Linguistics*. Vol. 2, ed. Eric Hamp, Fred W. Householder, and Robert Austerlitz, pp. 109–16. Chicago: University of Chicago Press.

———, and Halle, Morris. 1956. *Fundamentals of Language*. The Hague: Mouton.

Jameson, Michael H. 1961. "Mythology of Ancient Greece." In *Mythologies of the Ancient World*, ed. Samuel N. Kramer, pp. 219–77. Chicago: Quadrangle.

Jowett, M. A. 1937. *The Dialogues of Plato*. 2 vols. New York: Random House.

Jung, C. G. 1973. *Four Archetypes*, trans. R. F. C. Hull. Bollingen Paperback Series. Princeton: Princeton University Press.

Kapelrud, Arvid S. 1969. *The Violent Goddess: Anat in the Ras Shamra Texts*. Oslo: Universitetsforlaget.

Kerényi, Carl. 1961. *The Gods of the Greeks*. London: Thames & Hudson.

———. 1963. "Kore." In *Essays on a Science of Mythology*, ed. C. G. Jung and R. F. C. Hull. New York: Harper Torchbooks.

———. 1975. *Zeus and Hera: Archetypal Images of Father, Husband, and Wife*. Princeton: Princeton University Press.

Kirk, Geoffrey. 1965. *Homer and the Epic*. Cambridge, Eng.: At the University Press.

———. 1975. *Myth: Its Meaning and Function in Ancient and Other Cultures*. Cambridge, Eng.: At the University Press.

———. 1976. *The Nature of Greek Myths*. New York: Praeger.

Kitzinger, Sheila. 1974. *The Experience of Childbirth*. Baltimore: Penguin.

Kluckhohn, Clyde. 1942. "Myths and Rituals: A General Theory." *Harvard Theological Review* 35:45–79.

———, and Kroeber, Alfred L. 1952. "Culture: A Critical Review of Concepts and Definitions." *Papers of the Peabody Museum of Archeology and Ethnology*, no. 47.

Kolberg, O. 1857. *Pieśnu ludu polskiego*. Ser. 1. Warsaw.

Kramer, Samuel N. 1958. *History Begins at Sumer.* London: Thames & Hudson.

————. 1961. *Mythologies of the Ancient World.* Garden City: Doubleday.

————. 1969. *The Sacred Marriage Rite: Aspects of Faith, Myth, and Ritual in Ancient Sumer.* Bloomington: Indiana University Press.

Kretschmer, Paul. 1895. "Zum pamphylischen Dialect." *Zeitschrift für vergleichende Sprachforschung* n.s. 33:258–68.

Kroeber, Alfred L. 1948. *Anthropology.* New York: Harcourt, Brace.

Kuhn, Adalbert. 1886. *Die Herabkunft des Feuers und des Göttertranks.* Gütersloh: C. Bertelsman.

Larson, Gerald J. 1974. "Introduction: The Study of Mythology." In *Myth in Indo-European Antiquity,* ed. G. J. Larson. Berkeley and Los Angeles: University of California Press.

Latham, R. E. 1966. *Lucretius: The Nature of the Universe.* Baltimore: Penguin Books.

Lattimore, Richmond. 1963. *The Iliad of Homer.* Chicago: University of Chicago Press, Phoenix Books.

————. 1970. *Hesiod: The Works and Days, Theogony, The Shield of Achilles.* Ann Arbor: University of Michigan Press.

————. 1971. *The Odes of Pindar.* Chicago and London: University of Chicago Press, Phoenix Books.

Lawson, John C. 1910. *Modern Greek Folklore and Ancient Greek Religion: A Study in Survivals.* New York: University Books.

Leach, Edmond. 1967. "Magical Hair." In *Myth and Cosmos,* ed. John Middleton, pp. 77–109. Austin and London: University of Texas Press.

Le Mée, Jean, and Grüttner, Ingbert. 1975. *Hymns from the Rig-Veda.* New York: Knopf.

Lévi-Strauss, Claude. 1960. "Four Winnebago Myths: A Structural Sketch. In *Culture in History: Essays in Honor of Paul Radin,* ed. Stanley Diamond, pp. 351–62. New York: Columbia University Press.

————. 1962. *Le totémisme aujourd'hui.* Paris: Presses universitaires.

————. 1963. *Structural Anthropology,* trans. Claire Jacobsen and Brooke Grudfest Schoepf. New York: Basic Books.

————. 1967a. "The Story of Asdiwal." In *The Structural Study of Myth and Totemism,* ed. E. Leach, trans. Nicholas Mann, pp. 1–49. London: Tavistock.

————. 1967b. *The Savage Mind.* London: Weidenfeld & Nicholson.

————. 1969. *The Raw and the Cooked: Introduction to a Science of Mythology.* Vol. 1, trans. John and Doreen Weightman. New York: Harper Torchbooks.

Linton, Ralph. 1945. Foreword and two ethnological reports. In *The Individual and His Society,* ed. Abraham Kardiner. New York: Columbia University Press.

Loebel, Edgar, and Page, Denys. 1955. *Poetarum Lesbiorum Fragmenta.* Oxford: Clarendon Press.

Lord, Alfred B. 1953. "Homer's Originality: Oral Dictated Texts." *TAPA* 84:124–34.

Lowie, Robert H. 1972. "Association." In *Mythology,* ed. Pierre Maranda. New York: Penguin.

MacCulloch, J. A. 1948. *The Celtic and Scandinavian Religions.* London: Hutchinson's University Library.

Macdonnell, A. A. 1897. *Vedic Mythology.* Strassburg: K. T. Trübner.

Malinowski, Bronislaw. 1954. *Myth in Primitive Psychology: Magic, Science, and Religion.* Garden City: Doubleday.

Mannhardt, Johann W. E. 1875. *Der Baumkultus der Germanen und ihrer Nachbarstämme.* Berlin: Gebrüder Bornträger.

Martin, Larry. 1976. "A Reformulation of Nuer Concepts Underlying Marriage." Term paper, University of Chicago.

Masters, W. H., and Johnson, V. E. 1966. *Human Sexual Response.* Boston: Little, Brown.

Mead, Margaret. 1949. *Male and Female: A Study of the Sexes in a Changing World.* New York: William Morrow.

Meillet, Antoine. 1964. *Introduction à l'étude comparative des langues indo-européennes.* Preface by George C. Buck. University, Ala.: University of Alabama Press.

Moszyński, Kazimierz. 1968. *Kultura Ludowa Słowian.* Vol. 2. Warsaw: Ksiaźka Wiedza.

Müller, Max. 1861. *Lectures on the Science of Language.* New York: Scribner's.

Murray, A. T. 1960, 1963, 1960. *The Iliad.* 2 vols. *The Odyssey.* 2 vols. Loeb Classical Library. Cambridge, Mass.: Harvard University Press.

Murray, Gilbert. 1925. *Five Stages of Greek Religion.* Oxford: Clarendon Press.

Mylonas, George. 1961. *Eleusis and the Eleusinian Mysteries.* Princeton: Princeton University Press.

Nagler, Michael. 1967. "Towards a Generative View of the Oral Formula." *TAPA* 98:269–311.

————. 1974. *Spontaneity and Tradition: A Study of the Oral Art of Homer.* Berkeley: University of California Press.

Nagy, Gregory. 1973. "Phaethon, Sappho's Phaon, and the White Rock of Leukas." *Harvard Studies in Classical Philology* 77:137–77.

Nelson, Conny. 1969. *Homer's Odyssey: A Critical Handbook.* Belmont, Cal.: Wadsworth.

Neumann, Erich. 1972. *The Great Mother: An Analysis of the Archetype.* Princeton: Princeton University Press.

Newton, Niles. 1973. "Interrelationships between Sexual Responsiveness, Birth, and Breast Feeding." In *Contemporary Sexual Behavior: Criti-*

cal Issues in the 1970s, ed. Joseph Zubin, and John Money, pp. 77–98. Baltimore and London: Johns Hopkins University Press.

Nilsson, Martin P. 1950. *The Minoan-Mycenaean Religion and Its Survival in Greek Religion.* Lund: C. W. K. Gleerup.

———. 1972. *The Mycenaean Origin of Greek Mythology.* Berkeley and Los Angeles: University of California Press.

Oates, Whitney, and O'Neill, Eugene, Jr. 1938. *The Complete Greek Drama.* 2 vols. New York: Random House.

O'Flaherty, Wendy Doniger. 1973. *Asceticism and Eroticism in the Philosophy of Shiva.* New York: Oxford University Press.

Ortner, Sherry B. 1974. "Is Female to Male As Nature Is to Culture?" In Rosaldo and Lamphere, pp. 67–89.

Otto, Walter. 1954. *The Homeric Gods: The Spiritual Significance of Greek Religion,* trans. Moses Hadas. Boston: Beacon Press.

Page, Denys L. 1955. *Sappho and Alcaeus.* Oxford: Clarendon Press.

Parry, Milman. 1971. *The Making of Homeric Verse: The Collected Papers of Milman Parry,* ed. Adam Parry. Oxford: Clarendon Press.

Patai, Raphael. 1964. "Lilith." *Journal of American Folklore* 77:295–315.

Pauly-Wissowa. 1894. *Pauly's Real-Encyclopädie der klassischen Altertumswissenschaft,* ed. G. Wissowa. Stuttgart: Metzler.

Pomeroy, Sarah B. 1975. *Goddesses, Whores, Wives, and Slaves: Women in Classical Antiquity.* New York: Schocken.

Rawlinson, George. 1889. *History of Phoenicia.* London: Longmans, Green.

Redfield, James. 1975. *Nature and Culture in the "Iliad": The Tragedy of Hector.* Chicago: University of Chicago Press.

Renou, Louis. 1957. *Etudes Védiques et Pāṇinéennes.* Publications de l'Institut de Civilisation Indienne. Vol. 3. Paris: De Boccard.

Rich, Adrienne. 1976. *Of Woman Born: Motherhood as Experience and Institution.* New York: Norton.

Roche, Paul. 1966. *The Love Songs of Sappho.* New York: American Library/Mentor.

Rosaldo, Michelle, and Lamphere, Louise. 1974. *Woman, Culture, and Society.* Stanford: Stanford University Press.

Roscher, W. H. 1884–1937. *Ausführliches Lexicon der griechischen und römischen Mythologie.* Vol. 1. Leipzig: Teubner.

Rose, H. J. 1924. "Anchises and Aphrodite." *Classical Quarterly* 18:11–16.

———. 1948. *Ancient Roman Religion.* London: Hutchinson's University Library.

———. 1959. *A Handbook of Greek Mythology.* New York: Dutton.

———. 1969. "Religion." In *A Companion to Homer,* ed. Alan J. B. Wace and Frank H. Stubbings, pp. 463–78. New York: Macmillan.

Rosén, Haiim B. 1967. "Die Ausdrucksform für 'veräusserlichen' und 'unveräusserlichen Besitz' im homerischen Griechischen (das Funktionsfeld von Homer)." In *Strukturalgrammatische Beiträge zum Verständnis Homers,* pp. 12–41. Amsterdam: North-Holland Publishing Company.

Ross, Ann. 1967. *Pagan Celtic Britain: Studies in Iconography and Tradition.* New York: Routledge & Kegan Paul.

Rossi, Alice. 1977. "A Biosocial Perspective on Parenting." *Daedalus* 106:1–33.

Rougemont, Dennis de. 1939. *Love in the Western World.* New York: Harcourt, Brace.

Saake, Helmut. 1971. *Zur Kunst Sapphos: Motiv-analytische und kompositionstechnische Interpretationen.* Munich: Ferdinand Schöningh.

Sahlins, Marshall. 1976. "Colors and Cultures." *Semiotica* 16:1–22.

Sanday, Peggy. 1974. "Female Status in the Public Domain." In Rosaldo and Lamphere, pp. 189–206.

Sandys, Sir John. 1930. *The Odes of Pindar, Including the Principal Fragments.* New York: Putnam's.

Sapir, Edward. 1951. "The Meaning of Religion." In *Selected Writings of Edward Sapir,* ed. David G. Mandelbaum, pp. 346–357. Berkeley and Los Angeles: University of California Press.

Schadewaldt, Wolfgang. 1950. *Sappho.* Potsdam: Stichnote.

Schmidt, Carl E. 1885. *Parallel-Homer.* Göttingen: Vandenhoeck & Ruprecht.

Schmidt, Rüdiger. 1967. *Dichtung und Dichtersprache in indogermanischer Zeit.* Wiesbaden: Harrassowitz.

Schroeder, Leopold. 1887. *Griechische Götter und Heroen.* Berlin: Weidmann.

Scully, Vincent. 1962. *The Earth, the Temple, and the Gods: Greek Sacred Architecture.* New York: Praeger.

Sebeok, Thomas, ed. 1955. *Myth: A Symposium.* Bloomington: Indiana University Press.

Seltman, Charles. 1956. *The Twelve Olympians and Their Guests.* London: Parrish.

Slater, Philip E. 1968. *The Glory of Hera.* Boston: Beacon Press.

Snell, Bruno. 1960. *The Discovery of the Mind: The Greek Origins of European Thought.* New York: Harper Torchbooks.

Speiser, A. 1955. "Akkadian Myths and Epics." In *Ancient Near Eastern Texts,* ed. J. B. Pritchard, pp. 383–92. Princeton: Princeton University Press.

Stanford, W. B. 1968. *The Ulysses Theme.* Ann Arbor: University of Michigan Press.

Summers, Montague. 1933. *The Werewolf.* London: K. Paul, Trench & Trübner.

Thompson, J. 1939. *The Moon Goddess in Middle America, With Notes on Related Deities.* Carnegie Institute of Washington Publications no. 59. Washington, D.C.: Carnegie Institute.

Todorov, Tsvetan. 1971. *Poétique de la prose.* Paris: Seuil.

Turner, Terry. 1969. "Time and Structure in Narrative Form." In *Forms of Symbolic Action,* ed. Robert F. Spencer, pp. 26–69. New Orleans: American Ethnological Society.

Turner, Victor. 1967a. "Myth and Symbol." *International Encyclopedia of the Social Sciences,* pp. 576–82. New York: Macmillan and The Free Press.

————. 1967b. *The Forest of Symbols.* Ithaca: Cornell University Press.

————. 1969. *The Ritual Process: Structure and Anti-Structure.* Chicago: Aldine.

Van Gennep, Arnold. 1960. *The Rites of Passage,* trans. M. B. Vizedon and Gabrielle L. Caffee. Chicago: University of Chicago Press, Phoenix Books.

Vermeule, Emily. 1964. *Greece in the Bronze Age.* Chicago: University of Chicago Press.

Vernant, Jean-Pierre. 1965. *Mythe et pensée chez les grecs.* Etudes de psychologie historiques. Paris: Maspéro.

Vickery, John B. 1966. *Myth and Literature.* Lincoln: University of Nebraska Press.

Vygotsky, Lev S. 1962. *Thought and Language,* trans. E. Hanfmann and G. Vakar. Cambridge, Mass.: MIT Press.

Wace, Alan J. B., and Stubbings, Frank H. 1969. *A Companion to Homer.* New York: Macmillan.

Wackernagel, Jacob. 1916. *Sprachliche Untersuchungen zu Homer.* Göttingen: Vandenhoeck & Ruprecht.

Walcot, Peter. 1966. *Hesiod and the Near East.* Cardiff: University of Wales Press.

Ward, Donald. 1968. *The Divine Twins: An Indo-European Myth in Germanic Tradition.* Folklore Studies no. 19. Berkeley and Los Angeles: University of California Press.

————. 1973. "On the Poets and Poetry of the Indo-Europeans." *Journal of Indo-European Studies* 1:127–45.

Watkins, Calvert. 1969. Article "Indo-European and the Indo-Europeans" in *The American Heritage Dictionary of the English Language,* ed. William Morris. New York: American Heritage.

————. 1970. "Studies in Indo-European Legal Language, Institutions, and Mythology." In *Indo-European and Indo-Europeans,* ed. G. Cardona, H. M. Hoenigswald, and A. Senn, pp. 321–55. Philadelphia: University of Pennsylvania Press.

West, Martin. 1966. *Hesiod: Theogony.* Oxford: Clarendon Press.

Whitman, Cedric H. 1965. *Homer and the Heroic Tradition*. New York: Norton.

Wilamowitz-Moellendorf, Ulrich von. 1913. *Sappho und Simonides: Untersuchungen über griechische Lyriker*. Berlin: Weidmann.

———. 1931. *Der Glaube der Hellenen*. Vol. 1. Berlin: Weidmann.

Wilson, Karen. "Disintegration and Unity in Greek Myth and Art." Term paper, University of Chicago.

Index

The following index includes proper nouns, symbolically important words, and the more important Greek words, as members of these sets occur in the text proper, the footnotes, and the appendixes (except for a few items referred to only once in the latter two locations); the researcher can go from the index directly to the information. Particular attention has been given to "feminine" categories (for example, sister); on the other hand, some themes that pervade the book (religion, psychology) are not actually named very often in the text and so are underrepresented in the index. My thanks go to Lilian Doherty for critical assistance.